LUCK IS A TALENT

THE TRUE STORY OF A TRIAL LAWYER'S EXPERIENCE DEFENDING AN INNOCENT MAN CHARGED WITH MURDER

A MEMOIR

GARY V. JOHNSON

Luck Is A Talent

Copyright 2020 State Street Publishing

ISBN: 978-1-4951-4053-2

Publisher: State Street Publishing, Elgin, Ill. (847) 902-3664

Acknowledgements

Where to start? *Luck* was a book that took a number of years to write, and there are a lot of people who were generous, supportive and helpful along the way. They saw what I was trying to accomplish, and went out of their way to help me put this together. I'm indebted to all of them. There are only a handful of people I've met in my life that I trusted immediately, and my publisher, George Rawlinson (Can't Miss Press/ State Street Publishing), is one. Maybe it was partly because my friend and mentor Van Richards introduced us, but mostly it was George himself. You poured your heart and soul into *Luck*, George, and made it *our* project. So from the bottom of my heart, thank you for your hard work, encouragement, advice, honest critique, and guidance through the mysteries of book publishing. You turned *Luck is a Talent* into a quality product. And now you're a friend.

Thank you, Steve Buckley, and to your family, for your confidence in Cliff, Carol and me as your defense lawyers. You never allowed your wrongful charges and incarceration to diminish your humanity, and you always told the truth. You were one of three innocent men the State tried to kill, and you, Alex Hernandez and Rolando Cruz can take comfort in the fact that your ordeal was probably the single most important event, in a series of important events, that put an end to the death penalty in Illinois. Thanks, too, for being a friend.

Thank you, Cliff Lund, for having the faith in me to allow me to co-counsel the trial of Steve Buckley with you. You're a top-flight litigator, and I know you hate it when I say this, but you're still the smartest lawyer I've ever known. After all is said and done, you saved Steve Buckley's life and never really got acknowledged for it. Maybe this book will change that.

To my other co-counsel, and almost cell-mate, Carol Anfinson, thanks for agreeing to let me retry Steve's case with you. A lesser lawyer might have told me to go scratch, but you had the self-confidence and strength to let me on board. Your insight and fresh perspective were just what Steve needed. And thanks to your husband, Bruce, for bailing us out.

Tom Laz, and the late Frank Wesolowski, both of you deserve more credit than you ever got as part of a group of dedicated professionals who ended up seeing their clients exonerated. Even though we represented different clients, we were all pulling in the same direction. Your advice and calming influence throughout the case to a couple of rookie defense lawyers was invaluable.

Even though they weren't mentioned in the book, Public Defender

Investigator Chuck Hamm and private investigator Bill Vincent provided top-notch investigative work for Steve's defense. I'm grateful, and I know that Steve, Cliff and Carol are, too.

One of the smartest things I could have done was to join an incredibly talented and committed group of writers, led by Lisa Macaione, who encouraged, evaluated (always honestly, sometimes painfully so), and inspired. So thank you, St. Charles Writers Group, for making me a better writer and *Luck* a much better book. Many of the recommendations you made were in some way incorporated into *Luck* to improve its quality. Thanks, too, for making the 2nd and 4th Saturday mornings of every month so enjoyable.

After reviewing *Luck* and making suggestions, Don Evans, book doctor extraordinaire, insisted that I make certain changes, structural and otherwise, for the sake of the book. I resisted some of his ideas, mostly because I didn't think I could carry them out, and when I told him so, he twisted my arm. Well, you were right, Don. I could, and did, make many of those alterations, and *Luck is a Talent* is a better book for it.

If it appears, after reading *Luck is a Talent*, that I'm adept at grammar, punctuation, and other similar finer points of writing, it's only because editors Dave Gathman and Sue Samuelson went over the manuscript with a fine-tooth comb and cleaned up my mistakes. That was no small task. Thanks to both of you for making my writing look so good.

My book layout and cover design, along with the construction of my website, were the outstanding work of J.J. Bailey. To say they were professionally done is an understatement of the first order. Thanks, J.J., for making *Luck* and its website look so good.

The artist's rendition of the courtroom scene on the cover is the creative work of the extremely talented L.D. (Lou) Chukman. Though nowadays, at least in high-profile cases, cameras are allowed in courtrooms for videos and still pictures, I miss those old days when artists would portray the spirit of legal proceedings via drawings. Thanks, Lou.

And my book photograph was a result of the skill and efforts of photographer James Harvey. You didn't have a lot to work with, James, so thanks for making me look good.

Thanks to the best law partner a guy could ask for, David Camic, my hardworking assistant, Carla Richards (I wouldn't survive long in the legal world without her), and to Sandra Parga, Vic Puscas, Patty Andrews, Belinda Lozano, Chris Powell, and all the folks at Camic Johnson, past and present. You've been my work family for more than 25 years and have unfailingly supported me throughout. I can't imagine a better place to work. And David, you're the best cross-examiner I've ever known.

I don't think my employers during Steve's trial, Clancy, McGuirk and Hulce, completely understood what they were taking on when they allowed me, even encouraged me, to handle Steve's defense. Nevertheless, their support never wavered. So thanks Wendell Clancy, John McGuirk, Mary Ellen Hulce, and everyone at CMH, for backing me all the way. And a very special thanks goes out to my former assistant, the late Pat Conner, who constantly encouraged and logged many hours getting Cliff and me ready for court.

There are several people I consulted with to get their recollections of certain events in the book, and I would like to thank all of them. So I'm grateful to Tom McCulloch, Ed Cisowski, Carole Grahn, and, of course, Cliff and Carol. Steve Greenberg helped out with a lot of the Brian Dugan material. Thanks, also, to William Bodziak, who clarified some of the shoeprint information and provided other valuable resources. It also goes without saying that I'm thankful for his honest and expert evaluation of the shoeprint evidence in the case. He was one of the tide-turners.

Speaking of shoeprints, even though I've already expressed my gratitude in the book itself, Dr. Owen Lovejoy gets a standing ovation from me. He took time out from his work studying the origins of humankind to teach me about science in general and shoeprints in particular. His analysis and testimony, along with that of Joseph Nicol, to whom I'm also grateful, was spot-on and prevented Steve from getting convicted.

I wasn't kidding when I say in the book that the biggest payoff for me for my work in the Nicarico case was the new friendships I made in the process. So a special thanks goes to John Hanlon and Mike Metnick (both of whom I also consulted with on aspects of *Luck*), Jeff Urdangen, Tom Breen (who also let me go through his files), Todd Pugh, Larry Marshall, Nan Nolan, Matt Kennelly, Jed Stone, Bill Clutter, Scott Turow, the late Jane Raley, Ron Sadowski, and again to Tom Laz and the late Frank Wesolowski.

Included in this new group of friends are authors Tom Frisbie and Randy Garrett. *Victims of Justice* and *Victims of Justice Revisited* are the "go to" works on the Nicarico case, and always will be. Randy, thanks for taking all my crazy phone calls, and for all the help you provided me and other lawyers on this case. Your investigative work was incredibly thorough. Tom, thanks for writing a great foreword to this book for me.

Thanks to Texas-based lawyer Chip Babcock and his staff, who represented the *Chicago Tribune* in Tom Knight's failed lawsuit against them, for sending along transcripts and other pertinent information about the case.

I'm also grateful to DuPage County Public Defender Jeff York, and the members of his staff, for letting me go through the Buckley file in a conference room at his office. I hope I didn't leave too big of a mess. Flint Taylor and John Stainthorp, Steve's civil lawyers, thanks to you, as well, for letting me dig through your files and transcripts at your office.

Thanks to fellow writers Bruce Steinberg and Carolyn Schroeder for encouraging me as I got started in the writing process. Carolyn, I appreciated your positive attitude and fearlessness. I hope some of it rubbed off. And Bruce, your critiques of my early chapters were primers on writing that were critical to telling this story in the best possible way. Scott Turow, thanks for your encouraging words, as well, after reading a sample of *Luck*.

Kathy and Lan Nielsen, a free copy of this book is on its way to you. Transcribing the late Bill O'Connell's notes of the David Strand (not his real name) case couldn't have been easy. And not charging me was an extra bonus. Court reporters are some of the unsung public servants of the justice system.

Not wanting to have a fool for a client, I sought out legal advice on various aspects of *Luck* from Peter Storm. Thanks, Peter, for your professionalism and legal guidance.

There were a number of people from different backgrounds who read over the entire manuscript before final publication and made suggestions. I would like to thank my sister, Pat Lord, Bob Kovacs, John Barsanti and Van Richards for taking the time to look over and work over *Luck*. Your input was more helpful than I can describe.

My brother, sister and I were raised in an incredible environment by our two parents and our maternal grandmother. Thanks, Bob and Jeanne Johnson, and you, too, Mums, for making a wonderful life for us. As I note later, I was born with a pewter spoon in my mouth. I wish you could have read this book. Same to you, brother Bob (and my first client). Whenever I feel the need to be rebellious, I think of you. I miss you every day. And Pat, in the category of sisters, they just don't get any better than you. Thanks for your support for this project and for your sincere and well thought out critique of *Luck*.

Last, but not least, thank you God—for all of my good fortune.

Colleen's Dream

Colleen Drury is an amazing soul and friend of Amy's and mine. When she was diagnosed with ovarian cancer in 2007, Amy said cancer didn't realize who it had picked a fight with. It turns out even that tribute to Colleen's character was an understatement. Colleen fought for more than five years before the disease took her life at age 58. But she made sure that with her passing, the battle had just begun. Before her death in 2013, Colleen and her four daughters created Colleen's Dream, a charitable organization run by those same daughters and other family members. Colleen's Dream raises money for ovarian cancer research and education, all for the specific goal of achieving Colleen's dream—the prevention and eradication of ovarian cancer.

In honor of our dear friend, Colleen Drury, all profits from *Luck is a Talent* will be donated to Colleen's Dream.

Dedication

To my beautiful wife, Amy, whose good-natured, but persistent, prodding, encouragement and advice were instrumental to the writing of *Luck*. I couldn't have, and wouldn't have, done this without you. Also, to our wonderful children, Andrea and Philip. It's easy to be fearless when you have a family that loves and supports you.

Foreword

I first met Gary Johnson in the old Romanesque red brick DuPage County Courthouse in Wheaton, Illinois, while I lingered with other journalists in the hallways and courtrooms of that stately edifice once roamed by Clarence Darrow. I was among the reporters hoping for scraps of insight from Johnson and other lawyers about a death penalty case that would become the most significant in the county's history. Unfortunately for us, the lawyers at that moment were restrained by a judge's gag order and remained tight-lipped.

I was a reporter for the *Chicago Sun-Times*, and Johnson was a defense lawyer for one of three men originally charged with the 1983 murder of a 10-year-old girl from the nearby Chicago suburb of Naperville. Neither of us knew it then, but over the course of six trials and a series of hearings that lasted longer than most trials, this case would grow into a powerful argument against the death penalty, one that would help lead to the abolition of capital punishment in Illinois. The case continues to be cited in other states as they debate whether they, too, should end the death penalty.

In those early days of the case, Johnson was representing a young man from Aurora, Illinois, named Steve Buckley, who together with two other Aurora men had been charged with the murder. After two convictions and a hung jury in the first trial and a series of subsequent trials ordered by the Illinois Supreme Court, all three men would eventually be exonerated. Years after the charges were first brought, a fourth man named Brian Dugan would plead guilty as the sole perpetrator of the crime. Dugan's subsequent death penalty, along with those of everyone on Illinois' Death Row, later would be commuted to life in prison as doubts about wrongful convictions in numerous cases such as this grew too great to ignore.

In 1998, I and my co-author, Randy Garrett, published a book about the case titled *Victims of Justice*. An updated and more complete edition, *Victims of Justice Revisited*, came out in 2005. In those volumes we sought to lay out the narrative of a story in which many who devoted their careers to criminal justice sounded unheeded warnings. The doubters were many: the local police chief, one of the key detectives assigned to the case, an assistant Illinois attorney general assigned to write a prosecutorial appeal, the head of an Illinois State Police investigation into the case.

In this book, Johnson gives us the background on the case from his perspective—an instructive tale of events that often linger behind closed doors. Watching courtroom dramas on the screen or televised coverage of trials doesn't teach us about the myriad decisions, setbacks, and minor victories that take place before a judge begins and ends a day's session in the courtroom. Here are those details that round out a full telling of an epic legal saga. Written as a serious reflection years after the last weary court stenographer typed up the last of a seemingly endless series of transcripts, this account gives us unreported details of legal stratagems and courthouse tactics, along with some of the human details of a great courtroom drama.

Johnson also shares with us his own story—that of a young lawyer who happened into a criminal case that would make headlines for years as trials came and went, new evidence emerged and judges and jurors wrestled with an increasingly voluminous set of facts. He writes without seeking to inflate his record. Rather, he invites us to share in his extraordinary experience. These pages are an education for those interested in going into the law and a rewarding read for those already well versed in it. It's a companion narrative for those familiar with the case and a litany of surprising twists and turns for those new to the story. In these pages, we learn why Johnson and his co-counsel found themselves behind bars on behalf of their client. His delving into the arcane forensic field of shoeprint identification is a fascinating story that merits multiple retellings.

Today, the transcripts are gathering dust, if they haven't all been entirely digitized, and the old courthouse has been converted into condominiums. But here are the unrevealed scraps of information that we journalists waiting in the hallways were eager to hear, and the reader should feel privileged to learn them.

With this accessible and thoughtful book, Johnson has done a favor for those who seek a greater understanding of how legal careers, the criminal justice system and the death penalty work, behind the scenes and in the trenches.

-Thomas Frisbie

Table of Contents

Preface

"The duty of a public prosecutor is to seek justice, not merely to convict."

- Included in Rule 3.8 of the Illinois Rules of Professional Conduct after the various prosecutions of Stephen Buckley, Alejandro Hernandez and Rolando Cruz.

"We now hold that the suppression by the prosecution of evidence favorable to an accused upon request violates due process where the evidence is material either to guilt or to punishment irrespective of the good faith or bad faith of the prosecution."

- Brady v. Maryland 373 U.S. 83 (1963)

"He [the prosecutor] may prosecute with earnestness and vigor— indeed, he should do so. But, while he may strike hard blows, he is not at liberty to strike foul ones. It is as much his duty to refrain from improper methods calculated to produce a wrongful conviction as it is to use every legitimate means to bring about a just one."

-Justice George Sutherland, Berger v. United States, 295 U.S. 78, 88 (United States Supreme Court, 1935)

"Most people don't like lawyers. Yet I know many lawyers— a lot of them former students of mine—and I like almost all of them. Lawyers have many qualities that make them good people and enjoyable companions. They are smart, and their training enables them to use their intelligence efficiently and rationally. Lawyers are open-minded: they will give a well-reasoned argument a fair hearing, and sometimes can be persuaded by it. They are interested in upholding principles, not just in taking the path of least resistance. And lawyers, almost to a person, have great senses of humor. Further, not only are individual lawyers likeable; the importance of lawyers to our society should not be underestimated. Try to imagine a society without lawyers. Now picture whether it would look more like the United States, or like any one of a number of countries that recently have dissolved into chaos."

-Professor David McCord, Drake University Law School

I suppose I'm exposing myself to accusations of being a hypocrite, or at least to being inconsistent. I can't tell you how many times I complained about not wanting to be known as a "one-trick pony" after I was one of the lawyers involved in the successful defense of Steve Buckley, one of three men initially charged with the abduction, rape and murder of 10-year-old Jeanine Nicarico. Even though the Nicarico prosecution was one of the most important criminal cases in Illinois history, I didn't want it to define me. Besides, at the risk of also being accused of false modesty, it sure helps when your client is innocent. To make matters worse, after it became clear someone else had committed these crimes, and not the original three defendants, I wrote an open letter to the DuPage County State's Attorney via the *Chicago Tribune* encouraging him to allow the real killer to plead to a life sentence, as opposed to receiving the death penalty, so we could put this case behind us once and for all. Yet now, with *Luck is a Talent*, I'm writing a book about it.

In my defense, the passage of time has changed things. Even though the story of the Nicarico case was thoroughly told, and quite well, in the books *Victims of Justice* and *Victims of Justice Revisited*, those were works of investigative journalism that, for very practical reasons, could not have completely covered my side of the story, or Steve's. It's a story that should, and now can be, told. This book, in part, is an attempt to do that. It's an "inside baseball" book that details the case from the perspective of, and emphasizing, Steve's defense—the ups, the downs, the all arounds. You, the reader, will quickly realize I'm pretty open about the things we did well in Steve's defense, and the things we did poorly. There were plenty of both.

That's not to say that other parts of the case are not covered in *Luck*— they are. If you include all the criminal and civil litigation in Nicarico from start to finish, the case lasted about 28 years, and had multiple investigations, trials and hearings, along with extensive local and national media attention. After my defense of Steve, I played a sideline role in some of those events. But as I previously noted, this is primarily a behind-the-scenes book about Steve's defense and my experiences as a lawyer. Though from time to time I deal with the serial prosecutions of Steve's equally innocent co-defendants as they affected Steve's case or my participation in it, I didn't represent them, so less emphasis is placed on that part of the story.

Luck is a Talent is about more than just my participation in the Nicarico case, however. Over the years, my wife, Amy, and others, have heard some of the stories and events that have occurred in my 40-some years as a lawyer, many of which they found amusing or interesting. "You should write a book about your experiences," they said. "Yeah, someday, maybe," was my knee-jerk answer. But as reflexive as my responses were, I had always intended to do something with those stories. I just wasn't sure how to put them together. So when time and events opened the door to write about Nicarico, and since some of the very stories people found interesting were from that case, or in some way relatable to it, I decided to write about both in one book.

With that in mind, I need to make one thing perfectly clear. While part of the reason for the inclusion of these stories is to inject some humor into the book, I am by no means trying to detract from or make light of the tragic consequences of the Nicarico murder, or its subsequent prosecutions. The majority of what you are about to read deals directly with the Nicarico case from my perspective, and I have tried to treat the people and issues involved seriously and with respect.

There are a few other things you should be aware of before beginning. First, this book is written to the best of my recollection. I have always known how fragile memory is, but writing this has really driven that point home for me. There were a number of times I would recall an event that occurred, only to have court transcripts show something different. Also, I interviewed a number of people about historical events that we had jointly participated in, only to end up with two or three different versions of the same occurrence. We would almost always agree on the major points, but not always on smaller things. All I can say is that I've tried to recreate those events as accurately as possible.

Which brings me to my second point. I've quoted from court transcripts from the Nicarico case throughout the book. They are highlighted in bold print. For aesthetic reasons, I have not put quotation marks around them, unless the person speaking in the transcript is quoting someone else. Quotes from newspaper articles, blogs and other sources are not in bold type, but are attributed in the body of the book or in an endnote. All other quotes come from conversations that are based on my recall and sometimes the recall of others.

Third, I've included some legal concepts in the book that are part of the story. I've done my best to simplify them so they are understandable and to keep you from getting bogged down, but I'm afraid I've only been partially successful. So while the legal points are relevant to what occurred, don't obsess over them. They are merely intended to be helpful in setting up some of the conflict that occurred. There will be no exams on the topics I covered.

Fourth, this is a work of nonfiction—it's not a suspense novel. In parts of the book, I foretell what happens later on in the course of events. You should note the dates I provide since there is some bouncing around. The timeline near the end of the book might be helpful.

Finally, I'm pretty hard on some of the prosecutors who handled this case for DuPage County. But I'm not one of those defense lawyers who constantly fights with or doesn't get along with opposing counsel. Hell, I was a prosecutor, twice over. They have a difficult job and usually aren't paid anywhere near their worth. The vast majority are a credit to the legal profession. My problem with some of the prosecutors in the Nicarico case is they didn't act much like prosecutors or lawyers.

Chapter 1
Contempt of Court

November 12, 1986

I was alone in one of those old-fashioned jail cells. Unlike the more modern lockups, this one had bars from floor to ceiling. I could hear the correctional officers going about their work around the corner. The only place to sit was on a bunk bed. My suit jacket, shirt, belt and tie had been taken from me, so when I climbed onto the top bunk to lie down, I wasn't able to keep warm.

"If I was you, I wouldn't put my head *directly* on that mattress," warned an only slightly sympathetic jail guard. I sat up and scratched my head. There I was, a 33-year-old, never-been-arrested-before criminal defense lawyer, cooling my heels in the old DuPage County, Illinois jail.

I, along with my co-counsel, Carol Anfinson, had just been held in contempt of court by Judge Robert Nolan. It occurred during our defense of Steve Buckley who, along with Rolando Cruz and Alex Hernandez, had been falsely accused of kidnapping, raping and murdering 10-year-old Jeanine Nicarico of Naperville, Illinois. It was one of the most publicized cases in Illinois history. Steve's first trial had ended in a hung jury over a year-and-a-half earlier, and the events which led up to our being jailed happened as we were attempting to schedule a retrial date.

I paced back and forth in my cell. *Have we just irretrievably screwed up Steve's case?* I wondered. *No, Judge Nolan has badgered and bullied us long enough. We had to stand up to him somewhere along the line, and this was as good a place as any to dig our heels in. But how are we going to get a fair trial from that jackass now that he's tossed us in jail?*

Then I heard Carol's voice from her cell around the corner, out of sight.

"Who's Vasco da Gama?" "What's the Amazon River?" I listened as she kept rattling off questions.

"Hey, what's Carol doing over there?" I asked one of the guards.

"She's having coffee and watching *Jeopardy!*"

"What the ...? I want to watch *Jeopardy!*, too. And how about a cup of coffee for me?"

"Sorry. There's only one TV, and we can't let you share a cell with a female." As if I would try to do something untoward with my co-counsel. "You can have a book," the guard continued. There was no response to the coffee request.

He accompanied me to the lockup's extensive library—of about seven books. I chose *The Winds of War* and returned to my cell. Sitting on my bunk, I tried reading, but other thoughts—selfish thoughts—began to creep in. I had hopes of someday running for state's attorney in neighboring Kane County, and the consequences of the day's events began to sink in.

Fantastic, I thought. *I'm sure that mug shot they just took of me will make a great campaign ad for someone.*

My mind eventually went back to Steve's defense. I mostly thought about the pros and cons of trying to get Nolan off the case. The pros won.

After a little over an hour, a guard escorted me out of my cell. "We're taking you to the new jail, where you'll stay 'til you can post bond." DuPage County had just built a new sheriff's office and corrections facility a mile or so away, and that was where we were headed, but not before one more act of humiliation. I felt someone messing with my ankles and I looked down. I was being shackled.

How the hell did this happen?

Chapter 2
Boy, Have I Got a Case for You

July 1984 (28 Months Earlier)

The line of lawyers standing in front of the jury box railing, waiting their turn to have their cases called in Judge Richard Weiler's courtroom, was already long when I walked through the courtroom door. It had been about nineteen months since I left my job as a prosecutor for the Kane County State's Attorney's Office. I was now in private practice working as an associate in the law firm of Clancy, McGuirk and Hulce, where we concentrated in civil law—primarily personal injury. The judge allowed some quiet chatter among the waiting lawyers, ostensibly so we could resolve legal issues, while he was dealing with his business at the bench. In reality, most of the talk was social in nature.

Cliff Lund, a civil law attorney roughly my age whom I had known for about five years, was in line next to me. We exchanged greetings and he asked how things were going for me practicing civil law.

"It's growing on me. I'm still getting used to the idea that discovery in civil cases is so much more extensive than in criminal cases, where the stakes are often much higher. I do miss the criminal work, though. I'd like to get some criminal clients, but I just haven't been able to swing that yet."

"Really?" Cliff paused and chuckled. "Boy, have I got a case for you!"

"No kidding? Tell me about it."

"Well, you've read about the three guys charged with the murder of Jeanine Nicarico, haven't you?"

Everyone in the Chicago area knew about the Nicarico case. On February 25, 1983, 10-year-old Jeanine stayed home sick from school in unincorporated Naperville, Illinois. Since her two sisters were also in school, and both her parents worked, she was home alone. In the afternoon, she was kidnapped out of her house. Her body was discovered by hikers two days later on the Illinois Prairie Path. A reward was offered and authorities pleaded for people with information to come forward.

Over a year later, on March 8, 1984, three young men—Stephen

Buckley, Alejandro "Alex" Hernandez and Rolando Cruz—from the east side of Aurora, a large Chicago suburb adjoining Naperville to the west—were indicted for Jeanine's murder, as well as for kidnapping and sexual assault related offenses. The prosecution was seeking the death penalty for all three. The press coverage was extensive, and all of it was bad.

Although I was familiar with the public accounts of the case, I had not followed it all that closely. I thought it was odd that indictments were obtained more than a year after the offense, but less than two weeks before the Republican primary—at that time, the only competitive part of the election process in Republican-rich DuPage County—in which the incumbent DuPage County State's Attorney, J. Michael Fitzsimmons, was in the political fight of his life. As a matter of fact, Fitzsimmons went on to lose that primary to Jim Ryan, who would later also play a very significant role in the Nicarico case. I suspected politics had played a part in the indictments and I told Cliff that.

Cliff had represented one of Steve Buckley's sisters in the past and was in touch with the family. "The Buckleys are looking for private counsel to defend Steve. If you're interested, I definitely can get you involved. We could try the case together."

Interested?! I could barely contain myself. It was a chance to do the case of a lifetime. Plus, I would get to work with Cliff, a lawyer I held in high esteem. We immediately planned our initial steps. Over the next few days, I ran the proposition past the partners at my firm and they were supportive. Cliff conferred with the Buckleys, also with positive results. I called Steve's public defender, Ed Ward, and told him what was transpiring. Ed discussed the evidence with me and he didn't seem too unhappy at the prospect of private lawyers taking over the case.

Cliff and I visited Steve at the DuPage County Jail. It wasn't a lengthy visit, but it was enough for us to get a sense of our almost-new client. A 21-year-old high school dropout, Steve lived at home with his parents. He was the youngest of five children who had all been raised in a rough area on the east side of Aurora. He had a criminal history that included a burglary and a misdemeanor theft. His father, John, who had retired from Commonwealth Edison after spending more than 30 years there, was in poor health as the result of a couple of strokes. Steve's mom, Marilyn, was a homemaker. Steve came from a good family but a bad neighborhood.

I liked Steve from the get-go. He was open, direct and smarter than his lack of formal education let on. And when he told us, in very blunt terms, he had absolutely nothing to do with what had occurred to Jeanine

Nicarico, I tended to believe him. This initial sense of his innocence would solidify as we got further into the case.

Things were happening quickly. Everything was ready for Cliff and me to file our appearances—the formal method of a lawyer declaring representation of a party. Then reality began to set in. As I dug into the case, I got the feeling that we were about to grab a tiger by the tail. Never in my life, as it turns out, has one of my gut instincts been more spot-on.

"I have a feeling this thing is even bigger than it appears, and that it'll go on for years to come," I confided to my wife, Amy. She, too, supported my representing Steve. But we just had our first child six months earlier and I wanted her to be aware that any estimates of the amount of time this would consume were a little fuzzy. I had a similar conversation in a second meeting with the law firm partners. All agreed that, while the case would involve a substantial commitment, I was probably overstating its extent. Everyone was on board.

There was only one hurdle left to overcome. I was 31 years old. Although I had prosecuted some serious crimes during the latter part of my four years at the state's attorney's office, my defense trial experience consisted of one DUI bench trial. What qualified me, or Cliff for that matter, to represent a client in a case like this?

I was afraid.

Boy, Have I Got a Case for You—Sidebar

The Nicarico case would end up being a high-profile case on a local and national level. Aside from the massive interest by the Chicago-area media, it was featured on *60 Minutes, American Justice* and *48 Hours*, and more recently on the *Investigative Discovery Channel*. It was also written up in *The Washington Post, The Los Angeles Times, The Atlantic* and *Vanity Fair*. But I was also very briefly brought into a case—for about a week—of another nationally known defendant.

My contact with Drew Peterson[1] came when he was initially suspected of murdering both his wife and one of his ex-wives. Even at that early stage, the press coverage was overwhelming. He would eventually be indicted for, and in 2012 be convicted of, the murder of his ex-wife, for which he is now serving a long prison sentence. But at the beginning of the investigation, he was represented by my friend and outstanding criminal defense lawyer Fred Morelli.

During that same time period, Fred was also seriously considering a run for judge. The reason he got me involved was that if he did indeed make that run, he wanted someone to help out while he conducted his campaign. Also, if he got elected, he wanted someone to turn the case over to.

Fred and I were involved just long enough for some of the national media to know that we were Peterson's lawyers. During the latter part of our week-long representation of him in early November 2007, I started getting calls from a producer at *Good Morning America*. He told me that Peterson was going to be on the *Today* show, their competitor, and that he wanted to get Peterson on his show. I had learned from another lawyer with experience from these morning shows that they were intensely competitive. I assured this producer that my client would be doing no such thing, but over the course of one day, he called a couple of times and even popped in unexpectedly at my office to insist that Peterson was interviewing with *Today*. Again, I assured him that he was mistaken. That night, while I was at a meeting at Fermilab (Fermi National Accelerator Laboratory), the producer came to my home, unannounced, and spoke to Amy.

"Are you Mrs. Johnson, and is your husband Gary Johnson?"

"Yes."

"The lawyer?"

"Yes." Amy was both curious and a little nervous.

"Is Gary home?"

"No. I'm sorry. He's at a meeting. Can I help you?"

"Well," the producer said, "your husband is a liar!"

Amy was a bit perturbed. "Who are you, and why would you say that?"

The producer gave his name and title, then explained that Peterson was going to be on the *Today* show the following morning. "And your husband guaranteed me that he wasn't going to do that. Your husband is a liar."

"Well, I know he's not a liar, but I suggest you work this out with him." Then she closed the door.

Amy called me and told me what had transpired. I called the producer, who apologized to me for his conduct. As it turned out, he was right about one thing. When I got home that night, I saw an ad on NBC for the *Today* show, saying that Peterson would be on the show the following morning for an exclusive interview.

I watched the interview the next morning while I was exercising at the gym. In it, he and Matt Lauer had the following exchange:

Lauer: "What are you most frightened about?"

Peterson: "Basically, my legal defense. Uh, talking to lawyers Monday night, it could cost as much as a quarter million dollars to defend one of these cases. So, basically, I'm reaching out to attorneys of America for help. If anybody would like to take my case, ah, and help me out here, please, call. Let me know what you could do for me. Help me out."

Later that morning, I spoke with one of my law partners, Sandra Parga, by phone.

"What'd you think of the *Today* show interview?" I asked.

"Well, Gary, you're the only lawyer I know who's gotten fired on national television."

Chapter 3
Luck is a Talent

"Luck is a talent." At least writer William Somerset Maugham thought so. I hope he's right, because I'm not certain how talented I am. But just ask anyone who knows me, and they will tell you—if luck is indeed a talent, then I'm a damn Mozart.

Maybe It Was a Family Affair

I think I would have gotten into Illinois Wesleyan University—a school with a pretty competitive admissions process—on my own, but I'm not sure. I wasn't exactly a power student at Willowbrook High School in Chicago's west suburban Villa Park. I suppose it didn't hurt that both of my parents and my older brother, Bob, all attended college there.

When I got to IWU, I took my studies much more seriously and decided I wanted to go to law school. I wasn't driven by any kind of passion for the law. For me it was three more years of school and a way of delaying the inevitable reality of settling into a job. Since it was a dream of my parents that I attend law school, they were behind me all the way—emotionally and financially. I worked during my college and law school years, but my folks actually relished taking on the responsibility of bankrolling my higher education. I never had to worry about money. What I'm trying to say is that, while maybe I wasn't born with a silver spoon in my mouth, it might have been at least pewter.

I Don't See Any Real Way You're Getting In Here

During the law school application process, one of the schools I wanted to attend most was a bear to get into—Vanderbilt. With the credentials I had, students today would call such an application a "stretch." Back then I simply called it an extreme long shot. I had been told that the dean of the law school was an IWU graduate, so I applied. You can imagine my surprise when I received an invitation, in the form of a postcard, to have a personal interview with the dean. Such interviews with prospective students were very rare. As a matter of fact, I had never heard of this happening to anyone else. *If they want an interview with me*, I thought, *I must have a real shot at this.*

I scheduled an appointment. On the designated day, I got a lift from my home in Villa Park to O'Hare and flew down to Nashville for an early Saturday morning meeting with the law school dean.

Decked out in a sport coat and tie, I hopped onto a bus to Vanderbilt, found the law school, then the dean's office, and at the appointed time, knocked on the door. No answer. After waiting a short time, the dean arrived. I introduced myself.

The dean frowned. "I wasn't aware I had any appointments this morning."

I ignored the bad sign and showed him my postcard. To my relief, he agreed to meet with me right away. The dean retrieved my application and spread it out on his desk. Law school applications are generally made up of undergraduate grades, LSAT (Law School Admissions Test) scores, and, sometimes, reference letters. Most of the emphasis is on grades and the LSAT. The Vanderbilt reference letters were on a form provided by the school, and they consisted mostly of boxes that needed to be checked. From my vantage point, it was easy for me to see which boxes had been marked by the IWU professors I had contacted. To my horror, they had provided honest—and therefore less than outstanding—evaluations! *What the hell?* I thought. *Where's the puffing*—a slang sort of legal term meaning permissible exaggerating in advertising—*you're supposed to get on these things?* Yet another bad sign.

"I'm looking at your grades and test scores," the dean said slowly as he was digesting the application. "I don't see any real way you're getting in here."

I suppose I would have appreciated his brutal honesty had it come before I trekked to Nashville. And I suppose I had no right to be disappointed, though I was. But I did have a right to be pissed.

Seeing "rejected" written on the proverbial wall, what I did next didn't really require much courage. I had nothing to lose. So I scooted my chair up to the front of the dean's desk, looked him squarely in the eye and waved my postcard at him. "Do you think," I said slowly, emphasizing every word, "you could have told me that over the telephone?"

"Well, ah, you never know. We still have to go over all the applications, and there's a committee, um, you know, anything can happen, I just don't ..."

"Yeah, yeah, sure," I said, wanting to end the interview as quickly as I could. "Don't worry about it. Anyhow, thanks for your time."

I spent the rest of the morning wandering around Nashville. I picked up lunch at a McDonald's before my flight out and made my way to Nashville's Centennial Park, where there is a full-scale replica of the Parthenon. Surprisingly, there were very few people at the park. I sat at the base of the Parthenon and, completely dejected, ate my lunch. Pathetic.

Of course, I didn't get into Vanderbilt. Instead, I went to law school at Drake University in Des Moines, Iowa. I spent three years living in a run-down old house with several other law students—a couple of whom are still like brothers to me—paying $60 per month rent. I got a great education, made lifelong friendships and had the time of my life. Very few people can say that about anything, let alone law school.

A Pop Quiz Helps Me Pass the Bar Exam

In late July of 1978, I took the Illinois bar exam. It was a two-day test. The second day was the multi-state portion of the exam, which most of the rest of the country also took, and consisted of 200 multiple choice questions. The first day was the Illinois section and was made up of 16 essay questions. You had to answer all of them. The morning session of day one went well for me. The afternoon was a different story. Each question was difficult. One in particular seemed to pose a real problem.

When the first day ended, I spoke to a number of fellow exam takers. The company that prepped us for the test had warned us not to discuss—during exam breaks—the responses we had given. Comparing answers and wringing your hands over completed and turned-in portions of the test were counterproductive. But it seemed that a lot of people were troubled by that one especially difficult question, so eventually someone brought it up, and soon it was being debated. As it turned out, the test preppers were right, because as the question was being discussed, you could feel everyone's angst increase. Though I didn't say so, thanks to my grim determination to attend a certain law school class at Drake on one particular Friday, I was certain I had answered the question correctly.

Thursday nights were lively at the bars near Drake. Law students usually imbibed at the West End, a tavern just off campus. One such night near the end of my third and final year, the West End was particularly crowded. Graduation was about a month away and the bar reviews and bar examinations for the various states would soon follow. I think everyone was coming to the realization we would soon be going our separate ways, so we were cramming some camaraderie in. A number of us were debating whether we would make it to Professor T.J. McDonough's 8 a.m. Bankruptcy class the next morning. I hadn't been keeping up with the reading in that class, so I figured I had better at least show up and absorb as much as I could before the final exam.

"I'm an iron man," I joked. "A little late-night partying won't keep me from being there." Nobody else made such a commitment.

The following morning, the "iron man" bravado was replaced by a headache. Going to Bankruptcy class didn't seem nearly as important as it had the night before. After all, I could always rely on *Bankruptcy in a Nutshell*—one of several law school shortcuts akin to *CliffsNotes* for literature—to get me through. Such a strategy was not uncommon for law students. Some upperclassmen relied exclusively on these kinds of shortcuts for all their courses. But I stumbled ahead and made it to class anyhow.

Bankruptcy was a course taken mostly by third-year students, many of whom had been out with me the prior evening. One result was that a ton of third-years cut Bankruptcy that day. Another was that Professor McDonough was beside himself.

McDonough was one of those law professors who scared the shit out of first-year students. I had been no exception. He was large—about 6'1" and well over 300 pounds—and loud. I remember in my first-year Contracts class, when I had told him that I hadn't seen the movie *A Man for All Seasons*, nor read anything about Sir Thomas More, the Lord Chancellor of England in the 1500s and the movie's protagonist, he mocked me in front of the entire class. "You, sir, are culturally deprived!" he yelled. He was mellower with upperclassmen, most of whom weren't afraid of him anymore, but he still maintained a presence.

"Where is everybody?" McDonough bellowed at the more-than-half-empty Bankruptcy class. Nobody answered. "This is bullshit! Where the hell is everybody?" he yelled again. Still no answer. Then he seemed to get hold of himself.

"I don't know why I'm yelling at *you*. You're here!" He looked around the classroom. "I'm gonna give you all a pop quiz, and it'll be easy! You'll all do well, and you'll get extra credit—just for being here and finishing it!"

Since law school grades normally are based only on one test, a three- or four-hour final exam at semester's end, the quiz idea seemed strange to me. It must have shown, because McDonough looked in my direction. *Oh, brother*, I thought, *what does he want with me?*

"Mr. Johnson," McDonough zeroed in. "Do you want a leg up on your missing classmates?"

I felt bad for my absent classmates, most of whom were friends. Plus, I didn't think I would fare well on a pop quiz, no matter how simple, in a class in which I had been slacking. "No, thanks. I'm good. That won't be necessary."

"C'mon, it'll be easy. What about you, Mr. Stump? Wanna leg up?" McDonough shifted his attention to Gary Stump, the one person who didn't need any extra help. He ended up graduating first in our class.

"No. That's okay. I'm fine the way things are," Stump replied.

"Too bad. You're getting a pop quiz. It'll be easy and I guarantee you'll all do well. Here's the quiz: Just write out the facts of Smith v. Jones, one of the cases we went over yesterday." (I don't recall the actual name of the case). "Put your name on your paper, and turn it in."

Not bad, I thought, *that is easy*. Except for one thing—I hadn't read Smith v. Jones. So I figured if he was going to force this quiz on us, I might as well try to do well.

"Professor McDonough," I shouted out. "Can we have a few minutes to read the case?" I was worried that he might be upset with my admission that I hadn't read the previous assigned materials, but I got one final reward for showing up to class that day.

"You've got five minutes!"

Five minutes was plenty of time to digest the abridged version of the case the textbook provided. I read over the facts and got them on paper with time to spare. With the extra time, I read the court's holding and reasoning. It was a case about bankruptcy as it related to a business law concept known as "piercing the corporate veil." One of the advantages of incorporating a business is that the owners (shareholders) limit their liability to the value of the stock they own. Not all forms of business carry that protection. However, if the company doesn't conduct itself sufficiently like a corporation, it might be possible to "pierce the corporate veil" and hold the shareholders personally liable, beyond the value of their stock.

It was a difficult case—the kind, when you read it, you would say to yourself, *Hmmm, I never would have thought of that, but that's an interesting principle which makes sense when you mull it over*. And because of the way I had been forced to internalize the concept, it stuck with me long enough to do a lot more good than just give me extra credit in Bankruptcy class.

When I saw the question on the bar exam—a question dealing with an obscure issue regarding piercing the corporate veil that was nearly identical to the case for which I had obtained extra credit in Bankruptcy just a few months before—I had to chuckle. *There are going to be some people who struggle with this question*, I thought. *But, thankfully, not me.*

****

Of all the people who took the Illinois bar exam that July, I might have been the next-to-last to learn my results. During my last year of law school, I worked two jobs—as a research assistant for one of Drake's law school professors and as a teacher in law-related courses at Des Moines Area Community College. The extra money was used to fund a trip to Europe one week after the bar was over. I went with one of my law school housemates, Dan Bonnett. We had been inspired by one of our older housemates, Bill Drury, who made a similar trip earlier—only he had done so by taking off a semester of law school. We were gone for nine weeks of backpacking and hosteling. It was the trip of a lifetime, but the exam weighed heavily on my mind. Even though I had gotten lucky on the "piercing the corporate veil" question, there was another question for which I had violated the "don't discuss your exam answers" rule. The feedback I got was not comforting.

While I was in Europe, I wasn't sure if I would get back before the bar exam results were in. We had been told that the exam would take roughly two months to grade, but there was no specific date given. Today, results are given over the Internet. Of course, in 1978, regular mail was used. And since back in those days the amount of communication with folks at home while traveling overseas was minimal by today's standards—in my case amounting to one five-minute phone call and a handful of letters sent to and mailed from various American Express offices—I had no way of knowing if the results were in.

When Dan and I arrived at O'Hare Airport in early October, my dad was there to meet us. Dan still had to catch a plane for the short trip to his hometown, Rock Island. I hugged my dad and he welcomed me home with some news.

"We got your bar results a little less than a week ago."

I was mildly surprised. "Did you open 'em?"

"I did," Dad said as he looked down at his feet. "Now I don't want you to get upset ..."

"Oh, no. I didn't ... son of a bitch!" I groaned.

Dad smiled. "I'm just kidding—you passed."

"Woo hoo!" I screamed, dancing around my backpack with both arms raised in the air. I looked like Rocky Balboa at the top of the steps of the Philadelphia Museum of Art. Within seconds, I think everyone at O'Hare knew I had passed the bar. Poor Dan—he had to wait several hours until he got to Rock Island to learn his fate. Later, he told me his mother greeted him at the airport saying, "Welcome home, Esquire!" Dan said it had been the longest three hours of his life.

Does This Qualify As Irony?

A price I paid for the Europe trip was that by the time I returned, it seemed all the good jobs were taken. I had a pretty decent resume, so I was frustrated when each of my roughly 50 job applications resulted in either a rejection or no response at all. I didn't even get a nibble. That is, until the mayor of St. Charles, Illinois intervened.

I was still in law school when my parents moved to the far western Chicago suburb of St. Charles in Kane County. As luck would have it, they moved next door to the mayor, Fred Norris. Mayor Norris set me up for an interview with Kane County State's Attorney Gene Armentrout. I met with Gene and some of his staff, and we hit it off immediately. Sometimes you just know when you're in the right place, and that's how I felt there. Problem was, they had no openings. But Gene told me he would keep my resume handy, and would contact other county state's attorneys' offices and recommend me. At least it was a start.

Within days I got a call from the DuPage County State's Attorney's Office, a place that had politely rejected me just weeks earlier, requesting an interview. From what I could tell, they had openings in both their criminal and civil divisions. In Illinois, state's attorneys' office criminal divisions prosecute violations of state criminal laws, while the civil divisions defend their counties in lawsuits and advise department heads and elected county officials. In two sessions, I met with the State's Attorney, Michael Fitzsimmons, his First Assistant (the second in command) and the Chief of the Civil Division. I told Fitzsimmons I preferred to be a prosecutor in the criminal division, but I would take civil if that's what they wanted.

It appeared to me that I was on the brink of being hired into the criminal division, but I had to first meet with the chief of that division, Tom Knight. Fitzsimmons told me to wait in their lobby, and he would have Knight interview me as soon as he was available. I waited for a while until it appeared that the office was about to close. When a young man I had not yet met came bounding down the stairs with gym equipment in hand, I piped up.

"Are you Mr. Knight?"

"Yes, I am. What can I do for you?"

"I was supposed to be interviewed by you for a possible job."

Knight was genuinely embarrassed. "Nobody told me you were here. I'm really sorry, but I'm already late for a racquetball game. Do you mind if we do this later? You can call my secretary and schedule something." I agreed, and the next day I scheduled an appointment with Knight for the following week.

I didn't keep that appointment. Shortly after I scheduled it, I got a call from Gene Armentrout. He had an opening in his criminal division and wanted to know if I was interested. About a month later, on January 2, 1979, I was sworn in as an assistant Kane County State's Attorney.

The odd twist of my nearly becoming a DuPage County prosecutor wouldn't reveal itself until some six years later.

****

I did represent one person while unemployed and during the early stages of the job application process. He was my first client, the story of which will be expanded upon in Chapter 4.

Luck is a Talent—Sidebar

I occasionally wonder what would have happened if fate, in the form of a last-minute job opening in Kane County, hadn't interrupted the interview process at the DuPage County State's Attorney's Office. I only had one interview left in DuPage—with Chief of the Criminal Division Tom Knight—the very lawyer with whom I would fight tooth and claw in the Nicarico case some six years later. I was pretty sure I was close to getting a job offer. I was even making plans to move into DuPage County, something that was encouraged of DuPage prosecutors at the time, to live with my Aunt Ilse and Uncle Rey in Wheaton until I could afford an apartment.

Patrick King, the prosecutor who would assist, or second chair, Knight in our trial, had only a year or two less experience than me. What if I had taken the job in DuPage, and it was me, instead of Pat King, assigned to be Knight's second chair? How would I have responded after I had internalized all the evidence that, as a defense lawyer, would cause me to be convinced that Buckley and his co-defendants were innocent? Would I have had the guts of John Sam or Mary Brigid Kenney, one a cop and the other an appellate prosecutor—both of whom will make appearances later in this book—who, upon realizing the wrongfulness of the Nicarico investigation and prosecution, made their feelings known to anyone who would listen, and ended up quitting their jobs rather than supporting the prosecution of innocent people?

Chapter 4
My First Client

Autumn 1978

"Are you sure you trust me with this?" I asked. "I really don't know what I'm doing. Not only have I never been to court before, but you would be my first client—ever."

I was with my older brother, Bob, in his backyard in Roselle, Illinois. Bob had a rebellious spirit, and that quality led to his getting arrested for DUI in Chicago the year before. He had pled guilty and was sentenced to one year of court supervision, a disposition in Illinois that allowed him to keep his driver's license.

Now he had to return to court to conclude his supervision. The problem was back then, at least in this one particular courtroom in Cook County, there was a requirement that the judge who sentenced you was the only one who could discharge the supervision. Twice Bob had gone to court on his own, but both times the case was continued because the sitting judge was not Bob's sentencing judge. Now Bob wanted my help—pro bono, of course. And the ink had yet to dry on my law license.

"You'll do fine. I really think all I have to do is show up with a lawyer and they'll let me go," Bob tried to assure me.

The big day arrived—my first day in court as a lawyer representing a client. I was decked out in the only suit I owned, and Bob was dressed in a sport coat. So far, so good. As Bob drove to the courthouse in Chicago, I relayed the only legal advice I felt qualified to give. "Treat the judge with respect," I said. "Everything is 'yes, sir' and 'no, your honor.' Got it?"

"You don't have to worry about me."

When we arrived in court, I tried to keep my jitters in check while I spoke to the prosecutor before the judge came out. I explained the history of the case to him, and he informed me that, once again, the wrong judge was in court that day. He said he would do what he could to help conclude the case.

When the judge took the bench, we were the first case called in a packed courtroom. Bob and I stood at separate podiums in front of his honor. I introduced myself as Bob's lawyer. The prosecutor told the judge that Bob was eligible to be released from supervision, and that was his recommendation. The judge read the file and then looked at my brother.

"I'm sorry, Mr. Johnson, it appears that you're ready to be discharged, but I can't do it. The judge who sentenced you has to release you, and he's not here today."

"Your honor, my client has been here twice before to be discharged, and he had the same problem both times. Couldn't you see your way to concluding this matter now?" I asked, as my very first argument before a judge.

"Your honor, this is a huge inconvenience for me driving in all the way from Roselle," Bob chimed in, maybe forgetting he had a lawyer. "I can't see why you can't let me off today." He had an edge to his voice.

"I'm sorry. You'll have to get another date when your original judge is back."

Bob wouldn't let go and continued to challenge the judge, becoming less and less deferential as the moments passed. Feeling that things were slipping out of control, and before Bob said anything we would both regret, I again asked the judge to make an exception to a rule that made no sense to me.

"I'm afraid I can't, Mr. Johnson," the judge said, speaking now to me. "You'll have to return."

I didn't know what else I could do. I was ready to retreat and go home when I looked over at Bob. He was stewing. Red-faced and pointing his finger at the judge, he ignored the high-powered legal advice I had previously given him. "Look, man, I've been here three times now to finish this thing up, and you guys just won't let me go. I'm sick of this. I'm not coming down here again."

The judge responded, angrily saying things I couldn't make out as he and Bob talked loudly over each other.

I tried to think of something to say, but I could only stammer. "What my brother, uh, I'm sorry, I mean my client, means is, uh ..." My voice trailed off and became irrelevant as I listened to Bob and the judge continue to argue.

Finally there was silence. The judge glared at Bob. "All right, Mr. Johnson. I'll discharge you. But the next time you decide to get drunk and drive, do it in Roselle, and not on the streets of Chicago."

I expected Bob to be happy with the result. I was. Despite the smart-ass remark by the judge, we had gotten what we wanted. *My first courtroom victory,* I thought. *Winning ugly, but winning!* But I couldn't have been more wrong. As we were leaving, Bob reached the rear of the courtroom first. He shoved the door open with both hands, then turned to me—resulting in his facing the direction of the judge and everyone in court. "What an asshole!" he blurted out in a voice loud enough for everyone to hear.

Instinctively, I shoved Bob, hard, through the doorway and out of the courtroom. I was afraid court personnel would drag us back in to face the wrath of the judge. "We gotta get the hell outta here," I said, grabbing his arm. So we sprinted, my first client and I, out of the courthouse and down the street to the parking lot. I overshot the car door, in Three Stooges-like fashion, before I backed up and got in.

As we sped out of the city, Bob, slightly out of breath, smiled at me. "You did pretty good in there today. Thanks."

Chapter 5
Becoming a Prosecutor

November 6, 1981

I wasn't completely aware of what I'd gotten myself into until we walked into the roll call room at the Kane County Sheriff's Office around 11 p.m. Deputies in both regular uniforms and SWAT team gear conversed and appeared anxious. Rifles lined the floor near a podium. A chalkboard contained some basic information about a raid that was to occur in several hours at the home of James McCrimmon. Everyone was waiting for details to be filled in at the meeting that would occur in a few minutes.

I swallowed hard and looked at my co-worker, John Barsanti. "What the hell did we sign up for?"

John was less nervous. "This is going to be great!"

I had been an Assistant State's Attorney for nearly three years, and John for about two. When John joined the office we became fast friends and both dove into all aspects of the job. That meant, in part, working with the police, giving them legal advice, and helping to develop cases. We had become friends with Kane County Sergeant Ken Ramsey, who was only a little older than us. Ramsey, who would later become the elected Kane County Sheriff, had it in for McCrimmon and he was the driving force behind the evening's events. The police had received information that illegal gambling-related activities were going to occur at McCrimmon's home just outside the city limits of Aurora, putting it in the sheriff's jurisdiction. A search warrant was obtained and the raid was planned. Looking back, it was a bit like killing a gnat with a sledgehammer. But back then, it didn't feel that way. John and I were involved to give legal advice, but I don't deny we were looking forward to being close to whatever excitement might occur. I had gone on a couple of police ride-alongs before, but this night would be something else entirely.

Ramsey convened the meeting and introduced John and me as legal advisors for the raid. The plan was to leave the sheriff's office in central Kane County and meet at a church parking lot a few blocks from McCrimmon's residence. There we would wait for the optimum time to execute the search warrant. The element of surprise was critical.

To my amazement, just before the meeting started, Ken approached John and me to inform us that we would both be driving squad cars to the meet location. "Just don't use the sirens or Mars lights," he said as he handed us keys to our very own police cars. *John was right*, I thought. *This was going to be great!*

The church parking lot was about eight miles from the sheriff's office. As I drove south down Kirk Road, then Farnsworth Avenue, I was a bit cautious at first. Then I noticed the power, not just of the whip-fast car I was driving, but of a car with Mars lights and other police regalia that made other drivers nervous. I was surprised at how quickly it went to my head. I picked up speed, first a little, then a lot. Traffic control lights and signs became more or less optional. Once or twice I was blocked by motorists in the two southbound lanes who weren't aware I was behind them. I kept my promise to Ken and didn't use the Mars lights or siren—not that I knew how—but honking the horn produced the desired result.

I made it to the rendezvous at the church without incident. I got out of the car and talked with Ken, John and a few others for a while. It was nighttime, when sound carries pretty well, and since we were only a few blocks from McCrimmon's residence, everyone was speaking in hushed tones. We had some time to kill, so John suggested that we wait in "his" patrol car.

Once in his squad, we were like a couple of kids in a children's museum. We were pressing buttons and turning knobs, all the time asking each other, "I wonder what this does?" or "What's that for?" Then John started opening up about a personal problem. Over the prior two years, we had grown close and confided in each other on a regular basis about all sorts of things. It was around the time of his divorce, and he was clearly upset and wanted to talk. Why he picked that very time to spill his guts to me about it, I'll never know, but spill his guts he did—at least until we heard a loud rap on the window of the squad. It was one of the deputies.

"Will you guys shut the fuck up in there! You turned on the car's speakers and now the whole neighborhood knows about Barsanti's woman problems!"

Fortunately, our childlike curiosity didn't compromise the operation. Still, mostly as a result of the McCrimmon guests' ability to discard evidence quickly, the raid itself turned out to be far short of a success. The police entered first, followed several minutes later by John and me. By the time we got into the house, there were dozens of people who had been detained, and contraband, in the form of small amounts of cocaine, cannabis, knives and evidence of illegal gambling, was scattered everywhere, making it impractical, if not impossible, to connect it to anyone.

All in all, 63 people, including McCrimmon, were arrested for various misdemeanors. They were driven in a school bus to the sheriff's office to be processed. But what started with a bang ended with a whimper. The charges against McCrimmon eventually were dismissed. Moreover, I don't believe the raid resulted in a single conviction against any of the others. Worse yet, McCrimmon filed a federal civil rights suit against Kane County, the Sheriff, the State's Attorney, John and me. There were a number of allegations in the suit, but one of the issues was John's and my conduct. We had made the mistake of participating in the search. It wasn't much—I recall going through a few drawers and feeling kind of odd about doing it. But it went beyond our role as legal advisors and affected the amount of immunity we would have in the suit. Pat Lord, who is my sister and was an Assistant State's Attorney for the Civil Division of the office, defended us. The way she put it, it was one of many times in my life she came to my defense. She did her usual outstanding job. Neither she, nor Herb Hill—McCrimmon's lawyer and a friend of mine—can remember what the lawsuit settled for.

****

Not every day at the state's attorney's office was as exciting as the McCrimmon raid, but I sure enjoyed my job and looked forward to going to work every morning. My intuition about the office proved accurate. Not only were the people with whom I worked outstanding, but the county's mixture of urban and rural areas made it a perfect place to learn how to try a criminal case. The major municipalities, Aurora and Elgin, were places that experienced big city, urban types of crime. While normally this wouldn't—and shouldn't—be a point of pride, as a criminal lawyer it allowed me to litigate serious criminal cases. Only nearby Cook County, which includes Chicago, could offer more in that regard. And since Kane had a smaller office and a fairly regular turnover rate, the dues-paying period that had to be endured before advancement to higher-level felonies was relatively short. It was a great time to be a prosecutor in Kane County.

I started out in the Traffic and Misdemeanor Division, where I prosecuted everything from speeding tickets and DUIs to assault, battery and sex abuse cases. Every day there were bench trials (where a judge determines the outcome), contested motions, plea negotiations and sentencing hearings. Later, I moved to Juvenile Court, where I was able to prosecute felonies charged against minors. I got to know lawyers and judges, and became familiar with the criminal justice system. It was basic training for a beginning trial lawyer.

I managed to advance to the felony division in a year. My first solo felony jury trial took place at 13 months. I was in the Priority Prosecution Unit, which handled more serious felonies, after just two years. By today's standards, that's remarkably fast—too fast, really. The gestation period for a fully developed prosecutor is, and should be, longer. Prosecutors wield a lot of power and need to learn how to use that power judiciously. Even seasoned veterans wrestle with issues concerning whether to charge an offense, what to charge, plea negotiations, whether to offer more generous pleas in return for testimony—otherwise known as "flipping"—from a co-defendant, and generally the best way to proceed with a case. Often I was prosecuting and trying felonies against lawyers with much more experience than I had.

I wish I could say that my meteoric rise was due to my precocious skills as a prosecutor and trial lawyer, but that wouldn't be accurate. A scandal in the office concerning the forging of names on a state-wide petition to limit taxes, along with collateral fallout that occurred afterward, led to a number of resignations. My superiors in the office could have replaced those assistants with more experienced prosecutors from other counties, but I had worked hard, and they were willing to take a chance on me. Fortunately, it was those very same supervisors who helped keep me from screwing up royally during those early years.

The petition-signing situation resulted in Gene Armentrout not seeking re-election. A new state's attorney, Bob Morrow, was elected two years after I started at the office, and he brought in a new First Assistant, Tom Sullivan. I'm friends with both Bob and Tom today, but back then, things got a little bumpy for me. They reluctantly promoted me to Chief of Priority Prosecutions—at the time, the third-highest position in the criminal division—when that spot opened up. I didn't realize it then, but their reluctance was well-founded. I was too inexperienced for such a job. As a result, while I did get to litigate higher-level felonies, my being a "chief" was a title without any authority. I had very little in the way of decision-making responsibilities.

Over my years as an ASA, I felt like I grew as a prosecutor, and I'm not just talking about litigation skills. I like to think that I learned the difference between criminals and people who just screwed up. When I had the authority to do so, I tried to treat them differently. My new bosses felt pretty much that way, too, but I admit to probably taking it to a different level. In the defense bar, I became known as a bit of a soft touch, meaning I supported giving more generous plea offers. That didn't help my situation with Bob and Tom. We didn't always agree on other matters, as well, and all of this led to some deterioration in our relationship. Looking back, I think I have to shoulder most of the blame for that. I could be pretty stubborn. So after four years as an assistant, I resigned my position to join the civil law firm of Clancy, McGuirk and Hulce.

Becoming a Prosecutor—Sidebar

When I resigned my position as an Assistant State's Attorney at the end of December 1982, I had a feeling I might return someday as the elected Kane County State's Attorney. There were a couple of reasons for this. First, I liked being a prosecutor and thought I could do a good job. It was a natural future step for me. And second, I have to admit I was pretty serious about a career in politics, and I thought being the state's attorney would be a good place to start.

Getting elected to such an important office required laying some groundwork, which I was happy to do. That included supplementing my criminal experience by practicing civil law at Clancy, McGuirk and Hulce, a highly regarded firm in St. Charles. That also meant continuing to stay active in Republican politics, which I had actually begun doing a few years earlier. So by the time I started making noise about running in mid-1987—the Illinois primary election was in March 1988—I felt I was ready for both the job and the election process to get the job. But with the incumbent state's attorney not seeking reelection, there were some other very good lawyers, also politically active, considering a run at what would be an open office.

Winning would be difficult.

Earlier in my career, when I was working in the trenches for the Republican Party, I became friends with Terry DesCoteaux. Terry was a very self-effacing but high-powered Republican political advisor, campaign manager and fundraiser who, despite her esteemed status, was not afraid to toil with us minions. Banking on an offer to help me if I ever decided to run for state's attorney, I asked for her help.

She agreed to sign on as an advisor, but I had other plans for her. I kept redefining her job until, before she knew it, she was my campaign manager. She never asked for a dime from me—not that I could have afforded to pay her if she had. But once Terry was on board, everything changed. All of my potential primary opponents, except one, decided not to run. She scared them off.

I won the Republican primary with 60% of the vote and had no Democratic opponent. Without deprecating the efforts of others who helped me win that race, including my own hard work, I owe that victory to my friend Terry.

****

One of the fringe benefits to the job as a prosecutor was exposure to colorful and eccentric people, including defendants, witnesses, lawyers and judges. In my second stint as a prosecutor, when I was the elected State's Attorney, that also included politicians and political workers. There was no shortage of interesting people.

My very first felony case, for example, involved a young man who attempted to burglarize a small sporting goods store in Aurora. He managed to enter the building and crawl on top of the drop ceiling over the store. When the ceiling gave way, he had the misfortune of falling onto a mannequin that didn't have the body form attached to it, thereby impaling himself on the standing rod. The alarm went off and the police arrived to find the burglar with the mannequin rod completely through his torso—he had been shish-ka-bobbed. He was moaning, and waving his arms and legs like an insect on a pin, begging the police to help him. Miraculously, he survived the incident without severely damaging any major organs. On the day he pled guilty, he could barely walk to the front of the courtroom. He got probation.

****

When I was in Traffic and Misdemeanor Court, my co-worker, J. Brick Van Der Snick—yes, that's his real name—prosecuted a guy who had set up his windshield wiper fluid apparatus to commit the crime of Illegal Transportation of Alcohol. While the usual way this crime is committed is to simply have an open container of liquor in your car, this character was far more creative. He filled his car's windshield wiper fluid container with vodka, then jerry-rigged the sprayer line to come inside the driver's compartment. Whenever he wanted a hit of vodka, he just put the tube in his mouth and pressed the wiper spray button.

****

In a murder trial during my first go-round as a prosecutor, I asked the janitor of an apartment complex, where the victim also worked, to do an in-court identification of the defendant. The defendant was employed by the company that provided washer/dryer facilities and services in the apartment complex. The janitor had not seen the defendant commit the murder, but he was asked to identify the defendant as the person who collected the coins out of the machines. We planned on connecting the defendant to the murder with other evidence.

Instead of identifying the defendant, he pointed to Van Larson, a lawyer who was in the courtroom to watch the trial. The crowded courtroom erupted with laughter. It was an embarrassing moment for the witness, me and even Van. Shortly after his testimony, and during a break in the trial, I walked outside to see the janitor by the railing on the third floor of the courthouse.

He was very upset at his mistake, thinking he had blown the case for us. In fact, he had not. We lost the case via a directed verdict (a concept I'll explain in more detail later, but essentially it involves the trial judge taking the case out of the hands of the jury and finding the defendant not guilty after the State has rested), but for a variety of other reasons. Nevertheless, the janitor was kicking his leg over the railing as if he were about to jump.

I don't think he was serious, but I did have to calm him down and satisfy myself that he wouldn't do anything rash.

****

Back in November 1980, one of the most anticipated TV shows in all of television history was the *Who Shot J.R.?* episode of the prime time soap opera *Dallas*. The prior season's cliffhanger finale had J.R. getting shot, but his assailant was unknown. The first episode of the new season would answer that question, and it seemed that everyone would be watching, so John Barsanti decided to have a *Who Shot J.R.?* party at his house. On the night of the party and the show, his house was crowded with prosecutors, defense attorneys, support staff, spouses and significant others.

When the episode aired, everyone crammed into his family room to watch. Before the show started, John hatched a plan he needed help with, so he conspired with another prosecutor, Dennis Schumacher, and me, to execute it. It worked beautifully. Just seconds before J.R.'s shooter was revealed, John, who was right outside the family room, signaled Dennis, who was in the hall, who in turn signaled me.

I was by the circuit breaker. Since I wasn't sure which switch would turn off the power to the family room, I just killed the power to the entire house. The place went black as pitch. After a few moments of dead silence, I could hear a lot of "What the hell?" and "What's going on?"

and "Where's John?" When I figured enough time had passed, I restored power to the house. It turns out, what John, Dennis and I had thought was cute, pissed off everyone else.

****

Another practical joke I took part in had slightly more serious consequences, and if one of the unintended victims hadn't been a friend, I would have been in for some well-deserved public embarrassment. It was the summer of 1988. I had already won the Republican primary for Kane County State's Attorney. The Democrats declined to nominate anyone, so I had clear sailing for the November election. That gave me time to work on other candidates' elections, including that of the Republican nominee for Kane County Coroner. She was running against the kind of candidate Kane County Republicans weren't quite used to—a nearly unbeatable Democratic incumbent.

I was in an office conference room with a group of people culling Republicans from voting lists for the purpose of sending out mailings and asking for money. In Illinois primaries, each voter has to declare which party ballot he or she wants to pull, and records are kept of those choices. A computer literally puts an "R" or a "D" next to each name and the year of the primary. Margie Taylor, an artist who created much of my campaign literature, was among those workers. Margie and I had become good friends as a result of her work on my campaign. I enjoyed her sense of humor, and we often commiserated over our increasing discomfort regarding the more-conservative politics of the Republican Party. She came across the primary voting record of Emil Punter, a talented photographer who did a lot of political work, including for me during my run.

"How has he voted?" I asked.

"He's been a good Republican—he's got all R's," Margie responded.

Then I got a harebrained idea. "Margie, can you doctor that up so that it looks like he's been pulling Democratic ballots for the primaries?"

"Let me see what I can do."

So Margie, cutting and pasting the old-fashioned way, created an authentic-looking document that made it look like Emil had nothing but D's after his name for as far back as there were records. In less than half an hour, Margie turned Emil into a Democrat!

"We should give this to him and tell him how disappointed everyone was when we discovered the party affiliation of the photographer so many of us used," I chuckled.

"I'm stopping by his house tomorrow," Margie said. "I'll show this to him and I'll let you know his reaction."

I didn't think about our little joke again until the next night when I came home from work. My wife, Amy, informed me that Margie had called in a panic, and that we were in some hot water. So I called Margie.

"Gary, you're about to get a call from Lorraine Sava, and she's really upset with us," Margie warned. Lorraine was the County Clerk, and as such, she was in charge of elections for Kane County. She and her husband, Walt, had been friends of mine in Republican politics for years. "I dropped by Emil's place today to show him his doctored-up voting printout and he wasn't in, so I left it in his door, along with a note saying how disappointed we all were—especially Terry DesCoteaux. So he went to Lorraine's office to complain. Things got out of control after that."

I told Margie this was my fault, and that I would handle it. She refused to let me take all the blame, but since it was my idea, I knew what I had to do—but I didn't look forward to it. I called Lorraine.

"For the love of God, Gary, what were you thinking?! You, for all intents and purposes, are the state's attorney-elect, and you pull a stunt like this! Do you know the chaos you caused?"

"No, other than Margie telling me that …"

"Well, Emil was in here complaining that we had inaccurate voting records. He showed me the voting printout that Margie had dropped off—all D's. Then I checked our records, which showed all R's by his name. We couldn't figure out what happened. But we were worried that if his records were messed up, there were other voting records that might have problems. We all but shut down the election office and contacted our computer people in Chicago. They came with some hardware and spent the better part of a day with us. By the time Margie and Emil talked and cleared this up, we spent a lot of time and money trying to fix a problem that didn't exist."

"Jesus, Lorraine, I'm so sorry. I didn't have any idea this would get so out of hand. Let me know what your office is out, and I'll reimburse you. I don't know what else I can do." I continued to apologize profusely.

"I forgive you, Gary, but I just can't believe you did this. It's a good thing I'm your friend."

Other than one more conversation I had with Margie, the subject was never brought up again.

****

I was elected Kane County State's Attorney and served just one term—from December 1988 to December 1992. From the beginning of my professional life, I had wanted to be the state's attorney, and to have a political career beyond that. But fairly early in my term, I had a change of heart. I kept it to myself, just in case I happened to change my mind again, but as my four years were drawing to a close, I announced that I wasn't going to seek reelection.

I've never been able to give an adequate explanation as to why I chose not to run again, not even to Amy, so I don't expect to succeed here. There were several factors, but two topped the list. Most importantly, I came to conclude that I wanted to continue my career as a trial lawyer. Being the elected state's attorney was no way to do that. During my term, I completed seventeen felony trials, almost all of them juries. While I believe that helped me stay in touch with the many issues confronting prosecutors working in my office, for an office the size of the one I was in charge of—one which needed a full-time administrator—that was way too many. That I selfishly indulged my desire to do so many trials as the state's attorney was probably a sign telling me to get back into private practice and be a litigator. Furthermore, if I served only one term, I would return to private practice just days before my 40th birthday—a perfect time, I thought, to change gears.

I also knew that if I were to continue my career as a politician, I would have difficulties with the Republican Party. People who know me today are surprised to learn I held office in various Republican organizations. But as I got older, the party got more conservative, and I got to be pretty liberal. Still, to this day, with only one exception that I will explain later, you will see only "R's" after my name on the election rolls. I live in the heavily Republican far western suburbs of Chicago.[2] I pull Republican ballots in primaries so I can support high-quality Republican candidates in local elections, some of whom happen to be friends of mine. I won't name names, but some of them also occasionally cringe at Republican politics.

I was happy with the job I did as state's attorney. I accomplished a number of goals, the most important of which was to foster the most ethical and effective prosecutor's office I could. I'm confident I could have won reelection, maybe even without opposition. But that isn't to say that everyone was happy with the way I had done my job.

I have a theory that if a state's attorney in Illinois is doing his job well, he will have antagonized just about every major voting group in his constituency at one point or another, making reelection a challenge. After one term, I was well on my way down that road. A good example of that is that a substantial number of Aurora police officers were upset because my office had prosecuted two of their own for excessive use of force.

This turned out to be a problem for John Barsanti—who was my First Assistant and who handled those prosecutions from beginning to end—when he ran to succeed me. John was the best prosecutor I ever knew, and I endorsed him, but the Aurora police, and however many other police officers or citizens they could convince, refused to support him. He lost the Republican primary election by 102 votes—a razor-thin margin for a large suburban county—so it's safe to say that those prosecutions cost him the election.

Thankfully, 12 years later, the voters of Kane County elected John as their state's attorney.

****

The one primary election in which I did pull a Democratic ballot was one of the very earliest of the primaries for which I was eligible to vote. My motives were, from a Republican perspective, actually pure—I wanted the weaker Democratic gubernatorial candidate to win so he would be a pushover for the Republican. I should have told my mother.

Mom was an election judge at my polling place in Villa Park, and although a moderate Republican, a strong Republican nonetheless. She happened to be the person to whom you announced which ballot you preferred. And after I arrived, in the period of about 30 seconds, she probably violated nearly a dozen state and federal election laws.

"Hi, Mom. I'll take a Democratic ballot." I didn't expect there would be a problem.

"But you're a Republican."

"Yeah, Mom. Please, I'd like a Democratic ballot."

"I'm not giving you a Democratic ballot. You're a Republican." She was absolutely serious.

"Mom!"

"No."

By now I'm looking around, knowing vaguely she shouldn't be pushing a specific ballot on me, and hoping the other election judges or voters weren't paying attention. Plus, my mother was embarrassing me.

"C'mon, Mom, you can't do that. Please! I'll explain later." I was talking softly, barely moving my lips.

I finally got my ballot. More importantly, my mother wasn't charged with any crimes.

****

I nearly ended my career as the Kane County State's Attorney with an incident even more embarrassing than the doctored-up Emil Punter voting records fiasco that started it. In the winter of 1992, Mary Robinson, the lawyer who, you will learn later, represented me on the appeal of my DuPage County contempt holding, was having a party at her Elgin law office to celebrate her appointment as the head of the Attorney Registration and Disciplinary Commission. In Illinois, the ARDC is the arm of the Illinois Supreme Court that disciplines lawyers for various forms of misconduct. At her party, I had two small Styrofoam cups of beer—the equivalent of little more than one twelve ounce beer. As I was driving home, another motorist made a left-hand-turn in front of me at an intersection in South Elgin where we both had a green light. I slammed on my brakes, but couldn't stop in time. We collided. After the other driver and I determined nobody was hurt and we were both insured, I went to the gas station at the corner to tell them to call the police, which they had already done.

So there I was, the state's attorney, waiting for the police to arrive to investigate an accident I was in, and I had beer on my breath. It didn't matter that the accident was not my fault. And it almost didn't matter that I was fine to drive. If the police smelled the odor, they would have asked questions and requested that I do tests—not something you want your state's attorney doing. What to do?

As the police arrived, I bought a Coke at the gas station to help cover the odor of alcohol. That turned out to be a mistake. While I was waiting outside, I saw South Elgin Police Sergeant Larry Jones, a friend I had known for years. He would later become Chief of Police and Village Manager. He poked his head out the window of his squad, and called to me.

"Gary, hop inside my squad and wait this out in here."

"That's okay, Larry, I'll just stay out here." I didn't need the close quarters of a police squad car to enhance the odor of alcohol on my breath.

"Are you crazy? It's freezing out there! Get in here. Stay warm."

I didn't feel I had too much of a choice to again decline his invitation without looking strange. It was freezing out. So I got into his squad on the passenger side front seat. I hadn't seen Larry in quite a while, so he was inquisitive not only about the accident, but also about how I was generally. It was about then the Coke started making me belch, which only made my predicament worse. I was worried that he thought I was acting weird when I constantly looked away, toward the passenger window, and answered his questions in as few words as possible.

Fortunately, neither Larry, nor anyone else, said a thing. At first I wasn't sure if it was Larry just giving me a pass. But I saw him years later, when he was the Village Manager of South Elgin, and told him the entire story. He said he didn't suspect a thing, or even think that I had acted all that strangely.

****

My friend and former law school housemate, Bill Drury, is a superior civil litigator and trial attorney in Phoenix, Arizona. He has noted that, with the advent of mediation and arbitration, among other things, young civil lawyers aren't getting the necessary experience from or becoming skilled in actual trial work. He's right, and while criminal practitioners are still doing a lot of trials (though as I write this, those numbers in my legal neighborhood are down, too), most of those are being done by prosecutors and public defenders, at least on the state level. Hiring good, or potentially good, trial lawyers is a bit of an art form.

So just what is it that makes for a good trial lawyer? What are the special qualities a lawyer should possess that will make him or her effective in a courtroom? As the state's attorney, I always insisted on, at some point in the interview process, meeting prospective prosecutors. And while I was looking for all the things you would expect when hiring a lawyer—brains, desire, work ethic, career goals, ability to work well with others—I would always try to find that extra, undefinable character trait I thought was necessary to be good in court.

Frank Wesolowski, the DuPage County Public Defender who would defend Alex Hernandez at his first trial, ran into trouble when the press reported that he had asked prospective P.D.s whether or not they were Republican. Since DuPage County was heavily Republican, and the DuPage circuit court judges who controlled Frank's job were Republican as well, the story raised suspicions. I asked Frank about this, and in the context of his searching for good trial lawyers for his office, his answer made sense. He told me that the reports saying he asked if potential employees were Republican were not true. He would, he said, ask if they were politically involved—he didn't care which way—just whether they were involved. He wanted people who cared, who were passionate enough to declare a side and advocate for it. If the applicant were a Democrat, that was fine by him. But he wanted fighters.

While I understand Frank's rationale, asking about political activity is a little dangerous, and I wouldn't recommend it. But he had the right idea. I think Mike Metnick, who would also represent Alex later on down the road, had the best philosophy, and it's one which I've adopted. Mike was an outstanding trial lawyer from Springfield, Illinois, and he headed up a top-flight criminal defense law firm. He would ask young lawyers if they ever competed in something. It could be sports, but it didn't have to be. It could be music, politics, chess—anything. He wanted people with a competitive spirit, who knew how to fight, win, lose, not give up—all that good stuff that would serve a lawyer well in court.

Later, when the issue was raised in the press as to whether I, as Kane County State's Attorney and a Republican, displayed any political party favoritism in the employment of assistant state's attorneys, I raised a few eyebrows with my response. "I'd hire a Communist if he or she could prosecute a case," I said. And I meant it, too.

Chapter 6
Becoming a Defense Lawyer

My fears concerning my representation of Steve persisted, but before they could get a good grip on me, a lot of wheels had already been set in motion. The Buckleys had scrounged up some money for a relatively small, all things considered, retainer—with the rest of the legal fees not to be paid until years later when Steve's parents had both died and their house sold. The partners at Clancy, McGuirk and Hulce seemed excited that the firm was getting involved. Cliff, unaware of my skittishness, was eager to get started. I had already informed a number of people that it looked like Cliff and I would be representing Steve. And, most importantly, Steve was counting on us to represent him. In the end, I was more afraid of backing out of the case than of going ahead.

On July 25, 1984, Cliff and I entered our appearances on behalf of Steve Buckley. We obtained the discovery—police reports, witness statements, lab test results, etc.—from Steve's old lawyer, Assistant Public Defender Ed Ward, and got to work. We also became acquainted with the lawyers for Steve's co-defendants. Assistant P.D. Tom Laz was representing Rolando Cruz, while the Public Defender himself, Frank Wesolowski, was representing Alex Hernandez.

Several things immediately became obvious. For starters, there were rumblings—not public, but within the legal community—that Buckley, Hernandez and Cruz were innocent. We had heard, and it was confirmed as we went through the discovery, that the evidence against them was both tenuous and suspect. These rumblings would become louder and more specific as the case developed.

We also noticed the State was pushing hard to have the case tried quickly. State's Attorney Michael Fitzsimmons had lost his primary election to Jim Ryan and had therefore become a lame duck. The chief of his Criminal Division and the driving force behind the prosecution up to that point, Tom Knight, would be leaving the office when Fitzsimmons's term ended in early December. The trial had originally been scheduled for September 10, 1984. There was no way Cliff and I could be ready in such a short period of time. We requested, and received, a continuance of the trial to January 7, 1985.

Since the trial would not get started before the change in administrations, the Nicaricos, who had developed a strong attachment to Knight, became concerned that Knight would not be prosecuting the case. As a result, some DuPage County residents, mostly from the Naperville area, circulated petitions requesting that Ryan keep Knight on for that sole purpose. I don't know how many signatures they got, but the number was impressive, to say the least. I had heard rumors that Ryan and Knight had not gotten along in the past, so I held out hope that Ryan would weather the pressure and let Knight go. Not only would that be beneficial in that a prosecutor less familiar with the case would take over, but I had the naïve hope that a fresh perspective might take the case in a different direction. My hopes were dashed when Ryan agreed to keep Knight on to try the case.

Unfortunately, that didn't put an end to the pressure to get the case tried in a hurry. I got the sense that the judge, Edward Kowal, and the State wanted to get these young men tried, convicted and sentenced to death as soon as practicable. That was borne out by the fact that the trial date was just 10 months after the indictments were returned. Considering this was a high-profile, three-defendant, death-penalty case—and the State and police took more than a year to obtain an indictment—that's lightning fast.

We also began to internalize something we already knew—the negative publicity surrounding the case was overwhelming. Even if you didn't read the newspaper articles or listen to the television news reports, just looking at the photos of Jeanine and the three defendants, which seemed to be used in every story, would cause a bias. Jeanine's picture accurately portrayed the 10-year-old, dimpled, cute little girl that she had been. Right next to her would be the Buckley, Hernandez and Cruz booking photos, otherwise known as mug shots. Hernandez's and Cruz's photos confirmed their ethnicity. And Steve, who on his best day would never be asked to be on the cover of *GQ* magazine, was sick when he was arrested and looked absolutely horrible.

Each story emphasized geography and implied demography, with Jeanine coming from the upper-middle-class, almost exclusively white, DuPage County suburb of Naperville, and the defendants coming from the racially mixed and lower-middle-class east side of Aurora in Kane County. Of course, the brutality of the crime, along with the fact that she was taken from her home—every family's worst nightmare—was regularly reinforced. A motion for a change of venue, requesting that the trial be held in another part of Illinois, would be near the top of our "must do" list.

Another motion that needed to be filed was to sever Steve's case from that of his co-defendants. The concept of judicial economy will allow for co-defendants to be tried together as long two conditions exist. First, there can be no conflicting defenses. An example of this would be if Co-defendant A's defense is that he did not commit the crime, but that Co-defendant B did. Second, with some exceptions, there can be no pretrial admissions made by one co-defendant that implicate another co-defendant, with the co-defendant making the admissions declining to testify at trial.

In our case, the defense for all three defendants was that each had absolutely nothing to do with the crime. But the police reports indicated that both Hernandez and Cruz had made, to one degree or another, incriminating statements. The veracity, authenticity, and in some instances the very existence of these statements would be litigated, and eventually repudiated. For the time being, though, they had to be dealt with procedurally. Even though some of the statements referred to Steve in an incriminating fashion, we were confident that our co-defendants' defenses—that they had nothing to do with what had occurred to Jeanine—pretty much eliminated the possibility of either of them pointing the finger at Steve. However, since the law provided that admissions made by a defendant in a joint trial are admissible only against the defendant making those admissions, and not against any of his co-defendants, this made for a strong case for a severance. More on this later.

Lastly, when Jeanine was kidnapped, the front door of the Nicarico home had been kicked in, leaving a shoeprint. That shoeprint was the centerpiece of the case against Steve. In the discovery, the State had provided reports from a couple of expert witnesses who gave qualified opinions stating that a shoe that belonged to Steve "could have" made or was "similar to" the print on the door. They needed more, and they knew it. They finally found a witness who was willing to opine that Steve's shoe, to the exclusion of all other shoes in the world, made the print on the door.

I was about to learn more about shoeprints than I ever thought possible.

****

People have asked me if it was easy becoming a defense lawyer after spending years as a prosecutor. After all, both sides work with the same laws and rules of evidence, and they both employ the same basic set of trial skills.

Flip side of the same coin, right? That's mostly true, but not totally. While my experience and skills as a prosecutor were transferrable to the defense side, there were differences in attitude, mindset and strategy that took time to learn and get used to.

For the defense lawyer, major decisions need to be made that prosecutors do not have to make. For example, should the defendant testify, or even put on a case? Should the case be tried to a jury, or just the judge? Are there any pretrial motions to suppress physical evidence or statements, due to the police acting unconstitutionally, that need to be made? Since the prosecution can't appeal acquittals, and defendants often appeal convictions, the defense lawyer has to make sure that he or she makes a good record for the potential appeal. It has been said that defense lawyers sometimes try their cases more to the appellate court than to the trial court.

Finally, there are two specific and major skill differences between the two sets of lawyers. Since prosecutors spend most of their time building cases at trial, they become adept at presenting evidence and direct examination of witnesses. Defense lawyers generally spend more time trying to locate weaknesses in those cases, which requires them to become more skilled at cross-examination. Of course, exceptions abound, but it's valid as a general rule.

I knew I had some work to do to fine-tune the attitude and skills I needed to transform myself into a halfway decent defense lawyer. And I didn't have much time to do it. So, as it turned out, there was one good thing that came about as a result of the State seeking the death penalty against Steve. I needed help understanding the law and strategies of defending a capital case, and I asked around for advice. Kane County had experienced a fair number of homicide cases for a suburban county, but there hadn't been much in the way of capital litigation there since the U.S. Supreme Court had refined—after a several-year hiatus on executions—the constitutional requirements for imposition of the death penalty.[3] There were no Kane County lawyers I could turn to.

Someone suggested that I talk to Robert E. Lee of the Cook County Public Defender's Homicide Task Force. How could I pass on a name like that? So I made an appointment and drove to Chicago to meet him. Thus began my formal education as a criminal defense lawyer.

****

Bob Lee had the metabolism of a hummingbird. He paced back and forth, smoking cigarettes and drinking coffee, in an office that was only slightly larger than a walk-in closet and which was filled with boxes and files. He was eager to hear more about the case he had already read about. As I laid out the facts to him, he suggested strategies and ideas as to how to proceed.

"In capital cases," he explained, "most of the time you have to decide whether your goal is to win at the guilt-innocence stage, or if you're just trying to save your client's life at the sentencing stage. You have to be prepared for both, but in determining strategy, the emphasis will be on one over the other."

"We're convinced that he's innocent, so that's the approach we want to take," I responded.

"Good. Now all of your decisions, especially whether to take a bench or jury trial, and if a jury, who you accept as jurors, will be made with that goal in mind."

We went on to discuss ways in which the Illinois death penalty laws of that time, along with certain U.S. Supreme Court rulings, compli- cated the process. For starters, death penalty cases had two stages. At either stage the defendant could choose whether to have a jury or a judge make the required findings. The guilt-innocence stage came first. If the defendant was found guilty of murder, next came the sentencing stage, which itself was divided into two parts. The first part of the sentencing stage was to determine whether the defendant was statutorily eligible for the death penalty. In Illinois, examples of statutory eligibility included murdering more than one person, under certain circumstances murder during the course of another felony, murdering a police officer or fire- fighter in the line of duty, contract killings for money, to name a few. In our case, DuPage County was seeking the ultimate punishment based on the part of the statutory eligibility section that allowed for the imposition of the death penalty if the murder victim was under 12 years old and the victim's death resulted from "exceptionally brutal or heinous behavior indicative of wanton cruelty."[4]

Both the defendant's guilt and his statutory eligibility for the death penalty had to be proven beyond a reasonable doubt and had to be, if de- cided by a jury, unanimous verdicts. If the defendant was found guilty of murder, but not eligible for death, his life would be spared and he would receive a prison sentence. If he was found eligible for death beyond a reasonable doubt, the sentencing process continued. The second and last part of the sentencing stage dealt with aggravation and mitigation—all the good and bad things about the defendant, his life, and the case itself. If a unanimous jury or the judge, depending on what option the defendant chose, found that there were "no mitigating factors sufficient to preclude the imposition of the death sentence," then the death sentence would be imposed. However, if the judge, or as few as one juror if a jury was ruling, found otherwise, then the death penalty would be averted.[5]

Another complicating factor arose from the case of *Witherspoon v. Illinois*.[6] There, the U.S. Supreme Court held that the State had a right to challenge the eligibility of prospective jurors by inquiring as to their personal feelings about the death penalty. Initially, the prospective juror would be asked if he or she agreed with the death penalty as a potential punishment. If that juror disagreed with capital punishment based on general, moral or religious grounds, further inquiry was allowed. If it was then determined that the prospective juror's attitude toward the death penalty would either cause him or her to automatically, without regard for the circumstances or the law, vote against the death penalty, or fail to be impartial at the guilt-innocence stage, that potential juror would be excused by the court. The prosecutors would not have to use one of their valuable peremptory challenges—those discretionary and limited-in-number challenges that each party can use to eliminate a juror for almost any reason, with only a few exceptions. The process was called *Witherspooning* or "death qualifying" the jury.

"Think about it," Bob Lee said. "Eliminating jurors with strong anti-death-penalty attitudes gets rid of jurors who usually have open minds about criminal justice and who might be more favorable to the defense. Even if the potential jurors' attitudes aren't strong enough to get them disqualified by the judge, the prosecutor will know that they are at least vaguely against the death penalty, and then use peremptory challenges to excuse them. You're going to want to try to avoid the *Witherspooning* process."

"How do I do that?"

"What you need to do is take a jury trial for guilt-innocence, then waive your right to a jury at the penalty phase and have the judge decide that. If you make that waiver *before the trial*, then the judge knows ahead of time that the jury won't be deciding on life or death. Bingo!! No need to death-qualify the jury."

Robert E. Lee was on a roll and even more animated than before, and I wasn't going to leave while he was. I went on to tell Bob that the initial research that I had done on the State's "star" shoeprint expert showed that her opinions, in this case and others, and her approach to shoeprint comparisons, were based on garbage science that had been disputed in the forensic community.

"You'll need smart jurors, maybe even jurors with some science in their backgrounds. People who will take a critical look at her methods,"

Bob suggested. This opinion would later be seconded by forensic scientists I spoke to.

All in all, I spent the better part of an afternoon soaking up what knowledge and experience I could from this veteran defense lawyer. In later years, when the death penalty in Illinois came under fire for its high number of wrongful convictions, one of the attempts to solve the problem was through fairly extensive mandatory continuing death penalty legal education. That afternoon, thanks to the generosity of Robert E. Lee, I got that education. Feeling a lot more confident, I thanked Bob and left. He invited me to call if I had any questions or if I just wanted to talk.

I didn't see Bob Lee again until about 20 years later, when I ran into him at one of those death penalty seminars. I effusively thanked him again, in front of a number of his colleagues, for his help. I think I embarrassed him. Sadly, Bob Lee died suddenly in May of 2012. I wish I would have known—I would have wanted to pay my respects.

Speaking of respect, there's one more thing.

Here I am, with the nerve to write a book about my experiences, particularly with the Nicarico case. The folks with the Cook County Public Defender's Homicide Task Force litigate cases like that all the time, just without the fanfare, and for what many private attorneys might consider chump change. I don't know how they do it. They are truly the elite of criminal defense lawyers.

****

It felt good to be practicing criminal law again, and I was really getting into the idea of being a counsel for the accused. Tom Laz, Rolando Cruz's lawyer, loaned me some tapes on the art of cross-examination, which I soaked up. I read transcripts of prior cross-examinations of the State's controversial shoeprint expert, and learned what I could from them.

I picked up some criminal defense practice tips in books published by veteran defense lawyers. For inspiration, I read *Gunning for Justice*, a book Cliff loaned me, written by famed criminal defense lawyer Gerry Spence. I applied for, and got, the job of conflict defense counsel for Kane County—a job that would start just before the Nicarico trial would begin. As conflict counsel, I would be appointed by Kane County judges to represent indigent criminal defendants in cases where the Public Defender had a conflict of interest—usually in multiple-defendant situations.

Despite all of this, in the end, I would be learning the criminal defense side of lawyering on the job—more accurately, on the case—Steve's case. And there would be times when that would be all too apparent.

Becoming a Defense Lawyer—Sidebar

Though what I'm about to say may be an over-generalization riddled with exceptions, I'm comfortable enough to make the assertions—so here goes. There are basically two paths to becoming a criminal defense lawyer, at least on the state court level, with each one imparting strengths and weaknesses that the other doesn't have.

One route is to become a defense lawyer, either in private practice or at a public defender's office, from the beginning. Though these lawyers never get to be directly involved in the prosecution of a case, and they don't have much experience working with police, from the start they are immersed in the education and mindset of defense work. They "grow up" learning defense skills, particularly cross-examination, dealing with clients, and learning what it takes to put on a defense. Most importantly, they become immediately accustomed to the concept of vigorously defending, within the bounds of ethics, defendants they sometimes believe or know to be guilty. And as an interesting corollary to that, they are also more accustomed to answering the oft-asked questions "How can you defend a person you know has committed the crime?" and "How can you defend someone like that?"

The other path is to start off in law enforcement, usually as a prosecutor, like I did, or occasionally as a police officer, as my law partner, David Camic, did. These defense lawyers have worked directly with police and victims. They've prepared search warrants and advised police concerning their investigations. As prosecutors, they were required to work under a slightly different set of ethical and discovery rules (see the Preface to this book) that are designed with the goal of preventing erroneous convictions. As I noted earlier, they spent their prosecuting years emphasizing a slightly different set of skills than lifelong defense lawyers. Lastly, prosecutors had to become comfortable exercising power that, especially in their early years, might be too much for some of the younger ones to handle appropriately.

While you could argue that being a former prosecutor gives that type of defense counsel the advantage of being able to better know what the other side is thinking, that's a skill that also can be learned by the defense lifer through his or her experience. Besides, trying to predict what the opposing counsel is thinking is more a function of the individual lawyer and the particulars of the case than anything else.

As a side note, an interesting phenomenon sometimes occurs when either a longtime prosecutor or longtime criminal defense lawyer becomes a judge. You might automatically think that the former prosecutor would be more State-oriented and trusting of the police, and vice versa for the defense lawyer. In my experience, that's not necessarily true. A pretty decent percentage of judges who come from one or the other of those backgrounds tacks the other way when they get to the bench. I'm not sure why. It might be a function of becoming jaded. But defense lawyers who are thinking of substituting a given judge out of a case—in Illinois a defendant can automatically substitute one or two judges off a case, depending on the severity of the crime—would do well to look beyond whether the judge was formerly a prosecutor or defense lawyer before making any decisions about changing judges.

Parenthetically, a couple of the best criminal judges I've practiced in front of never spent a day in a criminal courtroom as a lawyer.

As you might guess, neither pathway to becoming a quality defense lawyer is superior to the other. They're just different. And over time, as the defense lawyer ages and gains experience, differences that may have been apparent at the start of this trajectory seem to evaporate.

As to which side is more rewarding, the simple answer is "I just can't say." As a prosecutor, I enjoyed working for a cause larger than me—one that tried to dispense justice fairly to both defendant and victim. Sounds corny, I know, but it was the way I felt. Similarly, the cause I currently work for on the defense side is also bigger than me. Advocating for clients and protecting their rights, irrespective of whether they are factually guilty, partially guilty or innocent, is immensely rewarding. Equally as corny, I suppose, but that's the way I feel.

****

Of all the hot-button issues in the field of criminal justice, the death penalty, abolished in Illinois in 2011, may be the hottest. I haven't always been for its abolition nationally, but I am now, and I have been for a number of years. Maybe it was my experience in the Nicarico case that turned me around—I don't know for sure—but it was about that time.

That also means I was personally against the death penalty when I was the elected Kane County State's Attorney and my office sought the death penalty in two cases during my four-year term. I even prosecuted one of those cases personally. So I was grateful at the time, as I am now, that we failed to get the death penalty in both of those cases. It's just not a sentence that I believe to be appropriate. If that exposes me to allegations of hypocrisy, well, I don't totally disagree. I rationalized it some—arguing to myself that I was elected to be a prosecutor and that was one of the tools given to me. I also knew, at the time, most people in my county were in favor of capital punishment, so I added that to the mix. Besides, I thought, who better to have control over Kane County's death penalty decisions than me—someone reluctant to use it. If I came out totally against the death penalty when I ran for the job, I tried to justify to myself, I might have lost to someone who would have used it indiscriminately. Pretty good arguments all, but they don't totally exonerate me.

I agree with all the ethical, religious and constitutional (dealing with the Due Process and Equal Protection clauses, as well as the 8th Amendment's ban on cruel and unusual punishment) arguments against the death penalty. I also understand the arguments of proponents, which rely heavily on the now-debunked proposition that capital punishment acts as a deterrent. It also includes their less popular pitch that capital punishment allows society to have its "pound of flesh." I suppose I get that, too. But it's difficult for the pro-capital punishment crowd to get around the penalty's racial bias, arbitrariness of usage, lack of deterrent effect, cost and other similar arguments. That's where my respect for the other side's position begins to slip away.

In the end, though, the anti-death penalty argument that trumps them all—the one that I think should terrify everyone and require us to call for an end to capital punishment—is wrongful convictions. Our justice system is made up of human beings and human beings are prone to mistakes. That's especially true in murder cases, where the public is often angry and the pressure for justice in the form of vengeance is high. As you will see in the coming chapters, the Nicarico case is a textbook example of that, as well as the refusal to admit past mistakes and wrongdoings.

When I get into a debate with capital punishment proponents, I like to push them into a discomfort zone. I start by explaining there are roughly 2,700 prisoners on death row in the United States (according to the Death Penalty Information Center,[7] there were 2,743 as of April 1, 2018). Then I ask them what they think the percentage of wrongful convictions is in capital murder cases. At this point, I get all kinds of answers, but they generally range from as low as 1 percent to as high as 10 percent. My own best guess, and I admit it's a guess, is between 3 and 5 percent, and I offer that opinion to them. Then we do the math together to estimate the number, by my estimate and theirs, of totally innocent people on death row. That means we're talking about roughly between 27 and 270 people.

After that, I offer a giant concession. "Let's say, for the sake of this little debate, it's only one person—just one innocent person. All the others are guilty." By the way, not a single person I've ever done this with thinks that there isn't at least one innocent person on death row. Then I take the hypothetical further by saying, "Tomorrow we end all appeals. We line up all 2,700 prisoners on death row—all 2,699 guilty ones, along with the one who is innocent—and we kill all of them." Then I ask the question: "Are you comfortable with that? But before you answer, please keep in mind that, if we don't carry out the executions, we're not talking about releasing the 2,700. Their sentences would be reduced to what their punishments would be without the death penalty, which in all cases would be very lengthy prison terms or life in prison."

The responses I get to this hypothetical are pretty mixed. Although nobody likes the idea of an innocent person being executed, some proponents still say that is an acceptable error rate and it wouldn't affect their opinion much. About the same number express a substantial level of uneasiness. Then I ask the same hypothetical question with the percentage of wrongful convictions they had originally estimated. That brings about even more discomfort, but I must confess, I don't really know if I've changed any minds overall. Who knows, though—maybe I've planted a seed.

Chapter 7
Shoeprint

Autumn 1986

I sat at the conference room table at FBI headquarters in the J. Edgar Hoover Building in Washington, D.C., tapping my fingers on the table, but otherwise silent, looking at William Bodziak, one of the world's premier shoeprint experts. Since Bodziak was not just a forensic expert, but also an FBI agent, I had been forced to slog through a ton of red tape that goes along with interviewing FBI agents. An FBI lawyer assigned to monitor the interview had temporarily left the room with DuPage County First Assistant State's Attorney Robert Kilander, who had taken over the prosecution of Steve Buckley for his upcoming retrial. They were gone for several minutes, so Bodziak and I just sat there, silent. It was roughly a year-and-a-half since Steve's trial had ended in a hung jury, thereby setting up the retrial. I felt awkward; Bodziak was mildly perturbed.

"This is just wrong," Bodziak said, breaking the silence. "You shouldn't have to have the prosecutor of your client here when you interview me."

The folks at the FBI had assured me that the same rules would have applied had Kilander wanted the interview. Somehow, I didn't think he would have had to go through what I did just to speak to an agent. And I knew for damn sure I wouldn't have been invited along to participate, as Kilander had. But if this was the way it had to be, so be it.

"Listen," continued Bodziak. "I'm going to take over this meeting. I'll explain everything, and when we're through, I think I will have answered all of your questions."

"I can live with that." I put the list of questions I had prepared inside my folder and waited. After a couple of minutes, Kilander and the FBI lawyer reentered the room.

True to his word, Bodziak took control of the meeting. "Let me go over my findings and how I reached my conclusion." Bodziak proceeded to produce a number of exhibits—photos of the Nicarico door, the accompanying shoeprint, photos and overlays from Steve's shoe, among other things. Using the exhibits, over the next 20 minutes he discussed

the evidence and detailed the differences between the print from the door
and Steve's shoes, and stated his opinion: "In conclusion, Mr. Buckley's
shoe could not have made the print on the Nicarico door."
Music to my ears.
"Any questions?" Bodziak asked.
Kilander asked a few questions, mostly regarding Bodziak's difference of opinion from Ed German, a shoeprint examiner who had testified
for the State at Steve's trial. Bodziak explained he had discussed his findings with German, and that he simply disagreed with him.
"Mr. Johnson, do you have any questions?" Bodziak asked again.
I asked a couple questions concerning what German had said to him,
got answers, then I paused. "That's all I have. Thanks, Mr. Bodziak."

****

In the lead-up to and during Steve's trial, the prosecution went to
extraordinary lengths to connect Steve's shoe to the print on the Nicarico
door. Those efforts are described here and in subsequent chapters.
They got so excited over a clue that after a first, uncritical glance appeared to advance their argument, they forgot to take a second look. And
when other experts—mostly, but not all, from the defense side—took that
more analytical look at the evidence and exposed obvious errors in the
State's position, the police and prosecutors ignored them.
By the time the State's shoeprint theory deteriorated into complete
rubbish, which occurred in the months leading up to the date of Steve's
retrial, they had inextricably married themselves to the false proposition
that Steve Buckley kicked in the Nicarico front door.

Then, several years later, this happened.

February 1, 1990

"She [Jeanine] **was in her own home, behind her own locked
door, having a bowl of ice cream and watching TV** when Rolando
Cruz kicked in the door, **went downstairs, and took her from her
home, from the sanctity of her own home. She had a right to be
safe in her own home.**" (Emphasis supplied.)

- Richard Stock, Chief of the Criminal Division of the DuPage
County State's Attorney's Office, during his closing argument
at the death penalty hearing for Rolando Cruz, subsequent to his

being convicted for the second time of the murder of Jeanine Nicarico. The first conviction had been overturned by the Illinois Supreme Court.

1984
Dr. Louise Robbins

The shoeprint—it was a collection of dust left on the Nicarico door when Jeanine's assailant had kicked it open to gain entry into the house. It left a distinctive print of a right shoe that was clear enough to have significant evidentiary value. The police were able to locate a pair of new boot-like type of shoes, sometimes called "chukka boots," that had the kind of sole that created the print.

About a month after Jeanine was murdered, the police made their first contact with Steve. Alex Hernandez, in an attempt to get the reward money being offered, told the police that a guy named "Ricky" had made statements admitting to killing Jeanine, and he, Steve and Mike Castro were in a car with him when the statements were made. It was a lie, and after Steve (and Mike Castro, as well) denied knowing about any Ricky or his supposed statements, the police showed him the shoe they possessed with a sole like the print on the Nicarico door. "I have a pair of boots just like that," Steve said. Wanting to help the police as much as he could, he voluntarily turned his shoes over to them. Steve's mother packaged them up in a paper bag. Seeing the soles of Steve's shoes were, in general terms, similar to the print on the door, the police were excited. And with that, Steve became a suspect.

In the discovery, the State provided reports from three shoeprint analysts. Ed German, a shoeprint and fingerprint examiner from the Illinois State Police Crime Lab, opined that Steve's shoe "could have" made the print on the door. Robert Olsen, from the Kansas Bureau of Investigation, reported that Steve's shoe and the door print were "similar in general class characteristics" (also called manufactured characteristics, these include sole tread design, markings and general measurements). The reports were unclear as to whether these examiners claimed to find any "accidental" characteristics (evidence of cuts, scratches or other flaws that might be found in the sole of a shoe that occur with usage). Without matching accidental characteristics, qualified and properly trained forensic shoeprint experts will not conclude that a shoe, to the exclusion of all other shoes, made a specific print.

Looking at the print on the door, as well as various enhanced photos of the print, it's inconceivable that anyone could credibly claim to see any accidental markings. So the State had to find somebody who would say that Steve's shoe definitively made the print on the door without the benefit of matching accidental characteristics.

Enter Dr. Louise Robbins, a forensic anthropologist from the University of North Carolina-Greensboro, who testified throughout the United States and once in Canada as a shoeprint expert. She had developed a new and controversial theory that every person's wear patterns on the soles of his or her shoes, and any resulting shoeprints, were as unique to the individual as their fingerprints. This novel concept made matching accidental characteristics unnecessary to concretely connect a shoe to a print. Her report stated that, while she could find no accidental characteristics on the door print, the wear on Steve's shoe matched the wear patterns on the print. She concluded that Steve's shoe, to the exclusion of all other shoes in the world, made the print on the Nicarico door.

At this stage, Cliff and I weren't all that concerned with the German and Olsen opinions—they were too inconclusive. The Robbins opinion was another matter. Her opinion gave the State its only piece of significant physical evidence.

Dr. Owen Lovejoy

The State's case relied on a shoeprint and its interpretation by Dr. Louise Robbins using untested and questionable techniques. I needed help. So, on a whim, I called Dr. Ernie Isadore, a local podiatrist for whom I had done some collections work. I figured it was a longshot that he knew anything about her, so I was surprised by his response.

"Oh my goodness, you're about to be done in by a person whose methods are really being questioned," he said. "You need to call Dr. Timothy White out at UC Berkeley. He'll tell you all about her."

In the field of anthropology, evolution and the origins of the earliest humans, Dr. White was world-renowned. I called and explained the situation to him. He confirmed what Dr. Isadore had said was true, but that the person I should talk to was Dr. Owen Lovejoy at Kent State University. Dr. Lovejoy was another world-class anthropologist, who had also done shoeprint comparisons, and was fully aware of Dr. Robbins's methodology.

I immediately contacted Dr. Lovejoy and that's when the floodgates opened. He not only completely debunked her unsubstantiated theory that wear patterns on shoeprints are as unique as fingerprints, but he connected me with other shoeprint experts and anthropologists who also strongly disputed her opinions and philosophy. They, in turn, introduced me to lawyers who had encountered her in court. As it turned out, she had gotten away with giving questionable and often outrageous testimony in numerous cases, angering mostly defense attorneys, but at least one prosecutor as well. I was provided with transcripts of her testimony in some of those cases.

In the end, we were able to put together an impressive list of shoeprint experts to contradict the State's witnesses' conclusions concerning the print on the Nicarico door. They included, among others, Dr. Lovejoy, and Joseph Nicol, a forensic expert who was instrumental in creating the Illinois State Police Crime Lab. These experts were also of the opinion that there was no scientific basis for Dr. Robbins's theory as to the uniqueness of shoeprints.

We requested the court conduct a *Frye* hearing prior to trial. *Frye* hearings are based on the case of *Frye v. United States*,[8] which held that before an expert can testify to a new scientific principle, that principle must be generally accepted in the field from which it comes. In our case, that field would have been either shoeprint comparisons or forensic anthropology.

As far as we could tell, Dr. Robbins was the only person in the world, much less from those two fields, who was asserting this wear pattern shoeprint uniqueness theory. We lined up Lovejoy, Nicol and other experts to testify at the hearing. The State moved to strike our motion and avoid the hearing altogether. Judge Kowal granted their motion—no pretrial hearing would be held.

Judge Kowal's rationale for denying us a *Frye* hearing was that we could accomplish the same thing by cross-examining Dr. Robbins on her theories and techniques at trial, and that, along with testimony from our experts, would be sufficient. Of course, that's nonsense. There was no way Dr. Robbins would repudiate or even cast doubt on her own opinions or theories, no matter how skillfully she was crossed.

Since we could expect little or no help from the State's other experts, and since our experts would not testify until the State had rested, after Dr. Robbins had given her opinion, Judge Kowal's ruling was useless to us. We needed a pretrial determination, before Dr. Robbins testified, on the *Frye* issue.

Had Steve been convicted, I'm confident that would have been considered reversible error.

Eventually, in 1987, a *Frye* hearing of sorts was conducted. Sadly, I'm ashamed to say, it wasn't done in court as we had hoped. It was put together by some of the world's leading forensic shoeprint and anthropology experts. More on that later.

As it turned out, Dr. Robbins wouldn't be the only source of controversy regarding shoeprint evidence.

****

I consulted with a number of outstanding shoeprint experts from the fields of criminology, biomechanical engineering and anthropology, but it was Dr. Lovejoy who really helped me understand shoeprint evidence. I, like many lawyers, had spent my academic life taking the minimum number of science courses necessary to obtain whichever degree I was seeking. By way of a visit to his lab at Kent State and plenty of phone calls, Dr. Lovejoy patiently educated me on the scientific method, and how it applied to Dr. Robbins's unfounded and untested theories. He pointed out discrepancies and errors in all the State's experts' conclusions. He performed numerous and varied tests with Steve's shoes and the other shoeprint evidence to which he was given access.

From those tests he was later able to describe to the jury, as he had to me on previous occasions, the differences between the print on the Nicarico door and the sole of Steve's shoe. He connected me to many of those other experts for their perspectives. I learned from all of them. They either agreed with Dr. Lovejoy's conclusions that Steve's shoe could not have made the print on the Nicarico door, or they concluded that it was highly unlikely or very improbable that Steve's shoe made the print. Furthermore, I learned that these experts were part of a substantial and growing number of scientists who believed that Dr. Robbins's techniques and opinions were not based on any credible scientific principles.

When Cliff and I first took Steve's defense, conventional wisdom was that of the three defendants, the State's case against Steve was the strongest. After all, the shoeprint was the only piece of physical evidence that, in conjunction with the State's expert witnesses, connected a defendant to the crime. All the experts we consulted with had a hand in changing that negative for us to a positive, but Dr. Lovejoy more than anyone else.

Most importantly, he gave us confidence.

Early December, 1984
John Gorajczyk

"I was expecting your call, Mr. Johnson, and I'm relieved you finally got ahold of me." With those words from DuPage County Crime Lab shoeprint examiner John Gorajczyk, spoken just five weeks before the trial was set to begin, whatever nervousness I had in contacting him was gone. But despite Gorajczyk's feeling of relief that we had found out about his part in the investigation, he was reluctant to talk. I suspected he was under some pressure from his superiors at the lab. As unfair as it sounds, the criminal discovery rules back then did not require witnesses to talk to lawyers, even in capital cases. But I could tell he wanted to talk. We just had to figure out a way.

The night before, Tom Laz, Cruz's lawyer, had called. He was excited. "Gary, Gary, I have great news! You gotta get on the horn with John Gorajczyk right away. Phil Gilman just told me that Gorajczyk examined the shoeprint evidence right after they got it and said Steve's shoe didn't make the print on the door. You should see if he'll talk to you."

Gilman was a former lab director and forensic scientist at the crime lab who had recently quit after he let it be known that he didn't like the way that the Nicarico case was being investigated. I called Gilman, and he confirmed Laz's account.

After my phone call to Gorajczyk, I contacted the new lab director to get permission to speak to John and others at the lab. That permission was denied. Cliff and I discussed our dilemma. We had to figure out a way to interview Gorajczyk. We agreed that if we failed, we would subpoena him to testify without meeting beforehand. We would put him on the witness stand cold.

Our next step was to file a motion to dismiss the charges against Steve due to the State's failure to comply with the *Brady* rule, which we alleged amounted to a violation of the Due Process clause of the 14th Amendment.

Based on the United States Supreme Court case of *Brady v. Maryland*,[9] it—along with a specific discovery rule from the Illinois Supreme Court[10]—requires the prosecution to disclose to the defense any exculpatory evidence it is aware of. Not surprisingly, Judge Kowal denied our motion, but he did throw us a bone. He ordered John Gorajczyk to be interviewed by Cliff and me.

From that interview, we learned some shocking facts. First, Gorajczyk was asked to take a look at the shoeprint evidence by the DuPage County Sheriff, Richard Doria, himself. Gorajczyk then conducted what he described as a "preliminary examination" that resulted in a "preliminary conclusion." His findings were that Steve's shoe did not make the print on the Nicarico door.

Once he told the Sheriff and others at the lab of his results, he requested more time to further examine the evidence. He got a "we'll get back to you" type of response, and the shoeprint evidence was then sent to the Illinois State Police Crime Lab, never to be seen by Gorajczyk again.

Although he stated that he had never spoken directly to prosecutors about his findings, it was common knowledge at the lab what they were. Gorajczyk didn't write up a report because he did not conduct a full examination—it was just preliminary. Clearly, the Gorajczyk shoeprint findings should have been turned over to us. But on what theory? The shoeprint was the main pillar of the case against Steve, and Gorajczyk's opinion was, without question, exculpatory. *Brady* and the discovery rules required that the State provide the results to us, but only if the prosecutors knew about it. Knight claimed that he hadn't learned of the Gorajczyk examination until after we did.[11] That's an assertion I personally find difficult to believe.

But even if Knight and King weren't aware of Gorajczyk's findings, the discovery rules also required prosecutors to "ensure that a flow of information is maintained between the various investigative personnel and [their] office sufficient to place within [their office's] possession or control all material and information relevant to the accused and the offense charged."[12]

The members of the crime lab were investigative—they were actually deputy sheriffs. The Sheriff himself knew of the test results, straight from Gorajczyk's mouth. So did numerous people at the lab. Detective John Sam, one of the lead investigators on the case, and a name you will hear me praise in forthcoming chapters, also knew of Gorajczyk's opinion. That leads me to conclude that other investigators also knew.

It's hard to believe all those at the DuPage County Crime Lab and Sheriff's Office who knew about Gorajczyk's examination collectively just forgot about his conclusions. So would they have intentionally kept those results from Knight and King? That's equally unrealistic. But if they did, why did they?

The police weren't controlled by *Brady*,[13] but for the love of all things holy, *this was a death penalty case!* Didn't they, at the very least, have a moral responsibility to release this information to the prosecutors, who would then have been required to turn that over to us?

And, finally, once Gorajczyk had come to his preliminary conclusion, why didn't his superiors allow him to complete his examination so that his conclusions wouldn't be qualified as "preliminary?" You can bet the ranch they would have if he had said the shoe matched.

As far as I'm concerned, there are no satisfactory answers to any of these questions, and our not knowing of the Gorajczyk findings until we stumbled on them was unforgivable.

February 1, 1985

John Barsanti was being prepped by prosecutors Tom Knight and Pat King prior to his trial testimony in Nicarico. Preparing a witness to testify is common, even recommended, so that the testimony can be presented as efficiently as possible. John's testimony concerned whether or not Arthur Burrell, a witness who would testify against all three defendants, had been given lenient treatment in Kane County as a result of his cooperation with the prosecution in our case in DuPage County. At one point, Pat King showed some documents to Knight and asked if they should be disclosed, apparently pursuant to the *Brady* rule.

"The only Brady I know has got a hole in his head," replied Knight, in a likely reference to President Ronald Reagan's former press secretary, James Brady, who was shot in the head in 1981—and miraculously survived—during John Hinckley's attempted assassination of the president. There was some laughter, and the issue was dropped, at least while Barsanti was present.*

Fayva v. Payless

Our shoeprint experts were able to find multiple differences in the manufactured characteristics between Steve's shoe and the door print. But the difference that was most obvious, at least to me, was on the heel portion of the print and Steve's shoe. Though both had arched rays, they were arched in opposite directions. We had contacted Tom Riley, the owner of the company from Hingham, Massachusetts that imported the shoes/boots that had this kind of sole. He told us the type of sole involved had a name—New Silver Cloud. The sole was manufactured at numerous factories, mostly in China and Spain. Mr. Riley also informed us, and later testified at trial, that each factory made the soles with slight variations, so that while at first blush they looked similar, with just a little bit of scrutiny, you could easily distinguish them. The differences in the arched rays were just one example of that. To punctuate this point further, we purchased, from a Fayva shoe store in Aurora, five or six pairs of New Silver Cloud-soled shoes that had heel rays that arched in the same

---

* This account of the meeting between Barsanti, Knight and King is based on an affidavit of John Barsanti filed with the Circuit Court of DuPage County.

Tom Knight and Pat King have said they have no recollection of Knight saying this, and that no *Brady* material was withheld. Thomas Frisbie and Randy Garrett, *Victims of Justice Revisited* (Evanston: Northwestern University Press, 2015), 106.

direction as those on the Nicarico door. Steve had bought his shoes from a Payless shoe store. Obviously, Fayva and Payless obtained New Silver Cloud-soled shoes that had been manufactured in different factories.

William Bodziak

In my conversations with Dr. Lovejoy and other shoeprint experts, one name kept coming up as being considered the best in the business regarding shoeprint evidence—FBI forensic examiner William Bodziak. Dr. Lovejoy, in particular, kept hounding me to get the prosecution to agree to allow Bodziak to examine the evidence. I spoke to Tom Knight about this, but he informed me—accurately, as it turned out—the FBI had a policy that once another lab examined evidence, the FBI would not look at it. I was disappointed. I was confident that an expert with the reputation of Bodziak, who had both figurative and literal distance from the case, would exclude Steve's shoe.

Bodziak wouldn't be able to stay out of the case forever, but, unfortunately, his involvement wouldn't come until after Steve's trial.

Chapter 8
Race to Trial

The speed with which the Nicarico case was brought to trial, considering it was a multi-defendant case with complex issues and the possible imposition of the ultimate penalty, still amazes me. At the time, though, the Nicarico family and their supporters thought we defense lawyers were dragging our heels. Nothing could have been further from the truth.

Years later, before the abolition of the death penalty in Illinois, but after a number of wrongful convictions in capital cases came to light, the Illinois legislature and supreme court developed statutes and rules with enhanced protections for death penalty cases. One of those rules required defense counsel to file a "Readiness Certificate" prior to going to trial.[14] It fell short of giving defense counsel carte blanche to veto or continue a trial date, but considering the refreshing atmosphere of caution the new procedures provided, it was a powerful weapon. If we'd had that in the Nicarico case, it's likely that at least one of us, as defense counsel, would have balked at signing such a document so early on, and the trial would not have occurred only 10 months after the indictment. But without those kinds of protections, things moved very quickly, and Cliff and I had a lot to do—reading voluminous police reports, conducting our own investigation, preparing motions, talking to witnesses—and not much time to do it. For me that included road trips to Springfield, Illinois; Greensboro, North Carolina; Hingham, Massachusetts; and Kent, Ohio to interview Ed German, Dr. Robbins, Tom Riley and Dr. Lovejoy, respectively.

Beyond that, there were regular pretrial hearings on a variety of motions, including our attempts to get Steve's case severed from his co-defendants and get the trial moved out of DuPage County.

Steve Buckley was busy, too.

Solitary Confinement

As you can imagine, as a result of the charges against them, Buckley, Hernandez and Cruz weren't the most popular inmates among their peers in the jail. Within a month of his arrest, Steve got sucker punched in the jaw by another prisoner, and he was put in solitary confinement for his own protection. This was fine with Cliff and me because it reduced the possibility of Steve being the victim of a jailhouse snitch—an inmate who gets close with a fellow prisoner, learns facts of that prisoner's case from a variety of sources, then, often falsely, claims that the prisoner made admissions to him. In return, a snitch will usually get a reduced sentence.

As it turned out, this problem would rear its ugly head for Steve later on anyhow. But Steve wanted out, and his jailers obliged and returned him to the jail's general population. That worked until some of the prisoners in his pod complained about not wanting a child rapist and murderer in their midst, so back to solitary he went. All in all, Steve spent roughly three years in jail, with two of them in some form of segregated or solitary confinement.

To stave off boredom, Steve started to read books. He read anything he could get his hands on. He loved *Huckleberry Finn*, and he particularly enjoyed the novels of Stephen King. But Steve didn't stop there. At the time, the DuPage County Jail didn't have a GED program, but Steve convinced a priest at the jail to intervene with jail administration to have the priest's teacher friend come to the jail so Steve could take some classes and get his certificate. He passed the GED test on his first try. When other inmates heard what Steve had done, many of them also requested and received GED schooling. Steve had become a bit of a trailblazer.

When Cliff and I visited Steve at the jail, we would often discuss the books he was reading, along with religion and current events. Steve had some strong, well-thought-out opinions. As I said earlier, Steve was smarter than his lack of formal education indicated. And when it came to his defense, he had a lot to say and contribute there as well—often with a healthy dose of compassion that wasn't betrayed by his normally blunt demeanor.

"Those poor people," Steve would often say, referring to the Nicaricos. "I feel sorry for them. But I didn't have a damn thing to do with what happened to Jeanine."

Motion for Change of Venue

Early on, Cliff went to work preparing for our motion to change venue by assembling hard copies of the media coverage—mostly print and television reports regarding the investigation, arrests and court proceedings of the case. Wisely, he included the extensive petition drive to retain Tom Knight as lead prosecutor as part of the motion. The quantity of news reports was massive, and we feared the prejudicial effect on the three defendants would be substantial. We firmly believed that if ever a change of venue needed granting, this would be it.

Negative publicity was the only legal reason we had for requesting a venue change, but there was another equally valid, but non-legal reason for the request. DuPage County is a wealthy, and, by reputation, one of the most conservative counties in Illinois. Jurors who would be drawn from that jury pool would likely be tough on criminal defendants. So we wanted to get out.

A change of venue, if granted, can be accomplished in two ways. The trial could be held in another county in Illinois. In our case, this would be inconvenient for the court and the various witnesses, lawyers and other court personnel, who were mostly local to the DuPage and Kane county areas. Or we could select a jury in another county, then bring that jury to DuPage to hear the case. That option would probably result in sequestration—where the jurors are more or less locked up in hotel rooms—and would be a huge pain for them and their families.

In order to get the venue changed, we had to show more than just harmful publicity. We needed to establish actual prejudice existed and that we had a reasonable apprehension of not getting a fair trial.[15] Steve didn't have the funds to put together a survey that would show whether the pretrial publicity created actual prejudice, so we had to argue that the bad publicity was so pervasive that actual prejudice must have occurred. The law grants the trial judge broad discretion on this issue, so, of course, Judge Kowal ruled against us. But he did leave the door open. If the jury selection process exposed the necessary prejudice, he would reconsider.

Death Penalty Motions

There's a saying among those familiar with capital litigation: "Death is different." It may sound a bit silly, but for judges, prosecutors and especially defense lawyers (and, of course, their clients), death is indeed different. I've litigated a few death penalty cases over the years, and after each one I would swear up and down that I would never do another one.

Criminal lawyers on both sides often lose sleep over their cases, but when the death penalty is involved, the pressure is magnified. And even though it's not supposed to make a difference, when you add to the equation your firm belief that your client is innocent and could be executed for a crime he didn't commit, well, let's just understate it and say that it takes some of the fun out of your job.

But even though Cliff and I were both terrified, fear is also a great motivator, and it gave us the impetus to be aggressive on Steve's behalf.

So one of the things we did was file a raft of death penalty motions, all of which had been heard and denied in many prior cases. These were motions that were mostly worked up by the Illinois State Appellate Defender (appointed counsel for indigent defendants on appeal) and passed along to trial lawyers. Even though the denial of these motions in other cases had been affirmed by the Illinois Supreme Court, we were encouraged to file and argue them despite knowing we would lose. The theory was that the Illinois Supreme Court could change its mind, or the U.S. Supreme Court might eventually weigh in and change Illinois capital punishment law.

Among other things, the motions challenged the constitutionality of the death penalty itself and the procedures utilized in capital cases, the unfairness of the death-qualification process (*Witherspooning*) of the jury, the unfair application of death penalty laws when race was a factor, and the arbitrariness of the seeking and imposition of the death penalty. Even though we lost each and every one of these motions, they weren't bullshit. I believed, and do to this day, that the death penalty violates the 8th Amendment's prohibition against cruel and unusual punishment, and that the death penalty procedures in Illinois, when the penalty was in effect, also violated both the due process and equal protection clauses of the U.S. and Illinois constitutions.

Motions for Severance, to Dismiss, and Plenty of Friction

Cliff and I understood that the most important pretrial issue to be dealt with was our motion to sever Steve's case from those of his two co-defendants. In other words, we wanted separate trials. Laz filed a similar motion on behalf of Cruz. Wesolowski would also seek severance-related relief for Hernandez, but a while later.

Back when Steve's case was about to be tried, judges and prosecutors tended to disfavor severance motions because they required multiple trials for the same crime, and that runs contrary to a principle called "judicial economy." Things have changed somewhat today, I think, partly because of two Illinois Supreme Court rulings on this issue from the Nicarico case.

In certain cases, there are very important legal concepts counterbalancing the resistance to split trials. Evidentiary and constitutional legal principles hold that an incriminating statement (an admission or confession) is admissible against the person making the statement, but only that person and nobody else. A problem arises when that incriminating statement names other people who also happen to be co-defendants. If the party making the admission doesn't testify at trial, then the non-admitting co-defendants cannot cross-examine the defendant who made the statement. This violates the Confrontation Clause of the 6th Amendment to the United States Constitution—which requires a criminal defendant "to be confronted with the witnesses against him"—as well as evidentiary hearsay rules. One way, the best way, to cure that problem is to sever the case of the defendant who made the statement from the other defendants.

An example of this problem can be shown in the following hypothetical: If Defendant A confesses to the police that he committed an armed robbery with Defendant B, Defendant A's statement is admissible only against himself, and not against Defendant B. This poses a problem for Defendant B if he is tried jointly with Defendant A.

The incriminating statements alleged to have been made by Cruz and Hernandez were varied, wild, difficult to believe, and sometimes named individuals other than their co-defendants. But since some of the statements of Hernandez and Cruz also referred to each other, and to Steve—none of Steve's statements referred to his co-defendants, or himself, in an incriminating way—and since we were certain that Hernandez and Cruz were not going to testify, a severance was necessary. That way, for example, Hernandez's alleged statements could be used exclusively against himself, and not be admitted against Steve in his separate trial.

Unfortunately, the law provided a possible alternative to a severance. If the incriminating statements could be redacted, or edited, to eliminate any reference to co-defendants, the statements could be admitted, as edited, without a severance.

We objected to the redaction option for several reasons. First, given the nature of the case and the various alleged statements, we didn't believe that the statements were capable of being redacted sufficiently to eliminate all reference to co-defendants. This was especially true because we knew that the State was going to go out of their way to try to establish the inaccurate proposition that the three defendants were friends. Second—and this reason for a severance didn't become apparent until later—over time we learned that Laz and Wesolowski were unwilling, at the pretrial stage, to waive a jury for the sentencing phase of the trial. That meant that if there was one jury for the three defendants, it would have to be death-qualified. Our plans for a pretrial waiver of a jury and taking a bench trial for the sentencing phase only, thereby allowing us a non-death-qualified jury for the guilt-innocence phase of the trial, would be thwarted. We would have to work with the same death-qualified jury as Hernandez and Cruz.

Lastly, we just wanted to put some distance between Steve and his co-defendants. We felt that Steve might be brought down by the statements that were attributed to them, no matter how they were redacted.

Of course, the State vigorously opposed a severance, claiming they could sufficiently redact the statements to cure the problem. So it came as no surprise to us when, on August 29, 1984, Judge Kowal denied our severance motions. We promptly requested a list of the State's proposed redacted statements. Judge Kowal indicated that was his desire as well, without specifically ordering it. That began a difficult and bitter four-month process during which the State would stubbornly resist proposing clear and appropriate redactions.

It was a battle they would win in the short term. But the long run was another story.

****

Many times during the litigation of a serious criminal case, friction develops between prosecutor and defense counsel, and even the judge. I would venture to say that some of that can be a healthy thing for the whole process. But Tom Knight and I took it to a whole 'nother level. In and out of the courtroom, dealing with Knight was a miserable experience.

The marathon redaction fight we had with Knight wasn't the only source of irritation. Out of court, Knight and I rarely spoke. When we did, there was always tension. When I scheduled an appointment with him to examine the physical evidence the police had collected, I was made to wait about 45 minutes, only to discover not all the evidence was there to be viewed. So we scheduled another, then another appointment, with the same result each time—me waiting. I learned to bring work to fill the time.

After not getting the Gorajczyk shoeprint results from the State, I was angry and became suspicious. We had also discovered that a Du-Page Sheriff's deputy had dusted the interior of Steve's car for Jeanine's fingerprints and searched for other trace evidence—such as hair and fibers—and checked the car's tire tread for comparison purposes, all showing no connection between Steve and the crime. Those findings should have been memorialized in writing and turned over to us. They weren't. If the opposite had occurred, if they had found something incriminating, we would have been knee-deep in reports and expert opinions. And I personally don't care who was hanging on to that information—police or prosecutors—it should have been written up and released. Was there other information beneficial to the defense that we weren't getting? Each complaint we raised in court of not getting discovery was automatically and immediately responded to with a spurious similar complaint from Knight about us, creating a false equivalency as far as that issue was concerned.

I guess it's safe to say Tom Knight and I didn't much like each other.

****

Unlike my experience with Tom Knight, I've almost always stayed on good terms with my opponents in criminal cases. As a matter of fact, during my first stint at the state's attorney's office, there was a camaraderie that existed not just among prosecutors, but also between prosecutors and defense lawyers—mostly from the public defender's office—that didn't compromise our roles as adversaries. I can't tell you how many jury verdicts I sweated out at local bars with my opponents. We weren't always completely sober when juries returned their verdicts. While I'm not endorsing drinking alcohol when waiting on a jury—important legal issues can crop up during that period of time requiring you to keep your wits about you—it did make the process a little less agonizing. And the socializing didn't stop there. It occurred on a regular basis. It's a wonder my marriage survived.

The days of that level of socializing are over. And to be fair to the sour relationship Knight and I had, coming from different counties, we didn't have much of a history to build on. Nevertheless, whether I'm in Kane or another county, my rapport with prosecutors has almost always been cordial and solid. Some have even been good friends. I have to admit that a hard fought trial can sometimes test those relationships. It is, after all, an adversarial process engaged in by very competitive people. But time usually heals whatever wounds we've inflicted on the other and we're soon back to normal. Sometimes, after a clean, intensely litigated trial, the lawyers who have done battle, whether they won or lost, will view each other with a newfound respect, and maybe even admiration.

It's a good feeling.

Much of the socializing and interplay between and among both groups of criminal lawyers occurs when we're in court waiting for our cases to be called. If you'll recall, that's how I originally got involved in the Nicarico case. Don't get me wrong, work gets done. Lawyers work out plea negotiations and continuance dates, discuss the status of discovery, and so on. Defense lawyers will often seek out advice from colleagues, with regard to both specific cases they are working on and the business aspects of practicing law. But a fair amount of friendly banter, and even some high jinks, also takes place. Sometimes the case before the bench will provide the entertainment. Occasionally, even judges get involved.

A person who took courtroom horseplay to groundbreaking levels was "Maureen."[16] Maureen was a highly regarded prosecutor in Kendall County, which lies just south of Kane. She was also a prankster with a wicked, and often blue, sense of humor. Over the years, we got to be pretty good friends—good enough for me to learn that I had to keep on my toes around her.

Back in the days before smartphones were used to keep schedules, even before the advent of Palm Pilots, lawyers used to keep their important dates—court appearances, conferences, meetings, jail visits, etc.—in diaries that required handwritten entries. Some still do. I used to keep a small diary that would fit in my inside jacket pocket, while most carried around larger, more cumbersome date books. In any event, most lawyers were pretty relaxed about keeping these diaries, along with their files, on the lawyers' tables located in court while the judge was hearing various cases on his call. And if you weren't looking, that's when Maureen would go to work.

I had heard that Maureen used to jot some pretty crazy, often off-color, tidbits in lawyers' diaries when they weren't paying attention. So when I caught her starting to write something in mine—she didn't get very far—I knew it was harmless. But Max Peterson wasn't so lucky.

Max used to be the Kendall County Public Defender and was an old-school trial lawyer who had pretty much seen it all. Over the years, he had litigated a lot of cases against Maureen and other assistants in her office. He was a perfect target for her.

"Am I free for a client conference next Thursday at 5 p.m. here at the office?" Max called out to his assistant in the next room while he was on hold on the telephone. Max kept his diary in front with his assistant so she could be in charge of his scheduling when he wasn't in court. Max's assistant would occasionally find some of Maureen's handiwork in his date book, and she would just chuckle and white it out so none of Max's clients would see it if they happened to be waiting in her part of the office. But she couldn't catch everything. So she wasn't shocked when the specific time Max had inquired about had a strange diary entry.

Max's assistant picked up the date book and walked into his office.

"I'm afraid you're not available then," she said.

"What? I thought I was clear that night. What do I have going on?" Straight-faced, his assistant showed him the diary.

"On Thursday at 5, you'll be busy giving a blow job to someone named Joe."

"Dammit! Maureen!" a heterosexual and embarrassed Max blurted out to his understanding assistant.

I wasn't able to escape Maureen's mischief for too long. Later on in her career she was the Acting Kendall County State's Attorney, having been appointed to complete the term of the elected State's Attorney, who had left office to become a judge. Her daughter worked for *Playboy's* Christie Hefner. Maureen informed me that, as a result, they would occasionally get some adult video porn *Playboy* no longer had a need for. Rejects, I guess. So I jokingly asked her for some. She said that would be no problem.

After some time passed, Maureen hadn't come through with the videos. "Hey, where's my porn, where's my porn?" I would occasionally pester, snapping my fingers at her, as we passed in the courthouse hallway.

"Don't worry, you'll get it," she would promise.

This went on for a while, and as time passed, I forgot about it, until one day when the courthouse was particularly busy. Maureen approached me and asked what courtroom I was in that morning. She had something she wanted to give me.

"I'm in 114."

"It's a huge call in there today," Maureen said, referring to the large number of cases up. "I'll be in there in a couple of minutes."

She was right. Courtroom 114, which handles traffic and misdemeanors, was packed. Not only were there defendants, but there were also plenty of police and lawyers conversing and waiting for the judge to take the bench. I stood in line, leaning against the barrier that separates the jury from the rest of the courtroom, waiting to talk to the prosecutor about my cases, when Maureen walked in. She had a fancy gift bag in her hand, with ribbons and fluffy paper on top, and she was sporting a shit-eatin' grin. Sensing something awful was about to happen, I tensed up as she approached me. To make things even more dramatic, the lawyers and police began to quiet down as they noticed the Acting State's Attorney walk toward me, gift bag in hand. All of a sudden, it was pretty quiet.

"Here's the porn you've been begging me for," Maureen announced, loud enough for everyone to hear. She proceeded to, slowly and dramatically, remove the fluffy paper and ribbons, followed by two pornographic videos. She even recited their titles as she took them out, and held them up for everyone to see. One of the titles made it clear that it was pretty hardcore stuff. She then put them back in the bag, replaced the paper and ribbons, and handed the bag to me. Red-faced and heart pounding, I had no place to escape. I sheepishly accepted the bag, and Maureen quickly pivoted and left the courtroom. As she left, the police and lawyers started to laugh—softly at first, then working their way up to a collective hearty laugh.

I like to think of myself as pretty much unembarrassable. But not that day.

One of my better acts of lawyering lasted only a matter of minutes and occurred when I was waiting in a Kane County courtroom, with a number of other lawyers, to have a preliminary hearing. For a felony to advance to trial, the prosecution is required to obtain a probable cause determination—specifically, a finding of probable cause that a crime was committed and that the defendant committed the crime. "Probable cause," often referred to as "PC," is a burden of proof that is less than the "beyond a reasonable doubt" standard that is used at trial. In Illinois, probable cause may be determined by a judge at a preliminary hearing, in which case the charging document is called an "information," or by a grand jury composed of grand jurors (as opposed to petit jurors who hear trials), where the charging document is an indictment. At either proceeding, the rules of evidence are significantly relaxed.

The prosecution gets to choose which path to take, and in the larger counties that can afford to utilize grand jurors regularly, they almost always go with the grand jury. The reasons are simple. At a preliminary hearing, not only does a legally trained judge make the probable cause determination, but the defendant and his lawyer are also present. The defense lawyer gets to participate, usually just by cross-examining the State's witness. The way the system works in Illinois, defense lawyers never put on a case of their own at a "prelim." A skillful defense lawyer can learn a lot about the State's case during such a hearing. On the other hand, at a typical grand jury proceeding it's just the prosecutor, his witness or witnesses, and the grand jury—no pesky defense lawyer to gum up the works. Prosecutors can almost always get the grand jurors to do their bidding, and that has resulted in the old adage that a prosecutor could get a grand jury to indict a ham sandwich.

Back in the 1990s, Kane County used both prelims and grand juries for probable cause determinations, and it was then I was pressed into service on short notice. As I was waiting to have my case heard, a preliminary hearing scheduled ahead of me was beginning before Judge John Petersen. Everyone was present and ready—except the defense lawyer, who was nowhere to be found.

"Where's your lawyer?" asked Petersen, an absolutely no-nonsense, conservative and demanding-of-both-sides type of judge.

"I don't know," the defendant responded.

"Well, we're starting without him, and I'm going to get you a lawyer."

Why Petersen didn't just wait and call some of the other cases that were ready to go and hope that the tardy lawyer would show up in the meantime, I don't know. He looked around the room and I made the mistake of making eye contact.

"Mr. Johnson, get up here. You're the defendant's lawyer for her prelim."

Now I could have declined—there was no way Judge Petersen could have made me defend this defendant at her prelim had I objected. Beyond that, the defendant herself could have objected on a number of grounds. But despite Petersen being such a strict judge and harsh sentencer, and having a cantankerous demeanor, I liked him. I always thought that if I needed a judge to make a tough, gutsy call against the State on a purely legal argument, he'd be one who could do it. Plus, I was a little afraid of him.

"Yes, Your Honor. Can I get a copy of the police report?"

"State, give him your synopsis and call your witness."

A synopsis is usually a one-page summary of the State's evidence that is given to a judge when determining bond. I read the summary the officer had prepared as I listened to his testimony. I don't recall what the charge was, but back in those days Kane County was starting to phase out preliminary hearings, using them only on lower-level felonies.

After the State had taken the officer through his direct examination, I began my cross. It quickly became apparent that the officer may not have had sufficient grounds to detain and arrest the defendant, thereby setting up the possibility for a future motion to suppress evidence that would jeopardize the State's case.

"Objection, Your Honor. Defense counsel is turning this prelim into a deposition," the prosecutor said.

"Response?" The prosecutor was making an appropriate objection, but I still had a response.

"No, Your Honor, I think this is relevant to PC."

Petersen glanced at me, and I recall a slight smile on his face. *You dragged me into this*, I thought, *so give me some room here.*

"Overruled."

I was allowed to go on awhile longer, and after it was over, Petersen ruled that there was probable cause. But he had given me enough leeway to establish that the testifying officer might not have had enough grounds to arrest my "sort of" client. The case was continued for further proceedings, which would likely include a motion to suppress evidence based on an illegal arrest.

****

Over the weeks and months after Judge Kowal denied our severance motion, Cliff and I regularly pressed the State for their proposed redactions. It was vital for us to see, in advance, how the State proposed that the admissions would be introduced. And we needed them in writing so the judge could look at each individual statement, make a ruling, and work out a final editing. We also wanted a record for the appellate court in the event of a conviction. I wondered how in the world they would edit the statements to eliminate any reference to co-defendants. Knight's stubborn lack of cooperation regarding the redactions and usage of the alleged statements by Buckley's co-defendants—made worse by Judge Kowal's lack of judicial intervention—added to the unpleasantness.

During that same period, other issues were also addressed that needed resolution. We were mostly unsuccessful, and on the few issues that Judge Kowal did grant us relief, there was almost always a motion by Knight to reconsider. That wouldn't have been so aggravating if it hadn't worked so often. Knight could, and would, wear Kowal down.

One motion we won was when Kowal ruled that the State's attempt to connect Cruz to the son of the Nicarico cleaning lady was too tenuous to be relevant and admissible. But for the most part, our motions were denied. Some were even stricken by Judge Kowal without a hearing. As noted earlier, our motion to have a *Frye* hearing, using our experts to call into question Dr. Robbins's methods and prevent her from testifying, failed. And there was the motion to dismiss, also denied, for the State's failure to notify us about John Gorajczyk's favorable shoeprint findings. Everything was a pitched battle.

The press picked up on the discord. Pucky Zimmerman, a reporter for the *Naperville Sun*, wrote the following about our December 18, 1984 pretrial hearing:[17]

"Prosecuting attorney Thomas Knight and Johnson exchanged

heated words more than once during Tuesday's pretrial hearing. At one point Knight stated that he was offended when Johnson hinted that the State was covering up evidence. They also argued over who's (sic) burden it was to prove or disprove certain legal points.

"All attorneys involved also complained to the judge that their opponents had still not disclosed all of the evidence each side had against the other. Public Defender Frank Wesolowski asked the judge to schedule a session between the counselors to determine what had and had not been submitted. ...

"Kowal ordered the attorneys to sort out their differences during a recess in which he would hear the remainder of his court call then report to him to settle the matter of disclosures. ..."

As the weeks and months passed, it became clear that Tom Knight had no intention of providing much in the way of appropriate redactions. Even Judge Kowal pressed him—a little—but Knight would just put him, and us, off. He would, however, speak in generalities. His early position was to point us to the statements set out in the discovery answers and the grand jury transcripts, and instruct us to eliminate the names of the co-defendants from the statements and replace them with "friends from Aurora," or "another person I knew." That solution was laughable—he might as well have gone ahead and named the co-defendants. It would have guaranteed a reversal on appeal.

At that acrimonious December 18 hearing, a previously quiet Frank Wesolowski summed up the prospects of agreement in the following exchange:

Judge Kowal:

We are going to recess in a few moments to take care of the rest of the 9:00 o'clock call. Before counsel leave, straighten this matter out, and if necessary come into chambers after that.

Mr. Wesolowski:

Judge, may I address the Court? I haven't said a word to you but my name. I brought this up before and I don't remember when. I'm stating to you that it will not be worked out.
It seems to me the last time I rose to address the Court on this question of redactions, I asked the

> **Court to schedule a session. I believed I even sug-**
> **gested that it might be fruitful and possible to work**
> **something out if we met, attorneys only, with the**
> **Court. I do not suggest that at this time. I do suggest**
> **that we—our next session be devoted to redaction,**
> **whatever the redaction means. I see no**
> **resolution, no possible resolution, other than**
> **a minimum of two separate juries.**

Judge Kowal wanted as little as possible to do with the editing process. He wanted the lawyers to work it out. He may as well have asked us
to secure a lasting peace in the Middle East.

By December 27, Knight had given up on using the phrase "a certain
named friend" to refer to co-defendants, and agreed to replace that with
"a certain named person." That sounds very accommodating, until you
consider how extreme and certain to cause a reversal his initial position
was.

And when you consider that the prosecution would go out of its way
throughout the trial to connect the three defendants up as friends, something we warned Judge Kowal about, the change didn't amount to much.
It wouldn't take a Rhodes Scholar to figure out that "a certain named
person" or "persons" was one or both of the other co-defendants. Plus,
some of the statements allegedly made by Hernandez and Cruz referred
to people other than their co-defendants.

At trial, we could either name those people, thereby making it even
more clear that the other "certain named persons" in other statements
were referring to co-defendants, or not name them, thereby causing
the jurors to think that those statements were also referring to the co-
defendants, when in truth, they were not. Our position was that the State
couldn't mention "others" at all.

So, referring to the previous hypothetical of one defendant making
a statement that implicated both himself and another, our respective
positions would run something like this: When Defendant A made the
statement that he committed an armed robbery with Defendant B, Knight
would have had it go in at the joined trial as "I committed the armed
robbery with a certain named person." Our position would have been that
the statement by Defendant A should go in as "I committed the armed
robbery." Period. End of sentence.

An actual example from our case might shed even more light on
the problem. In the discovery provided by the State, all the defendants
received notice that the State was claiming Rolando Cruz had made a

statement after he was arrested. The verbatim portion of that discovery went as follows:

> "The Defendant Cruz asked to talk to Lt. Robert Winkler, previously disclosed, and he told Winkler that he remembers Alex Hernandez and John Doe[18] coming to him and asking him if he would help them steal a car. He declined but showed them how they could hot-wire a car. Later they came back to him and asked him if he wanted to come have sex with a girl they had stashed. He refused. The next contact he had was after the body was found. John Doe told him that Alex had a good idea, putting everything in the creek. Next, he saw a (sic) Alex Hernandez and that Alex Hernandez told him that although he thought he knew everything, he didn't. Not everything was in the creek."

Remember, the law states that this alleged admission can be used against Cruz, and Cruz only. But in a joint trial with Hernandez and Buckley, this statement implicates Hernandez, unfairly prejudicing him. Knight initially wanted to replace the names of Alex Hernandez and John Doe with "certain named friends." He later modified that by saying the real names should be replaced with "certain named persons" or "a certain named person."

The dilemma in this instance for Frank, as Hernandez's lawyer, and Cliff and me, was that there were two other defendants in the courtroom, and the jury would be left to believe that it was or probably was these two defendants that Cruz was allegedly referring to, thereby circumventing the intent of the law. And the kicker was that in Buckley's case, the alleged statement didn't even refer to him, yet the jury wouldn't know that. So Frank felt there should be no reference to other people at all.

Cliff and I believed that since this one statement didn't mention Steve, and that would be helpful to our defense, it should be admitted without any editing. But knowing that other statements did include Steve's name, we also knew that our argument would change for those other statements, and that Frank's position was valid for him. Admittedly, in this and several other instances, our proposals would really butcher the alleged statements as set out in the discovery answer.

Now if you think our positions were not completely fair to the State either, or that they would give the jury twisted and distorted evidence, I would agree with you. As a matter of fact, I told the judge as much when I argued that many of the statements simply could not be edited fairly to all sides. But if the State wanted to try the cases jointly, which they claimed promoted their precious judicial economy, we felt it was the price they would have to pay. Personally, and speaking as a former prosecutor, if I were them, I would have agreed to the severance so that the alleged statements could be introduced without redactions, and been done with it.

On that December 27 date, we still hadn't received the State's proposed redactions in a condition that could be filed and presented to the judge for ruling. Knight had only orally and with handwritten notes relayed his proposals to us. But we felt the process was too slap-dash and unclear, so we wanted the statements typed and presented in writing so we could clearly show, statement by statement, what the State was attempting to do. As you can see by Cliff's argument, we were looking for some way, any way, to get a clear and enforceable ruling from the judge as to how the redacted statements should go in.

> *Judge Kowal:*
> **Then the only thing I can do is put you back into another conference between yourselves so that you know. And in the event you are not satisfied, come immediately before me and spell out where you feel that we have a Bruton[19] [severance] violation.**

> *Mr. Lund:*
> **The problem, Judge, is we have come to loggerheads. We can't reach any kind of accord concerning the redaction of these statements.**
> **What I want is not a handwritten copy from Mr. Knight that says here is what my proposal is. I want it typed out, that says Judge, here's what we intend to use and here's our proposed redaction. So I can hand it to you and say here it is, Judge, we have a Bruton problem.**
> **We go back and forth about what we talked about. All we want is in black and white what the proposed redactions are. We have been asking since August.**

> *Mr. Knight:*
> **They've got it. He wants me to sit down and type. I don't type very well. There it is, word for word. Except for the part where we changed three words.**

Mr. Lund:

> Fine. If Mr. Knight doesn't want to type it, we can go
> through each one of these right now, and show you
> how it is not sufficient. We have approximately 30
> to 40 odd statements here, we don't think they have
> been redacted.
> If he wants to tell the Court now, we'll show you
> where we don't think they satisfied the requirements
> of Bruton.

Mr. Knight:

> We have just had a motion, we have gone into the
> lunchtime already. You have ruled, Judge. I under-
> stand what you are saying. I think you understand
> what I am saying. They just don't like it.

Judge Kowal:

> The Court is also concerned, I don't want to get to a
> point of trial and find out that a severance has to be
> granted and we have wasted time.

Mr. Lund:

> Is it really too much to ask Mr. Knight to type these
> up? He has had back from August.

Judge Kowal:

> I don't know what access he has to a secretary. The
> alternative would be to sit down with him, and have
> a reporter present and reduce it. There are several
> ways of doing something of that nature.
> As long as you are apprised of what the statements
> are and I am apprised also.
> If you are indicating there is an objection to it, I want
> to know about it. In order to properly rule on an ob-
> jection, I have to know what the redactions are. Mr.
> Knight told us he has given them to you.
> If you want to go over it again, go over it again.

For Pete's sake, all we wanted was a ruling as to each specific statement, and for some reason Kowal wouldn't give us one. So my secretary
Pat Conner and I went to work and listed all the statements the State had

tendered in discovery, and beneath each one that we felt we understood how the State intended to edit it, we typed up the redaction. On January 3, 1984—just four days before the start of trial—we appeared before Judge Kowal again. We presented the redactions along with a second motion to sever. In that motion, we requested that, if the motion were denied, the judge should at least consider a separate jury for each defendant. Using this process, when it came time for the State to put on a statement by one of the defendants, only that defendant's jury would hear the statement. The other two juries would be excused. Although this would be cumbersome, it had been done before, mostly in Cook County, and it would solve the severance problem.

The result, after months of pleading, arguing, motions and conferences:

Motions for severance—denied;

Motion for separate juries—denied;

Request for court review of each statement in order to ensure fairness—refused;

Prospects for a fair trial—dismal.

Here's what we got:

> *Judge Kowal:*
> **Look, any statement made, first of all as I indicated before, is attributable to the author. There will be no indication in that statement, reference by name to anybody else.**
> **Now, there are certain statements that are required to indicate that he was with somebody or pointed something out. That can be done without indicating a name.**

> *Mr. Knight:*
> **Or the identity.**

> *Judge Kowal:*
> **And then we'll have the instruction that the jury will be told that they will only apply that statement to the author and no one else. Nor is any inference to be drawn from it.**
> **So I think we can cover that by instruction.**
> **Okay. Anything else?**

Not all errors made at the trial court level result in a reversal in the appellate court. No trial is error free, and some mistakes are expected. Criminal lawyers where I'm from often categorize these errors made as "Big E" or "Little E." Errors that are Big E are those substantial enough to cause a reversal, which usually, but not always, include a remand to the trial court for a new trial. Little E errors are those mistakes that likely won't cause a reversal. Sometimes they're called "harmless errors." But too much Little E can add up to Big E. Occasionally during the course of a case, when a prosecutor wants to get a certain questionable piece of evidence admitted, I'll say, in an effort to convince her to back off, "If that gets in, it'll be Big E." Sometimes I'm sincere, sometimes not. She'll often respond something to the effect of, "I'll take my chances." Sometimes she'll reconsider, but usually not.

Informing the judge that he's about to commit reversible error, which is done without the slang, is another matter. Do that too often, and it's like crying wolf. Defense lawyers learn to pick their spots.

In the Nicarico case, we went into the trial with only a vague idea as to how the co-defendants' statements would be introduced. Plus, we were confident that what we did know of the redactions was they were terribly unfair to the defendants. In the event of a loss, an appellate court would be asked to pass judgment and determine if what had occurred was error. And if it was, was it Big E or Little E?

****

The cases against all three defendants were thin. As I indicated before, the statements attributed to Hernandez and Cruz all had serious problems. They came from disreputable sources, didn't fit the facts of the case, resulted in leading the police on wild goose chases, and so on. And the shoeprint evidence against Steve shouldn't have been able to convince any fair-minded juror that he was guilty, much less guilty beyond a reasonable doubt. These aspects of the State's case would further deteriorate after the trial, but they were shaky to begin with. If this had been a garden-variety residential burglary, with the same evidence, convictions would have been difficult to obtain. But this wasn't just a residential burglary—it was also a murder and sexual assault of a 10-year-old girl. There would be gruesome pictures, grieving family members, and healthy doses of sympathy and emotion. Our fear was that the reasonable doubt standard, already a fluid concept, might get modified in the minds of the jurors to the benefit of the prosecution.

Still, from where I sat, the State needed more evidence, and under very questionable circumstances, they would get it. The most notorious example was what came to be known as the "vision statement." Less than a week before trial, prosecutors disclosed to Tom Laz that a detective (Tom would later learn there were two detectives) was claiming that Rolando Cruz had made a statement to him about a year-and-a-half earlier, in May of 1983, stating that he (Cruz) had a vision of certain details of what had occurred to Jeanine—details that could only have been known by the perpetrator. It was a very damaging piece of evidence against Cruz. Yet no reports were written—even though there were tape recordings and/or written reports of all their other conversations with Cruz. No grand jury testimony was given about it and there was no other evidence of the existence of the statement. One such taped statement made by Cruz even occurred the day after the alleged vision statement, with absolutely no mention of the prior day's damning vision statement being made. As defense lawyers, we were flabbergasted. If such an important piece of evidence truly existed, it would have been preserved or documented in some way. It was a portent of things to come during the trial for Steve as well.

Cliff and I were confident. For starters, we felt that the shoeprint evidence would work out well for Steve. Not only did we have the better experts, but we had the discernable differences between Steve's shoe and the print on the door. Also, Tom Laz and Frank Wesolowski agreed that if we could poke holes in the one piece of physical evidence the State had, it would tarnish the entire investigation and work to their clients' benefit. We let them in on the type of juror we wanted so that they would know what we were doing during jury selection. Beyond that, Steve had a very good alibi—a legitimate defense in Illinois that is used when asserting the defendant was not responsible because he was somewhere else when the crime was committed and otherwise had nothing to do with the crime, but a term that defense lawyers detest because it connotes a lame excuse.

****

My in-laws, Amy and I celebrated my daughter's first birthday a few days early because her actual birthday landed on the day we would begin picking the jury. Everyone enjoyed themselves except, of course, me. I was scared shitless about the impending trial. Beyond that, it wasn't lost on me that I was celebrating the life of my daughter while another family was still grieving the loss of theirs. But I was so confident in Steve's innocence that during the weeks leading up to the trial, I had this crazy idea the State was going to just dismiss his case, as well as the charges against

Hernandez and Cruz.

It was the first of a few naïve notions I would entertain regarding the Nicarico prosecution. I held on to that hope right up to the start of jury selection.

Race to Trial—Sidebar

Conventional Nicarico case wisdom says there are three people who stand out over and above the rest in the courageous stances they took to see that justice was done. In this case, conventional wisdom got it mostly right, but I'm going to add one a little later on who I think deserves to be in this gutsy group. They each went against the grain of what you would have expected them to do, and to one extent or another, they all paid a price for the positions they took.

The first of these legal heroes is John Sam. John was one of the lead detectives from the DuPage County Sheriff's Office assigned to investigate this case. He was involved in a number of interrogations of Steve, as well as other aspects of the investigation. He knew early on that the original three defendants had nothing to do with the crimes against Jeanine, and he told anyone who would listen they were chasing the wrong people.

That kind of independent thinking didn't sit well with his superiors. As a result, he was dressed down on more than one occasion by his employer, the elected DuPage County Sheriff, Richard Doria. Those conversations would go something like this:

"Tom Knight's not too happy that you're going around telling people you don't think these three guys killed Jeanine," Doria would say.

"I'm just trying to find out who committed this crime."

"Well, stop rockin' the boat."

"I'm not rockin' the boat. Besides, Tom Knight's not my boss," Sam would respond. "You are."

John Sam was correct about that, but in the technical sense only. Tom Knight was running the show, and John's reward for speaking his mind and following his own hunches was to get assigned to scope out convenience stores for underage drinkers. He was fed up, so before the trial, John resigned his position at the Sheriff's Office. He never worked as a police officer again. Today, he works for a heating and air conditioning company.

John was the very first person in this case to vocally criticize the direction of the investigation of the Nicarico case. With the possible exceptions of Phil Gilman, the DuPage County Lab Director who also

voiced concerns about the case, and John Gorajczyk, he stood alone—
well before the confessions of another person, admitting that he alone
committed these crimes, would cause a small army of lawyers, cops and
journalists to begin to turn the tide.

John Sam was meant to be a cop, and the citizens of DuPage County
were cheated out of one of the best. Since his resignation, John has
refused to receive most of the accolades thrown in his direction. I all
but begged him to go to Springfield a number of years ago to be feted
by a group that wanted to honor him for his contribution to the case. He
refused.

Chapter 9

Trial

Including jury selection, the Nicarico trial lasted seven weeks. It was one of the longer state trials in Illinois history. Most of it took place in one courtroom, but at the tail end, courthouse logistics forced us to move down the hall. Though the courtrooms were relatively large, they became cramped due to the number of lawyers and defendants involved. The courtrooms were also cluttered with physical evidence and banker's boxes containing the lawyers' files.

The prosecutors and the defendants, with their lawyers, each had a table. The prosecutors' table, as is almost always the case with jury trials, was the closest to the jury. I've often heard defense lawyers complain about that, and I occasionally do as well, based on the belief that being closer to the jury brings about the advantage of familiarity. In our case, doing otherwise would have been difficult to arrange since there were three defense tables. There is one benefit, however, to being farther from the jury. It makes communication with client and co-counsel easier and more private.

The audience section of the courtrooms—divided much like a wedding ceremony, with supporters of the defendants on one side and of the Nicaricos on the other—was far more populated than that at the average murder trial. On some days, the courtroom was packed. Since the Nicarico supporters outnumbered those of the defendants, when necessary they would take over any unused seating space on the "defendants' side." The press usually sat in the front areas of the defense section as well.

I wouldn't go so far as to say that the entire courtroom setting was intimate, but it wasn't spacious, either.

Jury Selection

The most mysterious part of a trial for me is jury selection. Prosecutors and defense lawyers are given a certain number of peremptory challenges, depending on the type of case and the number of defendants. Peremptory challenges allow a party to excuse jurors for, with a few exceptions, any reason that party sees fit. In our case, the law at the time allowed each defendant and the State 12 peremptories.

Not included in those challenges are what are called "challenges for cause"—where the court excuses a juror and neither party has to burn a valuable peremptory. Those are instances where the judge rules, based on the juror's answers to questions, that the juror simply cannot be fair or follow the law. Whenever a lawyer spots a potential juror he or she doesn't like, he or she will sometimes attempt to elicit information from that juror that will cause the judge to excuse the juror for cause in order to save peremptories.

I've only used jury consultants once in my career, and they were very helpful, but financial constraints preclude such a luxury in almost all criminal trials. That leaves it up to lawyer and client. So before every jury trial, I try to think about both the general and specific qualities I want in a juror. By general qualities, I mean things like the ability to be fair, be open-minded and have a willingness to follow the constitutional principles that go along with a criminal case—the burden of proof, the reasonable doubt standard, that the defendant doesn't have to testify or even put on any evidence, and so on. The specific qualities I look for depend on the facts of the case, the defendant, the complaining witness or victim—many things, really.

Overall, jury selection can be complicated because jurors are adult human beings, all of whom have been around the block a few times, so each individual comes to us with a mixed background. In the end, for me, jury selection really comes down to two things.

First, all the thinking, overthinking and sweating out the details of each juror—and oftentimes outsmarting myself—are not nearly as important as the gut reaction I have after having had a brief opportunity to communicate with them.

Second, all that allows me to do is to challenge the patently bad potential jurors—the ones who, for whatever reason, give me that strong feeling that they cannot be fair to my client.

There are things that lawyers are not supposed to consider when selecting a jury. In the not too distant past, prosecutors were accused of, and many times were, using their peremptory challenges to eliminate minority jurors for racial reasons, especially when the defendant was also a minority. But in 1986, the U.S. Supreme Court ruled that such discriminatory practices violate a defendant's 6th Amendment right to a fair jury and his 14th Amendment right to equal protection of the law.

The Court held that whenever prosecutors exercise a challenge on a prospective minority juror, there has to be a legitimate race-neutral reason. The Supreme Court outlined a process the trial court must go through if the defense lawyer raises the issue.[20]

The Supreme Court has expanded this principle in a number of ways, including to hold that jurors may not be excluded solely on the basis of gender, either.[21] And, focusing on the constitutional rights of prospective jurors themselves to be able to sit on juries, the Court has held that defense lawyers are subject to the same prohibitions.[22] All of this has helped considerably, but prosecutors who still want to strike minority jurors have found creative ways to come up with race-neutral reasons.

As a defense lawyer, I almost always take the issue of race head on. Since I practice mostly in suburban counties, there have been times when the jury venire (the group of potential jurors in the courtroom from which the jury is selected) is all, or almost all, white, and my client is African-American or Hispanic. I make it a practice to ask each juror if that situation will make it difficult for them to be fair. I don't really expect that they will admit to a problem, if one exists, but it does help those who have a problem to put those feelings in check if they are picked. If potential jurors take offense at that, I've only had one over the years vocalize it in court.

In 1995 I defended a young African-American man who was accused of being the driver and an accomplice, along with a number of other African-Americans, in the murder of a Latino whom they thought was a member of a rival gang in Aurora. As it turned out, the deceased was no such thing. He was merely a college student who had run out of fuel and was walking to a service station to pick up a gallon of gas to put into his car. Aside from being a gang case, there were also obvious racial overtones. During jury selection, a middle-aged Hispanic gentleman was considered as a prospective juror. I was nervous about this juror because I was afraid he, as a Latino, might identify with the victim and not be fair to my African-American client. But as I engaged him in conversation and fronted my concerns to him, my gut told me otherwise. He seemed thoughtful and fair. I even asked him if he understood the reason for my concern, and whether my client and I had anything to worry about in the race department. He smiled, said he understood my fear, but that we didn't have to worry about any ethnic connection he might make with the victim or his family, or the fact that my client was African-American.

I leaned over to my client and told him my concerns. But I also said I liked him, thought he would be a fair juror and thought we should keep him. My client liked him, too, and told me he wanted him on the jury. So onto the jury he went. At the conclusion of the trial, when the jury reached their verdict and the judge asked who the foreperson was, the

Hispanic gentleman raised his hand and delivered the verdict forms to the bailiff. I have to admit that made me nervous. Jury forepersons are, by definition, leaders on the jury, and their opinions usually carry more weight than that of other jurors. After the not guilty verdict was read, I went out of my way to make eye contact with the foreperson as I thanked the jury from the defense table.

In another murder case I defended in the late-'90s, I was one of five lawyers representing a young Latino who had killed a white police officer from Joliet, Illinois. Despite plenty of evidence showing that the young man had killed the officer in self-defense, his first trial ended with a conviction and a sentence of death. His verdict was reversed due to errors in the jury instructions, and a new team of lawyers headed up by outstanding Los Angeles trial lawyer Milton Grimes was brought in to defend the young man at his retrial. Milton is an African-American. The relevance of the races of the people I have identified here will soon be clear. Wanting a more experienced Illinois lawyer to assist with the defense, I was brought into the case at the last minute—just two weeks prior to the start of the trial.

At one point during jury selection, a youngish African-American woman was being questioned as a potential juror by Milton. Now her being black, as a general proposition for this kind of a case, was a very good thing. Milton was black and our client was a fellow minority, so she could identify with our side. She would also be aware of how minorities too often are treated poorly by the police and that there might be circumstances where a young Latino may have to defend himself against a white police officer.

During Milton's "voir dire" (the questioning of potential jurors) of her, however, we discovered the prospective juror had been living with a police officer from a local department for quite a few years. In my mind, that changed the whole equation, but I sensed by Milton's questions that he was going to accept her. After he was done questioning her, our defense team huddled at our table.

"I like her," Milton whispered to the rest of us. "We should keep her."

"Oh, c'mon, Milton, she's sleeping with a cop. They might as well be married. Way too risky," I chimed in.

Milton just smiled. "She's one of mine, Gary. When we're dealing with your people, you can have the final say. But this one's mine."

So we kept her. It turns out Milton knew exactly what he was talking about. The jury ended up acquitting our client of murder and instead found him guilty of involuntary manslaughter. Since he had already served more than the maximum allowable sentence for that offense, the judge reduced his bond so he could be released soon after the verdict.

The Nicarico trial, starting with jury selection, began on January 7, 1985. It took us a week to pick the jury, which for me was a record long time. Several factors complicated the process. Most importantly, the jury had to be death-qualified, or *Witherspooned*. That was a huge disappointment for Steve, Cliff and me. After it became clear that the three defendants would be jointly tried, we hoped Laz and Wesolowski would change their minds and do as we had planned and, prior to trial, waive a jury for the death penalty phase. That would have eliminated the need to go through the death qualification process and increased the likelihood of an open-minded jury. Since they didn't want to give up their right to have a jury decide on whether to impose the death penalty—should it come to that—and we were all forced to have the same jury, we were stuck. As a consequence, there was no longer an advantage to us for a pretrial jury waiver for the sentencing phase, either.

Other factors lengthened the jury selection process. That there were three defendants, as opposed to the typical one, to question and pass on jurors was one of them. The gruesome and emotionally intense nature of the crime, which caused in-depth inquiry by the lawyers, was another. Surprisingly, the massive publicity surrounding the case, which also was addressed during voir dire, didn't cause as many problems as we had feared. I was astonished at the number of potential jurors who had only a vague knowledge or recollection of the case. And many of those who had been regularly exposed to press accounts were apparently not as poisoned by them as we had suspected. Whatever remote chance we had of getting a jury from another county, which we had requested in our Motion for Change of Venue, evaporated.

Considering the circumstances, we pretty much got the jury we wanted. It was conservative, but that was largely a function of picking a death-qualified jury from the most conservative county in the Chicago area. From what we could tell, it was also a smart jury. At least, we hoped, smart enough to see through the junk science of Dr. Louise Robbins.

Opening Statements and Laying the Groundwork

Before opening statements began, Cliff and I made a final effort to blunt the effect of the joint trial and the uncertainty as to the way the evidence of admissions would go in. We asked the judge, again, to go over statements individually to see if they needed more editing. We basically got the same response as we had before—a "let's wait and see" attitude.

But we also asked the court to prohibit the State from introducing any evidence of a social relationship between Steve and his co-defendants. As with the redactions issue, by the time we were done arguing, we weren't clear as to where we stood. I wasn't confident.

Knight's opening was long and detailed, setting out his theory that Jeanine was murdered and raped in a multi-defendant residential burglary gone bad. Among many other things, he detailed the first statement Alex gave to the police when Alex claimed that a guy named "Ricky" admitted to being Jeanine's killer. Knight added that Alex was in a car with his "friends" Steve Buckley and Mike Castro at the time. My immediate objection resulted in a mild rebuke from Judge Kowal, but the connection had been made. Knight's opening drew a few other objections from me, as well as a motion for a mistrial, which was denied.[23]

The groundwork for an unconstitutional connection between Steve's co-defendants, their statements, and Steve had begun. This was the very basis for our multiple severance motions. But in comparison with what the State would do on this issue later in the trial, Knight's opening was tame.

This was the first opening statement I ever gave as a defense lawyer in a criminal case, and in it I struggled with some of the same issues I still struggle with today regarding openings—that is, how much information I should provide to the jury.

Conventional wisdom in the legal community, which I agree with, says that jurors make up their minds early, so a powerful opening is crucial. That usually includes laying out most of your case. By the same token, a combination of factors—mostly, not knowing for sure how a case will unfold and wanting to play some of your cards close to your vest—might dictate a different strategy.

What I didn't really understand at the time was that a good opening can accomplish both goals.

As far as my opening was concerned, it was brief, not strong, and not very informative. In a word, it was ineffective. I was off to an unimpressive start.

If I were to give an opening statement in the Nicarico case today, it would be much different. Today, I would use exhibits and go into greater detail to inform the jury what the evidence would look like—to at least get them thinking that there were plenty of facts to show that there was another side to this case.

What I've learned over the years is that the best way to get the jury to keep an open mind about a case is to give them a good reason to do so in the opening. That's something I failed to do in my first one.

State's Case

After the opening statements were completed, Knight and King—occasionally referred to as the "chess pieces" by defense counsel in private conversations—devoted a substantial period of time presenting evidence pertaining to the discovery of the crime, the locating of Jeanine's body, the sexual assault, the collection of physical evidence, and the specific cause of Jeanine's death.

They established that on February 25, 1983, 10-year-old Jeanine stayed home from school as a result of being sick. Since both of her parents, Tom and Pat Nicarico, worked, and her two older sisters also attended school, Jeanine stayed home alone.

Mrs. Nicarico, a secretary at a nearby elementary school, stayed in contact with Jeanine by telephone and twice in person, the second time being for lunch. Before Mrs. Nicarico returned to work after lunch, Jeanine told her that a man, later determined to be a gas company meter reader, had come to the door. Mrs. Nicarico gently reminded Jeanine not to open the door for anyone.

Jeanine's sister, Kathy, returned home from school around 3 p.m. to discover their home had been broken into and Jeanine was missing. Kathy immediately contacted a neighbor, and soon thereafter the police were at the scene.

They discovered that entry had been made into the Nicarico home by someone kicking open the front door. Though it was in the police jurisdiction of the DuPage County Sheriff—the Nicaricos lived just outside the city limits in unincorporated Naperville—it was an alert Naperville city police officer, sent to the scene when it wasn't clear which department had authority, who discovered the shoeprint on the door.

Other local police departments and the FBI joined the sheriff's office to form a task force to find Jeanine and her kidnapper. Two days after the abduction, several young men on the Illinois Prairie Path, a few miles from the Nicarico home, discovered Jeanine's lifeless body.

She had been severely beaten about her head and face with some type of blunt object. Jeanine had also been sexually assaulted as established later by semen found on the anal swabs used in the evidence collection process.

Although the State's theory was that this was a burglary gone bad committed by the three defendants, no items of any value had been taken from the residence.

Statements Allegedly Made by Hernandez and Cruz

After laying that groundwork, the State presented testimony from a number of witnesses claiming to have heard statements from Hernandez and Cruz. In theory, those statements should have been redacted sufficiently so that references to any co-defendant, either direct or indirect, would be eliminated. This was the issue Judge Kowal should have nailed down prior to trial, but had not. But even if the judge had given the correct and strict redactions necessary to survive an appeal, I don't think it would have made much of a difference. The prosecutors seemed to have no problem violating the already loose and amorphous rulings that Kowal had handed down on the issue. That was exactly what we had feared, was what the law prohibited, and had been the reason for the severance motions and the request for stricter redactions. Through this combination of insufficient redactions and the admission of inadmissible evidence, the statements allegedly made by Hernandez and Cruz unfairly prejudiced Steve. Hernandez and Cruz were themselves prejudiced by alleged statements that were only supposed to be admissible against the statement's maker.

Our multiple objections, and those of Laz and Wesolowski, made throughout the course of the trial, were mostly overruled. Cliff and I were frustrated that Steve was being dragged into the statements that Cruz and Hernandez allegedly had made. The State would end up paying a heavy price for their conduct, but that wasn't any solace at the time the evidence was going in.

Enhanced Shoeprint Testimony

During the months preceding the trial, I had read everything I could on the science behind shoeprint comparisons. As any lawyer should under these circumstances, I became very knowledgeable on the subject. And while I agree that the field is a subject for expert testimony in that a witness with superior knowledge, experience and training can detect things that the lay person cannot, it is distinguishable from other forensic sciences in that the juror can actually participate in the examination process. Unlike other sciences—for example, DNA testing with its blurred lines and confusing explanations and statistics, psychiatric evidence with its vague and unfamiliar concepts, forensic pathology/cause of death with the requirement of a doctor to explain how the death occurred, drug testing, with its need for complicated machinery to prepare charts for the expert to interpret—shoeprints are something the lay person can observe, interpret and understand. There were significant differences between the shoeprint found on the Nicarico door and the sole of Steve's shoe. The State's witnesses would have to concede these differences, but they would tie themselves up in knots trying to explain how these differences came to occur.

The State's first witness on the subject was Don Schmitt. Even though the court said he was qualified as an expert, he was no such thing. Schmitt was the DuPage County Crime Lab's quartermaster—he looked after the evidence in the lab. At some point in his past, he had done shoe-print work, but it wasn't much. When Steve's shoes were first brought to the lab, Schmitt made some inked prints of the right sole and compared them to the door print. He opined that Steve's shoe made the print on the door. Schmitt prepared no report and wasn't even going to be called as a witness. But when we discovered the John Gorajczyk evidence, the State threw Schmitt onto the list of witnesses. I think the State was trying to detract from the Gorajczyk debacle by attempting to show that when the shoe first came in, the DuPage County Crime Lab just had a couple of people take a look at it, come to different conclusions, and then sent it off to the "real" experts. They failed. Schmitt was a joke—Knight even admitted to his lack of expertise later in his closing argument—and that's how I was able to portray him in a cross-examination that I was extremely pleased with.

The next of the State's shoeprint witnesses would be another story altogether.

Pride Goeth Before the Fall

All lawyers have good and bad moments or days, and I'm no exception. There are times when I have done so well in court that I feel like I'm the reincarnation of Clarence Darrow. There are other times when I think the State of Illinois was foolish to grant me a law license. I'm not at all superstitious, except to this extent. Whenever I have one of those "Darrow-like" moments, I don't pat myself on the back or internally bask in the glory of my legal "greatness." It's definitely bad karma. It seems as though every time I do that, invariably, and very soon thereafter, I completely screw something up, do damage to my client's case, and embarrass myself.

After I took apart Don Schmitt on the witness stand, I never felt more confident about winning the case and my ability as a defense lawyer. Boy, was I proud of myself.

"I Think I Just Killed Steve Buckley"

Ed German was a fingerprint and shoeprint expert at the Illinois State Police Crime Lab when the shoe evidence was sent to him to examine. After he completed his analysis, his report was simple and very brief. He concluded that Steve's shoe "could have" made the print on the Nicarico door. Such an inconclusive opinion wasn't going to help the prosecution very much. Nevertheless, that's what I expected German to say when he testified. How much harm could he do, right?

As Tom Knight took him through his direct examination, a confident Ed German testified that the differences between the sole of Steve's shoe and the print on the door were explainable by the fact that there was significant movement and distortion on the door print causing those dissimilarities. He claimed to have found three accidental characteristics on Steve's right shoe—those marks on shoe soles caused by gouges, scrapes, cuts and the like—that were observable and matched the print on the door. Further, according to German, the manufactured characteristics matched up as well. He then opined that Steve's shoe probably made the print on the door.

German had enhanced his courtroom opinion from what was in his report—exactly what the State needed! Now, to be fair, prior to trial I had met with German at the State Crime Lab in Springfield, and he had told me then that he felt more strongly about the connection between Steve's shoe and the door print than the "could have" opinion he had written. Still, I didn't expect him to vary from his written report when he testified.

When German answered questions on direct examination, I could tell that he was experienced and skilled at testifying. He was glib and slick, and I could see that before I asked him the first question on cross.

Knowing these things, I should have handled the cross of German with great care. He was a dangerous witness. I should have had confidence in the fact that there were obvious differences between the print and Steve's shoe that were difficult to explain, that there was a built-in contradiction in his claiming of significant distortion on the print and then testifying that there were enough similarities to come up with his "probable" opinion, and that our experts would successfully contradict his explanations. Most of these things I could have tied up in closing argument. My cross should have gotten him to admit the patently obvious things helpful to Steve's defense, and then to sit down. But I had just destroyed Don Schmitt on the witness stand—why not Ed German, too?

That kind of hubris led to that day's downfall for me. Words here cannot possibly describe how poorly the cross-examination of Ed German went. During hours of testimony, German explained why he was not impressed with the differences I pointed out between the shoe and the print. The fact that our investigator had actually purchased shoes that had the New Silver Cloud sole with arcs in the heel that matched the arcs on the door, but went in the opposite direction of the heel arcs on Steve's shoe, was brushed off as insignificant. As my frustration grew, and no doubt showed, I got flustered and began violating the rules attorneys, especially defense attorneys, are supposed to follow during cross-examination. Those rules include controlling the witness and not letting him or her give lengthy responses. This is done by asking leading questions that are simple and which usually require only a yes or no answer.

Instead, I asked open-ended, wordy and complicated questions. German skillfully took those opportunities to buttress his findings with long-winded answers, often going way beyond what I had asked—only making matters worse for me, or, should I say, Steve. I let German repeat many of the conclusions that he had testified to on direct examination. I was unable to control him or the cross-examination. And when I failed at all of these things, I didn't have the good sense to find a graceful way to end the cross on some kind of positive note and live to fight another day.

It's entirely possible that the jury's opinion of German's testimony actually improved after I was done. It was a disaster, as the following two of my cross-examination questions clearly show.

>*Mr. Johnson:*
>
>**At some point, Mr. German, when the horizontal groove on the toe area hit the door it made a mark; did it not? At some point?**

>Mr. German:
>
>**Perhaps but not necessarily. I would not have expected it to be the same type of mark as this. If you look at the overall photograph of the door, even without the transparency, you notice in general the door is relatively dark compared to the concentration of dust that you have in the shoe area. I believe that at the time that People's Exhibit 8A [Steve's right shoe], the shoe that made the impression on the door, that there was a layer of dust on the bottom of that shoe, such as you would have on your shoe if you stood in some dust. And when the contact was made with the**

door, the dust was on the tops of the ridges and the tops of the tread design and also, of course, the dust was down inside in the lower areas also. So at the initial point of impact, when there was a very forceful smashing blow to cause the transfer of the dust, it transferred from both locations, from the upraised area and the lower areas because the dust was carried by this shoe. Then, after that time, it was evident by the slippage and the fact that subsequent impressions, not made at that time, the shoe slipped down. At that time the shoe slipped down, the dust was already transferred from the initial contact and then the shoe slipped down and when it left, it was pulled away, it pulled away dust on the ridges here and that's what left this type of impression.

Later in the cross-examination:

Mr. Johnson:

Okay. You are saying because of movement or distortion that these dark areas, which represent grooves, do not match the light areas in the photographs, which also represent grooves. They come down at a different angle, at least according to the two photographs, here, the overlay and the photograph, correct?

Mr. German:

It's a very long question, but, no, your interpretation is not correct. They are very nearly identical to my trained eye. I can see that there's very, very good correlation, especially in the areas that you are talking about. If we slip it back to the original position, you will see they very nearly conform, almost identical, considering the distortion, considering the fact it is a photograph of the shoe as opposed to the actual impression. It's a very good so-called registration. It's a very good overlay in this location.

My current law partner of 25 years, David Camic, and I have litigated a number of cases together, including two murder trials. He is one of the best trial lawyers I know and is a very skillful cross-examiner. Over time, we developed a system in court of warning each other—particularly when one of us is cross-examining an opposing witness—when we are treading into any kind of dangerous territory. We let out a soft but audible hiss, as if a rattlesnake were about to rise up and bite the cross-examiner. It's been pretty effective.

Cliff and I hadn't worked out such a system, though I'm sure there were times during my cross of German that he probably wanted to just tackle me, tell me to shut the hell up, and drag me back to our table. I know Laz and Wesolowski, whose clients' fates were linked to Steve's, felt that way. But honestly, that day, I don't think any of that would have worked.

German's testimony ended on a Friday afternoon. The bad news about that was that it allowed his opinions and explanations to sink into the jurors' minds for an entire weekend. The good news was that I could take the night off. After court, I met Cliff for beers at Scotland Yard, a tavern in St. Charles. I'm sure Cliff could tell how I was feeling. He bought us each a beer and I took a couple of gulps.

"Honest to God, Cliff, I think I just killed Steve Buckley," I sighed.

Cliff laughed, which actually made me feel better.

"It didn't go as bad as you think, Gary. German was slick, but maybe too slick. He wouldn't give you anything, and I'll bet the jury saw that. Don't let this get you down."

Cliff spent the next couple of hours talking me off the ledge, trying to boost my morale and confidence. He was only moderately successful. When I got home, I told Amy about my disastrous day.

"Was it really that bad?" she asked.

"Amy, I really got my ass kicked. I'll tell you what I told Cliff. I feel like I just killed Steve Buckley."

"What? C'mon, Gary. You've always bounced back from these things before. You will this time, too."

"I'm not so sure. It was that bad."

"Well," Amy said, following with the only piece of advice that made sense at the time. "You're going to have to."

****

Over the years, I've found a good source of criminal advocacy advice to be court reporters—the people who take down and transcribe, word for word, courtroom testimony, legal arguments, rulings and much more. They've helped me learn how to preserve the record for possible appeal, they've convinced me to slow down my speech—some of them claimed that I talk too fast!—and they've provided substantive assistance as well.

I recall one trial during my first stint as a prosecutor when I had a difficult time with a defense witness. After the day was over, I was packing up my file and grousing about the witness's testimony. Liz Lemke, the court reporter, heard me and chided me for failing to see anything helpful to my case in the witness's testimony.

"You're letting the negative stuff blind you to the things the witness said that you can use to your advantage." Liz went on to explain what I had failed to see—I can't recall what it was now—but she was absolutely right. "And that's true of every adverse witness who testifies," Liz continued. "There's almost always something you can find that will be helpful to you."

It was great advice, and I've carried it with me to this day. Amazingly, it even proved to be true with Ed German, and in a very big way—we just didn't know it at the time.

German had testified that when he wrote his report he worked for the Illinois State Police Crime Lab, and their rules restricted him from elaborating any further on a "could have" opinion. Knight argued, in his closing argument, that meant the ISP Crime Lab rules allowed shoeprint examiners to come to only one of three conclusions—that a shoe: 1) did make a print; 2) could not have made a print; or 3) could have made a print. The thrust of their position was that once German's opinion fell into the "could have" category, ISP Crime Lab rules would not allow him to describe or explain probabilities. However, since at the time of his testimony German no longer worked at the ISP Crime Lab, he felt he was no longer subject to their restrictions and was free to modify, or enhance, what was in his report.

It would take a few days and an alert Cliff Lund to reveal the importance of this information.

"Star Witness"

Dr. Louise Robbins was an associate professor of anthropology at the University of North Carolina-Greensboro. Anthropology is not a field normally associated with forensic shoeprint examinations, but she became involved in it after studying footprints at various archaeological digs. And her history there wasn't without controversy. On one such dig led by the famed paleoanthropologist Mary Leakey, Robbins confused a set of ancient hominid (early human and other primates) footprints for bovid (hoofed animal) prints. She was corrected by, among others, the dig team's maintenance man. Later, after conceding that they were hominid prints, she went on to claim to know the gender of the maker of one of a subsequent set of similar prints, and that another source of one of the prints had possibly been pregnant. Of course, these opinions were met with extreme skepticism.[24]

Eventually, Dr. Robbins developed an untested and controversial theory that each individual leaves a shoeprint as unique as a fingerprint. This allowed her to do something that no other qualified forensic shoeprint expert would do—that is, to connect a shoe to a shoeprint, to the exclusion of all other shoes in the world, without matching accidental characteristics.[25] Then she began pushing herself on the judicial system.

Although she had done some work for defense lawyers, she testified almost exclusively for the government. When prosecutors had nowhere else to go, they turned to her, and she never disappointed. By the time she got to the Nicarico case, she had been testifying for years throughout the United States and once in Canada, selling her shoeprint "uniqueness" theory. I discovered a small army of defense lawyers, forensic experts (anthropologists and shoeprint examiners), and one prosecutor who were more than eager to provide us with transcripts, strategies and suggestions as to how to handle her, along with moral support.

Judge Kowal had denied us our pretrial *Frye* hearing—where we would have attempted to exclude Dr. Robbins's testimony as not being generally accepted in the scientific community by using other experts and their writings—holding instead that we would have to establish that proposition based on the evidence presented at trial. Since our experts wouldn't be testifying until the State's case-in-chief was completed, forcing us to play by those rules, which all but required us to get her to criticize her own methods and theories, ensured failure as to that issue.

In some ways, after the Ed German fiasco, Dr. Robbins's testimony was anticlimactic. Before her testimony, I requested an opportunity to question her outside the presence of the jury. I figured if I could expose some of her wild ideas to Kowal, he just might not let her testify in front of the jury. I reminded the judge that he had stricken my pretrial motion to preclude her from testifying, so he should at least grant me this. Kowal refused. During cross-examination in the presence of the jury, she was forced to admit that a court in Canada, though allowing her to testify as to footprint testimony, would not let her give an opinion as a shoeprint expert. In another part of my cross, after denying that she ever claimed that she could determine a person's race from a shoeprint, Judge Kowal refused to allow my attempts to impeach her with prior testimony from a federal case out of Pennsylvania, where she testified that she was able to "suggest" a person's race by examining the sole of his shoe. And on it went. In the end, though, as expected, Kowal allowed her to testify.

Surprisingly, after all the hoopla over Dr. Robbins and her controversial theories and conclusions, her testimony was not terribly effective. I was incredibly well-prepared for Dr. Robbins's testimony, and overall, my cross punched holes in her testimony. I had learned my lessons from the Ed German screw-up.

But she did give the State the one thing it so desperately needed—a definitive opinion that Steve's shoe, to the exclusion of all other shoes, made the print on the Nicarico front door.

"Ask Him for His Notes"

The final shoeprint expert witness for the State was Robert Olsen, who was employed by the Kansas Bureau of Investigations. He was a professional colleague of Ed German, and from what I could tell, that's how he got involved in the case. Prior to trial he wrote a very brief report stating that Steve's shoe was "similar in general class characteristics" to the print on the Nicarico door. Suspecting that he, too, had modified his opinion without the State giving any notice to us, I asked about it just before he testified. Sure enough, he was now saying that it was "highly probable" that Steve's shoe made the print—quite a jump. We complained to Kowal, who only provided us with the remedy of requiring Olsen to give us an interview before his testimony. That interview turned up gold.

Cliff and I spoke to Olsen in the court reporters' room and we learned a couple of things. First, Olsen claimed to have changed his testimony as a result of changes in KBI regulations since he had written his report. He said this allowed him to be more specific on those occasions when his opinion fell somewhere between a shoe "could not" have made a given print and a shoe "did" make a print. Second, he brought with him a folder of papers and notes. Included in that folder were notes Ed German had written when he conducted his examination. We didn't, however, read the contents of the folder—I can't recall if Olsen wouldn't let us or if Cliff and I just decided to ask the judge for them later.

Olsen's direct examination followed. As Knight proceeded, I got the feeling that the jury was becoming bored with shoeprint testimony. That was fine with me, except that we had experts lined up to testify and we wanted the jury to pay close attention to them. Cliff must have sensed that I had completely forgotten about the notes, so during Olsen's direct, he nudged me and whispered, "Ask him for his notes." I waited for the right time and approached the bench so the jury couldn't hear, asking for the notes. There was no resistance—we were promised the notes, which we received during a break between direct and cross.

Now is probably a good time to tell you a little more about my co-counsel, Cliff Lund. Over the years, I've received a lot of praise for the defense of Steve Buckley. Whether I've deserved it or not may be debatable, but I'm happy to say that most people have been very positive. Sadly, and unfairly, Cliff has never really been recognized for his efforts in the case.

This is probably because I was responsible for most of the direct and cross-examinations at trial. But our joint venture in defending Steve was a true partnership. He and I contributed equally, and in different ways. We each had strong points that complemented the other. And one of Cliff's strengths was, and still is, his intellect.

Throughout my career, I've run into plenty of lawyers who are more intelligent than I am. I guess one of my strengths is that instead of being intimidated by them, I get a bit of a chip on my shoulder and try to out-lawyer the smarter lawyer. Almost always, with a little hard work, I can stay in the ballpark with these folks. But there are some people who are just so far ahead of the game that no amount of hard work will completely close the gap.

Cliff is one of those people. When Cliff and I would plan or strategize about any aspect of the case, I often just sat back and listened as he analyzed and spotted things I never thought of. And regarding those things I would have eventually figured out on my own, Cliff would get there well before me. He was always several steps ahead of everyone else. He's the smartest lawyer I've ever known.

During the recess, Cliff and I sat at counsel table and went through Olsen's file. After reviewing Olsen's notes, we quickly proceeded to Ed German's handwritten notes that were contained in the folder. These were documents we had not yet seen, because they weren't turned over to us in discovery. They were a couple of pages long and were attached to a copy of his report. One page was entitled "Footwear Evidence Worksheet" and was signed by German.

In a box entitled "Results of Comparison," German summarized the conclusions of his examination of Exhibit 2, which was the lab exhibit number for Steve's right shoe. Rather than paraphrase, here is what German wrote in its entirety in the "Results" box, with emphasis supplied in bold by me:

> *"Ex. 2 Rt. Shoe 'Could Have'*
> Poor quality questioned print—could have **at best**— similarities within acceptable parameters observed when considerable distortion and movement introduced during test impressions. **Another shoe very well could have made the questioned print—other than Exhibit 2 right shoe."**

Another shoe very well could have made the print?! That sure was different from German's trial testimony, when he all but said Steve's shoe made the print on the Nicarico door. And could have *at best*?! That meant German was awfully damn close to being in the next category he was allowed to use at the ISP Crime Lab—"could not have."

"Damn, look at this, Cliff!" I was excited, and pissed, at the same time. "We should have had these notes a long time ago. I can't believe he testified the way he did."

"We have to get German back on the stand. We have to get this before the jury," Cliff whispered.

"I think he's out of state," I responded. "I don't know exactly where he is, and when we find out, then we have to go through the out-of-state subpoena crap." Serving a witness with a subpoena in-state is a relatively simple process of serving the subpoena on the witness. If, however, the witness is in another state, to require his or her attendance in Illinois requires the court in Illinois—and, eventually, the court in the state where the witness is—to issue the necessary orders. It's a bit of a process, and is something you don't want to have to do during a trial.

"We'll work on that," Cliff said. "In the meantime, I think you can question Olsen about these notes—bring out their contents and let them sink in with the jury—based on *Wilson versus Clark.*"

Cliff was right. Based on the then-relatively recent Illinois case of *Wilson v. Clark*,[26] if an expert witness bases his opinion on the facts or opinions of others, and those facts or opinions are of a type reasonably relied upon by experts in his field, then those underlying facts or opinions can be brought out during either direct or cross-examination of the expert. It was something federal courts had been doing for a while, but it was somewhat new law for Illinois state courts. And while the principle of *Wilson v. Clark* is second nature to trial lawyers today, back then it was pretty cutting edge stuff. Leave it to Cliff!

Unfortunately, the *Wilson v. Clark* angle didn't pan out. But during the long and heated arguments for and against it, we were able to educate the judge on what the notes said. It was a turning point, of sorts. For the first time, I saw a change in Kowal. He appeared genuinely irritated, maybe even upset, at this new information. He had heard German's powerful testimony and was now confronted with very impeaching notes—notes we should have had before German testified.

We demanded that Ed German be required to return to Illinois to answer for these notes. Judge Kowal had absolutely no problem with that.

Other Evidence

The State presented other evidence in an attempt to connect Steve to Jeanine Nicarico's abduction, sexual assault and murder. And for most of it, the Liz Lemke rule—that our opponent's testimony had information helpful to our case—would again prove itself to be true. Some of their evidence would be helpful at trial, and some would be beneficial later, after trial, when the real murderer of Jeanine Nicarico would confess that he alone committed these crimes.

When Joann Johannville walked up to the witness stand, I sensed something unexpected was about to happen. Mrs. Johannville was an older woman who was a neighbor of the Nicaricos, and her husband owned an upholstery repair business located in a garage next door to the Nicarico house. Shortly after Jeanine was taken, Mrs. Johannville was interviewed by the police and FBI about a strange-looking person she had seen driving in her neighborhood while she was driving home from lunch with her husband on the day of the kidnapping. Their cars had passed each other going in opposite directions very close to the Nicarico house.

During a very brief direct examination, Mrs. Johannville pointed to Steve and positively identified him as the driver she had seen. The only prior "on-the-record" attempt she had made at an ID occurred at the grand jury, when she had been shown a ten-person photo lineup, with seven of the photos being of Hispanic men, thereby making it essentially a three-person photo lineup. All she could say at that time was that Steve's picture looked "most similar," and then she went on to declare that she wouldn't say that Steve's picture was the person she had seen.

I was surprised that Mrs. Johannville made a positive ID of Steve, but I was even more surprised that Knight had her testify at all. *Make 'em pay for putting this woman on the stand*, I thought to myself. And I think I succeeded.

Mrs. Johannville had given several prior statements, including a written one, to the FBI and the grand jury. The FBI even had an artist draw a composite picture based on her description that she signed twice, on separate dates. And all of it described a person so vastly different from

Steve that any fair-minded person would have concluded that, despite her in-court ID, the person she saw driving that car was anybody but Steve Buckley.

Steve had worn his hair long, almost down to his shoulders, and he had a mustache and mutton chop sideburns so long than many people thought he had a beard. The person Mrs. Johannville saw had no such head or facial hair. The little bit of skin that was exposed on Steve's face was pockmarked from acne, which was part of the reason Steve had facial hair—again not seen by the witness. At the time of the crime, Steve was 20, but the man Mrs. Johannville said she saw looked like he was from 25 to 35 years old, but closer to 35. The car she saw was not a car that the Buckleys owned and was never connected to any of the three defendants. And the capper of it all, in every one of her statements the man she had seen wore "granny" glasses—those small, round or oval, wire-rimmed glasses that much older women sometimes wear. Think "Granny" from *The Beverly Hillbillies*. In her grand jury testimony, that was the "main thing" she saw. Steve never wore granny glasses, or any glasses for that matter.

If that wasn't devastating enough, Mrs. Johannville's explanations for her in-court ID of Steve should have done the trick. She had to come up with an answer for the granny glasses, so she testified both that she now wasn't sure that the person she had seen was wearing glasses, and also "maybe" she had "transposed" the glasses from someone else she knew who wore that type of eyewear to the driver's face. As far as the composite drawn by the FBI artist, which looked nothing like Steve, she just declared that she was not, in fact, satisfied with it, despite her signing it twice. (The FBI artist who had drawn the composite later testified that, to the best of his recollection, Mrs. Johannville told him that, from her limited observation, the sketch appeared to be the person she had seen). As for the head hair, she claimed the person was wearing a hood that covered his hair, even though the composite showed no hood, but rather a stocking cap. Knight even helped us out on redirect when Mrs. Johannville testified that the photo of Steve—who was a pale kid of Irish extraction—which she had seen in the grand jury, made him look Hispanic. Finally, she claimed that despite seeing Steve's picture in the news on a number of occasions after his arrest, it was on one later occasion, about two weeks prior to trial, when she saw his photo "flickering" on the TV, that she concluded the driver of the car was Steve.

The jury had to be asking itself, "What could have caused her to testify the way she did?" At least, that's what I hoped they were doing.

The testimony of Frank Kochanny, an employee of the Illinois Tollway system, had some minor significance at the trial, but would play a huge role a little over a year later at a hearing dealing with statements made by the real killer of Jeanine Nicarico. He testified that at about 2:45 p.m. to 3 p.m. on the day Jeanine was taken, while he and his co-worker were working on the tollway near the Prairie Path, he saw a 1978 green Ford Granada with a hubcap missing and only a driver inside, attempting to turn around on the narrow path not far from where Jeanine was found dead two days later.

The result of this information, learned immediately after Jeanine's death, caused the police to search for a green Granada. But try as they might, they could not, in any way, connect Steve or his co-defendants to a green Granada, or any type of similar car. That's where Dean Schmunk came in. His testimony, which defied credulity for anyone familiar with the frailties of eyewitness identification, would have been laughable in another context. But this was a case where we feared that the jury would believe just about anything the State presented, so we had to take it seriously. He testified that on March 8, 1983, eleven days after Jeanine was taken, he saw a person driving a green Granada with a hubcap missing in Aurora. He claimed to try to follow the car to get the license number, but was unable to do so. So he went to a bar to call the police with this information—information he knew the police were looking for. The police never followed up on Schmunk's call. A year later, after Steve was arrested and his booking photo was publicized, Schmunk claimed that was the person he had seen, and he called the police the next day.

Defense Case

We were well into the trial by the time the defendants started presenting testimony. Though exhaustion was settling in, we put on a good case, if I do say so myself. For starters, we established a very good alibi. In Steve's case, the alibi could have been a problem because the police didn't contact him until about four weeks after the crime occurred. Under normal circumstances, going back that length of time and trying to recall what you did at a specific date and time would be difficult enough. The fact that Steve was a very young man who was unemployed and basically just bumming around every day of his life made things even more challenging. It's not like I could ask Steve to look at his work diary to see what he was doing on February 25, the day Jeanine was kidnapped. That led Steve to originally tell the police, incorrectly, that he thought he was babysitting for his sister, something he did on many Fridays. Thankfully, a series of important dates and milestones in the lives of defense witnesses established where Steve really was.

The first such important date and time was John Buckley's (Steve's dad) February 25, 11:00 a.m. dental appointment. Remember, the State's case showed that Jeanine was kidnapped from her home on February 25, sometime between Mrs. Nicarico's lunchtime visit with Jeanine and her sister Kathy's 3:00 p.m. return home from school. John's appointment was backed up by the dentist's business records in the form of an appointment book, as well as some scribbled notes by John himself on a diabetes pamphlet. The dentist had died, making the foundation for that business record difficult to establish.

"Foundation" is an evidentiary term meaning that for certain pieces of evidence to be admissible, they have to be shown to be authentic. So here is where I will throw out my one and only kudo to Tom Knight. He could have made the admission of the appointment book an issue, causing problems for us.

Though we still could have succeeded in pleading our case to the judge to admit the record—it was, after all, presented to the grand jury while the dentist was alive—we didn't have to fight that fight. Knight stipulated, or agreed, to the appointment book's foundation.

The alibi witnesses, Steve's parents, John and Marilyn Buckley, along with Robert Peterson, recalled that it was on the day of the dental appointment that Mr. Peterson, a work acquaintance of John's who hadn't seen him in years, came over to see how John was doing after a stroke he had suffered.

Times varied a bit, but the three of them saw Steve at the Buckley house between 3 p.m. and 3:45 p.m. Marilyn had seen him asleep in his room well before that. John and Marilyn testified that Steve had just gotten up for the day and was going to see a friend.

A number of Steve's friends testified that Steve had been out late drinking the night before at a bonfire party at a friend's house on the Fox River—explaining Steve's late rising time on February 25—and was out again on the evenings of February 25 and 26.

Birthday parties of two of the witnesses on the 25th and 26th (one of them celebrating a 21st birthday) helped his friends recall those dates. Through it all, they noticed nothing unusual about Steve. Also, nobody had ever seen him in a green Granada or wearing glasses.

Considering the circumstances of having to go back a month to know what Steve was doing at this crucial time, that's a good alibi.

****

Steve had informed us that after one of his interrogations, he returned to his car to find powder all over the interior. Steve correctly figured it was fingerprint powder, and it was everywhere. Also, the broken lock on his glove compartment had been fixed. He had been shown no warrant for the search of his car, and the police never asked him for consent, though I'm sure he would have given it, considering his level of cooperation. They just went in. We were given no report of the dusting for Jeanine's fingerprints.

As you now know, the *Brady* rule and the Illinois discovery rules required the State to turn over all evidence that tends to negate guilt. Certainly, the negative results from the search of Steve's car for Jeanine's fingerprints, and whatever other incriminating evidence—hair, blood, etc.—they were looking for, would qualify. So if the prosecution was aware of this information, it should have been turned over to us early on. No special requests should have been needed.

I don't recall exactly how we discovered that Deputy Ray Koch from the sheriff's office was the evidence technician who had conducted the search in Steve's car, but at the very least his name wasn't given to us without our scratching around and asking for it. And at trial, when he testified that he couldn't find a report, and that it was unusual for him not to have one, I was hoping it would impress upon the jury how unfair this whole investigation was. I hoped they realized that if there had been something helpful to the State found in Steve's car, there would have been plenty of recorded information prepared. The lack of a report caused Koch to have only a vague recall of dusting Steve's car for fingerprints and checking the tread on his tires. We then had to rely on the fact that the State didn't put on any fingerprint or tire print evidence to infer that no matches were found. That's simply not fair.

Steve, however, was grateful for Koch fixing the glove compartment lock.

****

The *Brady* rule played a part in an on-the-record—but outside-the-presence-of-the-jury—argument Knight and I got into, with Judge Kowal not quite understanding what the State had done. This argument was pretty emblematic of how poorly Tom Knight and I got along. Before I get into the details of the spat, a little background.

We had called former DuPage County Crime Lab Director Phil Gilman as a witness to testify that he had run a test on Steve's shoes to determine if there was any blood on them. The test was very sensitive, so if there was any, he would have found it. Absolutely no blood was detected. But on cross, Knight brought out that Gilman had found fibers and animal hairs from indeterminate sources on the shoes. This could have been a problem in that the Nicaricos had a dog, and if the jury believed that these were possibly hairs from their dog, it would benefit the State's case.

Again, and I don't recall how, we got word that the State had another expert examine the alleged hairs and fibers. If the results were negative for animal hair, thereby eliminating the possibility that they were from the Nicarico dog, obviously that would be *Brady* material—tending to negate guilt. We should have been informed of that.

The following is the verbatim court-reported argument, with the only correction I made being the spelling of the name of the forensic scientist who tested the hairs and fibers. Keep in mind two things. First, the cold, dispassionate written record does not completely reflect the angry tone of the voices or the volume of speech. Second, you will see Knight disrespecting Gilman in his arguments, which I suspect came from Gilman quitting the crime lab as a result of the handling of this case.

> *Judge Kowal:*
> **Good morning. I understand there is a motion before we begin?**

> *Mr. Johnson:*
> **It has been recently brought to my attention with regard to the Buckley shoe, State's 8-A and 8-B, they were analyzed further with regard to the animal hairs that were found to be on them, and I have not received a report on that, and I understand that those animal hairs may have been compared to the dog in the Nicarico house. If there has been such an analysis, I'd like to see a report.**

> *Judge Kowal:*
> **State, are you aware of any report?**

> *Mr. Knight:*
> **We have no report, I don't even think they were animal hairs, but he brought out the facts the guy examined the shoes, so the fact is that he thought there were animal hairs, I don't think they were, but that's all we are doing with it.**

Mr. Johnson:

With regard to those, any possible analyses that was done, I'd like to know if there was a further analysis of those fibers done.

Judge Kowal:

All right. If there is any existing report—

Mr. Johnson:

Judge, report or no report, I can't—I don't think the State can hide behind 'No report.'

Judge Kowal:

Just a minute. Let me finish. If there was any work done at all, whether positive or negative, it should be turned over. If, however, the examiner didn't do anything, obviously there is nothing to turn over.

Mr. Knight:

They did, they are not animal hairs. Gilman thought they were animal hairs, they put the witness on, and we are not doing anything more with it. The analysis is they aren't animal hairs, and that's why we didn't try to connect it up with anything else. They wanted to establish that he looked at the shoes and found nothing. The fact is, he thought they were animal hairs, but they aren't animal hairs.

Judge Kowal:

Your understanding is Gilman was the only one that did that?

Mr. Knight:

He is the one that thought they were animal hairs, but they are not.

Mr. Johnson:

I think the question ought to be answered was there a further analysis—

Mr. Knight:

I don't know why he constantly wants to cross-examine me, Judge. I told you, and I will speak to you. There aren't animal hairs. We didn't bring him on and put him on the stand. We weren't going to bring out they were animal hairs. They brought him in, they put him on and wanted to put this in front of the jury. We didn't bother to waste your time or the jury's time showing that, but once they did that, we had to at least bring out the fact that he found what he believed to be animal hairs on that. We aren't going to try to connect them up with the dog, because they aren't even animal hairs, much less the dog's hair.

Judge Kowal:

My suggestion is to get in touch with Mr. Gilman and see if he has made a report or what his findings were, if any, if he went in that direction.

Mr. Johnson:

I understand that, Judge. What I understand is that those fibers were tested and I don't care how they were tested, for what reason they were tested or what, I think I'm owed a report.

Mr. Knight:

What for? Judge, he brought the guy on the stand, put him on and asked him about an examination of shoes, which we were not even going to ask him about, because the guy erroneously concluded there were animal hairs on the shoes. They brought him in, why do we have any obligation at all? I'm just telling you that—

Judge Kowal:

You have no obligation to follow it up. All I can indicate is call Mr. Gilman and find out what work he did or didn't do, and then report to the Court, if you have any problem.

Mr. Johnson:
   I'd like to know has there been an analysis?

Judge Kowal:
   Well, call Gilman—

Mr. Johnson:
   No, Judge, by somebody else.

Judge Kowal:
   Other than Gilman?

Mr. Johnson:
   Yes, that's what I would like to know.

Judge Kowal:
   If there is any report that is available, it is part of the discovery and it should be turned over.

Mr. Johnson:
   In other words, you are not going to require the State to tell me whether or not such an analysis was made; is that what the Court is ruling?

Judge Kowal:
   My understanding is it was by Gilman and Gilman was on the stand yesterday.

Mr. Knight:
   No—

Judge Kowal:
   If there is anyone else—

Mr. Knight:
   We didn't trust what Gilman said, we had somebody else look at the shoes and the fibers, and they aren't even animal hairs. He is the only one that says they are animal hairs. They weren't. We aren't going to introduce it, we weren't going to introduce any of that. They just chose to put the guy on the stand and

asked him about his examination of the shoes. We aren't going to try to prove that, that hairs from the Nicarico dog were on the shoes, but the problem is we didn't know where they were going to quit with this guy. In other words, we didn't try to put any evidence on about something that isn't true. They are the only ones that did that.

Mr. Johnson:
My next question would be, Judge, I would like to have a report if one exists, and if one doesn't exist, I'd like to know who did the analysis so I could talk to them.

Judge Kowal:
Well, analysis of what?

Mr. Johnson:
The fibers.

Judge Kowal:
Well, is there a fiber analysis report?

Mr. Knight:
There is no report on it, Judge, at all.

Mr. Johnson:
I'd like to know who did the analysis.

Judge Kowal:
Alright.

Mr. Knight:
Under what theory? I would think—

Judge Kowal:
Do you know?

Mr. Knight:
If you want to know, Judge, it was McCrone Institute, Skip Palenik at McCrone Institute in Chicago.

Mr. Johnson:
Thank you.

Judge Kowal:
You have that information.

Mr. Johnson:
Yes.

Good grief! See what we had to put up with?

****

Even relatively short trials take their toll, physically and mentally, on the participants, and I'm no exception. To make matters worse, I don't usually eat as well as I should. I rely too much on PowerBars and I tend to overdo the caffeine. Former Kane County Public Defender Mike McInerney once joked that I would go to trial with coffee in one hand and Kaopectate in the other. Weight loss, not something I can afford, is a problem. So a seven-week trial as intense as the Nicarico case absolutely brutalized me. And it resulted in a near accident that would have been a major embarrassment.

Near the end of the trial, we called Tom Riley, president of a major footwear importer from Hingham, Massachusetts, to testify about the origins of the New Silver Cloud-soled shoes that were at the center of Steve's case. Riley was actually the creator of the New Silver Cloud design. No fewer than one million of these shoes had been imported to the U.S. by his company and others, with most of them going to the Midwest and other northern states due to their being warm, winter-type apparel. The soles were manufactured at various factories, and each factory would alter the design slightly, thereby explaining the variations in the New Silver Cloud soles. It also explained how the curves in the heel section of the soles were different when you compared Steve's shoe with the door print and other shoes. It was important testimony, so when Riley got in late in the evening on February 12 from Hingham, Cliff and I wanted to go over his testimony with him at his hotel.

Afterwards, Cliff and I went to my office to get some work done. At about one o'clock in the morning, we were surprised to see my father show up at my office.

"Dad, what are you doing here?"

"Are you guys okay? Amy was worried about you, and I hear that your fiancé is worried, too, Cliff."

"Sure, Dad, we're fine."

"You should call her, Gary. Cliff, your fiancé called Amy looking for you when you didn't come home tonight. Amy called here but nobody picked up. Since she couldn't leave the house because of Andrea [our one-year-old daughter], she called me. And to make matters worse, she said you got a telephone threat a while back. What the hell is that all about?"

"Yeah, Dad. Our receptionist told me about it. It was a message left overnight on the machine. I didn't want to hear it, so I just had her call the police to let them know. I guess someone was upset about this case, saying bad things would happen if I didn't lay off. But I don't think it was the real deal."

"Well, now you have me worried. Cliff, call your fiancé. Gary, call Amy. Both of you—go home!"

"Thanks, Dad. Sorry to put you through this."

It's easy to forget that long and difficult trials take a toll on lawyers' families, too.

The next day, when Riley was to testify, I was sleep-deprived. As always, coffee was my drug of choice, which almost led to my "accident."

Tom Riley hadn't been on the witness stand very long on the afternoon of February 13 when my insides started acting up. My old high school track coach had a word for my problem. He called it the "scoots." At first, I thought I could gut it out, so I forged ahead. Then I began to sweat, and I could only concentrate on saving myself from embarrassment. So I walked up to the judge, ignoring the proper protocol of waiting for opposing counsel to approach with me.

Here's how the transcript reads:

> *Mr. Johnson:*
> **Judge, I need a five-minute recess, please.**
>
> *Judge Kowal:*
> **All right.**

But that's not how I remember it. My memory could be faulty on this, or the court reporter may not have been able to take down my whispering—I was trying to be tactful—but I recall the judge asking if we had to do it right then, in the middle of my examination. I also recall telling the judge in pretty clear terms that it was an emergency. So when he gave me the green light, I flew—and I mean flew—out of the courtroom and into a nearby bathroom. Amy had come to watch that day and became concerned.

She told me that one of the prosecutors followed me out, maybe thinking I was doing something, I can't imagine what, they would object to. I can tell you this much—if that prosecutor had poked his head into the bathroom and taken a whiff, he would have understood completely.

****

The testimony from our shoeprint experts was relatively uneventful but, I feel, very effective. They had one advantage that the State's experts didn't have—they didn't have to perform impossible mental gymnastics to justify the multiple differences between Steve's shoe and the door print. Joseph Nicol testified that it was "very unlikely" and "very improbable" that Steve's shoe was the source of the print.

Dr. Owen Lovejoy stated, quite directly, that Steve's shoe simply did not make the print. They both relied on the obvious, observable and multiple differences that could not be rationally explained away.

Then there was John Gorajczyk, the shoeprint expert from the DuPage County Crime Lab, who came through and testified that, based on his preliminary examination, Steve's shoe did not make the print on the Nicarico door. Gorajczyk testified that the elected DuPage County Sheriff had asked him to examine the evidence. After Gorajczyk made his preliminary examination, and after informing his superiors in the crime lab and the Sheriff of his opinion, and after further requesting time to do a more thorough scientific examination so that he could better explain his findings, he was told they would get back to him. Of course, they never did get back to him, and the shoes were packaged up and sent off to the state crime lab and Ed German. Gorajczyk testified that because he wasn't able to conduct a full scientific exam, he didn't write a report or otherwise memorialize his opinion, and he couldn't recall exactly why he thought Steve's shoe did not make the print. He could only recall that was how he felt.

We had other shoeprint experts available to testify similarly, but we sensed the jurors were getting sick of shoeprint testimony. We felt our experts did an outstanding job on the stand, and that more was not necessarily better.

****

One of the biggest decisions a defense lawyer and his client have to make during a trial is whether to have the client testify. Cliff and I exhaustively weighed the pros and cons, and Steve agreed he would do whatever we thought was best. On the "pro" side of the ledger were two very important factors. First, despite the fact that juries are instructed by courts not to hold a defendant's failure to testify against him, jurors tend to want to hear from the accused. That's just basic human nature. Second, though there was no way of knowing for sure, we thought Steve would have done well testifying.

When Steve told us he had nothing to do with the Nicarico crimes, and corroborated the alibi witnesses who testified for him, he was very convincing. We certainly believed him. And even though Steve, a high school dropout, would not have been nearly as educated as his cross-examiner, he was far from stupid. He had acquitted himself well during the various police interrogations—Detective John Sam, one of his interrogators, believed he was innocent—but Steve also did well, at least on paper, during his three sessions without a lawyer answering questions from Tom Knight before the special grand jury.

On the other side of the ledger were a number of factors. First, under certain circumstances an opposing party can introduce evidence of a testifying witness's prior criminal history for the sole purpose of impeaching that witness's credibility (but not for the purpose of showing a propensity to commit crimes). Prior to trial, we filed a motion requesting that Steve's burglary and misdemeanor theft convictions not be admitted to impeach his credibility in the event he testified. We argued that with both convictions, but particularly the burglary, the jury might unfairly believe if he committed those crimes, he probably committed the current charges as well. Judge Kowal went along with us on the burglary conviction but said he would allow the misdemeanor theft to be used for impeachment. Even though, overall, we thought this was a good ruling for us, we were still concerned that the jury's knowledge of the theft conviction would play into the State's theory that this was a burglary gone bad. Second, any time a defendant takes the stand, it's a risk. He could say something or act in a way that would turn off jurors. Lastly, and most importantly, we felt we were ahead—that we were winning. We figured, why should we take the risk when, as things stood and by all rights, we should win. We opted for him not to testify.

I have a confession to make. There was one other factor that crept into my mind that didn't belong there, but was an unintended consequence of the joint trial. Not only did I believe Steve was innocent, but I also felt strongly that Hernandez and Cruz were, too. I was hoping all three would be acquitted. But I also knew that Hernandez and Cruz weren't going to testify. *Would Steve's testifying magnify the fact that the others didn't, resulting in hurting their chances?* I wondered. *Or would Steve doing well weaken the State's case overall, thereby weakening the case against Hernandez and Cruz also?* I recall the former being the way I thought it would come off.

Looking back now, that gut reaction to Steve's testifying was completely rooted in my inexperience. I'm sure I would feel differently today. Back then, though, that was my thinking. But I also knew our only responsibility and concern should have been for our client, Stephen Buckley, and the impact on his co-defendants should have absolutely no effect on our strategy. The other two had their own lawyers to protect their rights. And I tell you, here and now, this factor played no role in the final decision.

I don't think.

****

As the trial was winding down, Cliff and I made sure the issue of Ed German's notes remained a stone in everyone's shoes. Just before closing arguments were to begin, Cliff laid it out succinctly for the judge—we needed time to get German back to Wheaton. The out-of-state subpoena process was well under way. As a matter of fact, as Cliff was making his arguments to Kowal, German was apparently in front of a California judge regarding this issue. As an alternative, Cliff suggested either striking German's testimony or simply admitting his notes.

All along, Judge Kowal had been receptive to our plight regarding German's notes. So when Knight relayed, after speaking to German, that German was willing to come back, but not until the following week, Kowal made his disappointment clear. Holding up closing arguments for that long and keeping the jury waiting was not a good idea. There was nothing left to do to fill up that time.

When Kowal kept up the pressure that something had to be done, Cliff and I sensed we would be able to get some kind of stipulation from Knight—and we were right. And though we weren't totally happy with the stipulation, we got most of what we wanted. We didn't want to push Kowal so far that we would lose him.

After all was said and done, German's notes were allowed to go back to the jury. The stipulation we read to the jurors said that the exhibit admitted into evidence was Ed German's notes regarding his examination of the evidence, but that German continued his examinations and comparisons after the March 28, 1983 and April 1, 1983 dates written on the notes, all the way to his formal report of April 20, 1983.

As far as any additional notes that logic would dictate German would have taken had he actually done any additional work that would have supported his quantum leap from "could have at best" to "probably," well, I've never seen those notes. They have never been produced.

Closing Arguments

In Illinois—as it is, I assume, with almost all legal jurisdictions in the United States—the closing argument setup gives the prosecution a huge advantage. The State is allowed a closing argument, followed by the defendant's summation. After that is completed, the State is given a second argument, called "rebuttal," to answer the defendant's closing. The defense doesn't get a second chance to respond. It's a hell of an opportunity for the prosecutor to gain an edge.

The theory behind this is that the State has the burden of proof, and therefore should get the additional argument and the final say. The end result is that the initial closing argument by the State is relatively mundane, filled with going over jury instructions and the basics of the State's theory. The rebuttal, on the other hand, is often substantially more theatrical and emotional, and, most importantly, unresponded to.

Most prosecutors take great pride in their ability to give rebuttal arguments. I surely did, and I was pretty good at it, too. But the best I ever heard was my friend John Barsanti. Damn, could he argue! When it became known that he was at the point in any of his trials when he was going to give closing arguments, lawyers, defense and prosecutors alike, would crowd into the courtroom to listen. Like a long distance runner with a great "kick"—the sprint at the end of the race—he could make up a lot of ground with his rebuttal.

During our two days of closing arguments, the courtroom was crammed—mostly with Nicarico supporters, but with some defense well-wishers, too. My parents and Amy were there for my closing, as well as my sister, Pat, and my very first client, my brother, Bob. Plenty of lawyers, mostly DuPage County prosecutors, also watched. Most notably, in the front row, and I'm sure for the benefit of the jurors, sat a number of pre-teens—maybe friends of Jeanine, but I can't say for sure.

My argument, and Knight's rebuttal, were on the second day. My closing was the very first defense argument I would give to a jury. I was nervous, and I even admitted that to the jury during my summation. It lasted two hours and, if I do say so myself, it went well. I even heard through the grapevine that some of the prosecutors in attendance were very complimentary. "Johnson gave an ass-kickin' closing argument," was how it was put to me. But, then again, it's pretty easy to give a good close when you have so much to work with.

Whenever I give a closing argument, I always note the faces of the jurors. Sometimes it's easy to tell which jurors are with me and which are not. Those who like what I'm saying will occasionally give a very slight nod of the head or a smile. It's a great boost of confidence. Others will frown or refuse to make any eye contact. I figure I'm probably in trouble with those folks. Still others will look intently at me, giving no indication, other than they're listening. They usually do the same to my opponent.

The Nicarico jury was tough to read. One guy, who astonishingly had trouble staying awake at various parts of the trial, nodded off for brief periods of time during my argument. But he did the same during all the arguments. The other jurors were a mixed bag of very slight positive and negative reinforcement.

My argument centered around two themes. First, I noted that each of the main pieces of evidence against Steve had flaws so significant that they could actually exclude Steve. Incorporating that with the State's burden of proof, as I went through each piece of evidence I asked the jury where the State stood in their efforts to get a guilty conviction. Before addressing the shoeprint evidence, but after summarizing the alibi testimony, the testimony of Steve's cooperation, and Mrs. Johannville, this is what the jury heard from me:

> **Now that we know that we're looking for a person who's close to 35, who has no facial hair, who has short hair that a cap, like this,** [referring to the artist composite prepared by the FBI at Mrs. Johannville's instruction] **can cover up, who has shoulders too big for his face, has a clear complexion, wears granny glasses, and now that we know Steve Buckley cooperated 110%, and conducted life as usual on the 25th and 26th, now that we know that we have witnesses who saw Steve Buckley at his house on February 25th, 1983—now that we know all these things, where's the State now in their attempt not just to convince you, but to convince you beyond a reasonable doubt that my client is guilty? Where are they now?**

The second theme was to compare the character of the case to the character of a person. Was this case, like a person, someone or something you could trust? I argued the character of the case included that it was a very emotionally charged situation, with a community up in arms, and that someone had to pay. I contended that if Deputy Koch, who searched Steve's car without any legal authority, had found any evidence in the form of blood, hairs, fingerprints or tire prints, you would have seen reams of reports and plenty of testimony about what had been discovered. But when the opposite occurred, when they found absolutely nothing connecting Steve to the crime, Koch didn't even write up a report, and stumbled through his testimony due to a lack of memory. Were the defendants getting a fair shake? Could you trust the State's case?

I pointed out that DuPage County Sheriff Doria himself, not an underling, had requested that his shoeprint expert, John Gorajczyk, examine the shoes:

> *Mr. Johnson:*
> **"John, take a look at those things** [Steve's shoes and the shoeprint evidence] **and see if they're the ones."**
> **So, John does, and he comes to the conclusion that, no, there's no match. This is not the shoe. And he tells people. He tells Doria. He tells a number of other people that it's not the shoe. Then what happens? What happens to those shoes after John Gorajczyk has the gall to debunk their clue, their first clue? They're packaged up, and somebody else takes a look at them. "No, thanks, John. It's okay."**
> **"You want to do any more examinations, Mr. Gorajczyk?"**
> **"Yes, I'd like to have done further exams on the shoe."**
> **"No, thanks, John. It's okay. Somebody else can take a look at those shoes."**
> **What does that tell you about the character of this case? What does that tell you about the length that these people are going to go to to make sure somebody pays for this crime? Ladies and gentleman of the jury, we'd better make sure it's the right somebody here because there's only one thing that can make this terrible travesty worse, and you know what that is.**

After I finished, I felt good—good in that I thought I had given a convincing argument and that Cliff and I had done everything we could to defend Steve. There was also a sense of relief that, for the most part, the hardest work of the trial was over. We were both spent.

Cliff and I prepared Steve for Knight's rebuttal. "There'll be a lot of finger pointing, ranting, and raving, stuff like that, and unless it crosses the line or is inaccurate, we just have to pretty much eat it," we warned. "Just make sure you don't show any emotion when it happens."

As Knight was about to deliver his rebuttal, I had to remind myself of what we had just warned Steve of—that these arguments can be emotional, stirring and make you feel as though you are taking a beating. Occasionally, prosecutors have gotten so carried away with their rebuttals that they have said things that landed them in trouble with the appellate court, sometimes causing reversals. Tom Laz warned that Knight had a reputation for crying during his rebuttals, so he brought that issue up to the judge before closings in an effort to not have to deal with it in front of the jury.

Tom Knight did none of those things during his rebuttal. Instead, he chose his own more well-worn path to self-destruction. He violated the three defendants' 6th Amendment rights under the Confrontation Clause—the Constitutional basis of our pretrial request for a severance and our fight for appropriate redactions. Our objections were based on Knight's comments improperly connecting alleged statements made by Cruz and Hernandez to their co-defendants.

> *Mr. Knight:*
> **If Buckley kicked the door in, all right. What does that tell you about those admissions they've** [Hernandez and Cruz] **made? Not only are they friends—**

> *Mr. Johnson:*
> **Objection, your Honor. I object to that as contrary to the law.**

> *Mr. Laz:*
> **I join in that, Judge.**

> *Mr. Johnson:*
> **The last three statements.**

> *Judge Kowal:*
> **So far, it's proper argument. May continue.**

Mr. Knight:

> You've seen that they're friends. They live in the same neighborhood. They're all in the same proximity with respect to the victim's home. And I'm using it only in the direction of Cruz and Hernandez because the fact is they've made statements which are directed as admissions against them.
>
> Okay. But they're also friends of Buckley's.

Mr. Johnson:

> Objection, Judge. That inference is improper.

Judge Kowal:

> Confine—

Mr. Knight:

> This is only—

Judge Kowal:

> Confine it to the evidence now and relate it in that fashion.

Mr. Knight:

> This is only as to Cruz and Hernandez I'm talking about. Okay. They're friends. They're neighbors. Therefore, when they make admissions that they've committed this crime, it's much more—

Mr. Johnson:

> Objection.

Judge Kowal:

> Objection sustained.

Mr. Wesolowski:

> It's improper.

When the arguments were completed, Judge Kowal read instructions to the jury and sent them back to begin deliberations. Jury instructions are the law applicable to the case set out in lay terms. They include the elements of the offenses the State must prove beyond a reasonable doubt to obtain a conviction, definitions of legal terms, how to consider differ-ent kinds of evidence, verdict forms, and more. A copy of those instruc-tions is given to the jurors for use during deliberations.

The Nicarico trial started with four alternate jurors. Alternate jurors are selected and listen to the evidence just like the regular jurors. In the event a regular juror cannot complete the case—due to illness, family problems, things like that—they are replaced by an alternate. When the jury begins deliberations, the alternates are released. One of the best criminal judges I ever had the pleasure of appearing before, John Leif-heit, gave the released alternates a very practical explanation of their service. "You're like a spare tire," he would say. "We usually don't think much about them, but when we need one, we're sure glad it's there."

As a result of juror attrition, by the end of the trial only one alternate remained. Figuring that getting verdicts on three defendants may take a while, Judge Kowal released the alternate with instructions not to talk to anyone about the trial until the jury delivered its verdict. In the event that one of the regular jurors couldn't complete deliberations, the alternate might still be needed, and Kowal didn't want the alternate's opinions tainted by outside sources.

When alternates are released, unlike in the Nicarico case, judges usu-ally allow them to speak to anyone they want about the trial. Sometimes lawyers will discuss the case with alternates, as well as the regular jurors after a verdict is delivered. Often you can learn something about the case or your lawyering that might be useful in the future, and it's something I partake in occasionally, depending on how I feel. There are times, how-ever, when it's absolutely frightening to discover the path the jurors took to reach their verdict. I know some lawyers who would simply rather not know.

There have also been instances of prosecutors who, upset with a jury's verdict of acquittal, gave the jurors they were speaking to a hard time, criticizing them for what they considered to be an incorrect verdict. This has included discussing evidence that was not admitted or that was sup-pressed, in an effort to make the juror feel bad about the verdict. Justifi-ably, this has landed those prosecutors in hot water with their trial judges.

The Verdict

Cliff and I assumed the deliberations would take some time, so we informed the clerk where we were going so she could contact us and we went to a restaurant to get a beer, and later, dinner. In the bar area, *Animal House* was on television, so we watched it to pass the time. Later, the jurors were released for the night without coming to a verdict. The next day, a Friday, I went to the office to catch up on some work, and Cliff and I also prepared for a sentencing hearing in the event of a guilty verdict. We didn't get much done—we were both pretty wiped out. When evening came, we received word by telephone that the jury had reached a verdict. Cliff and I met Laz and Wesolowski at the courthouse.

When we arrived, the place was crawling with print, radio and television news media. Cliff and I, both a bundle of rubber bands at this point, sat on a bench outside the courtroom waiting as the Nicaricos and their supporters gathered at the other end of the hallway. I don't know what the holdup was—maybe they were waiting for someone, I don't know—but they just stood there for what seemed like forever. Knowing that Judge Kowal wouldn't take the verdicts until the Nicaricos were ready, and sensing the possibility that there might be only a partial verdict, I used the time to discuss strategy with Cliff.

"Cliff, if the jury is hung on Steve, the judge or Knight may want to give the *Prim* instruction. Should we object?"

A *Prim* instruction, sometimes given to a deadlocked jury, not so gently nudges jurors into coming to a verdict.[27]

"If they're hung, I wish I knew what the score was before making that decision. I'd only want to give it if I thought we had a majority of the jurors," Cliff said.

"That's going to be impossible to figure out. Let's wait and see, but I think we should play it safe and object. Plus, I think Kowal will give it over our objection anyhow if he thinks it'll get them to agree."

Then Cliff changed the subject. "I can't bear the thought of going through a sentencing hearing if we lose this thing. It'll be hard to fight through the let-down."

"You got that right. And I just get the feeling that whoever is convicted is going to have a hard time avoiding the rusty needle," I said, using the crude vernacular of criminal lawyers for death by injection.

The Nicarico group finally made their way into the courtroom, and Cliff and I followed. The deputies brought out Buckley, Hernandez and Cruz, who each sat at their separate tables with their lawyers. After Judge Kowal instructed the bailiff to bring the jurors in from the jury room, Steve whispered to us.

"What do you think?"

The answer we gave to this question, which was most certainly also asked by Steve at other times before the jury concluded its work, is the subject of some disagreement. Cliff recalls not knowing which way the jury would go, and I recall the same, but also discussing the deadlock possibility. Steve's memory is that we told him, based on the questions the jury had been asking the judge from time to time throughout their deliberations, it didn't look very good for him. It's possible Cliff and I could have been trying to keep Steve's expectations low. In any event, we talked briefly, and Steve had the final word, at least for that moment.

"There's no way they find me guilty. This is America. I didn't do anything."

The courtroom was silent as the jurors made their way into their seats. Conventional wisdom says that if the jurors look at the defendant after they take their seats, that's a good sign for the defense. If not, the opposite is true. I can't remember where the Nicarico jurors looked, but I can remember this: my stomach was in my throat as the clerk read the verdicts.

Hernandez and Cruz were found guilty of murder, aggravated kidnapping, residential burglary, and various sex-related crimes. While I was surprised the jury came to this conclusion on such flimsy, questionable evidence, the atmosphere throughout the trial eliminated much of the shock. I felt bad for Hernandez and Cruz, and Frank and Tom as well.

As for Steve, the jury couldn't reach a unanimous verdict, and they made it clear that further deliberations would be fruitless, so they hung. The *Prim* instruction was not given. A hung jury ends with the judge withdrawing a juror, so the technical conclusion is a mistrial, which is how Judge Kowal handled it. It does not bar a retrial if the prosecutor so desires. There was no question in my mind that the State would retry Steve.

Later, I talked to Michael Callahan, one of the jurors. He told me that the vote on Steve went back and forth from 7 to 5 to 8 to 4 in favor of guilty, and it ended with the 8 to 4 vote. He also informed me that he was not impressed with the shoeprint evidence the State presented, so at least to some extent, our jury selection goal of selecting smart jurors who would not simply take the State's shoeprint evidence at face value paid off. Callahan said that when deliberations started, he knew he would never vote for a guilty verdict against Steve, and that he would do what he could to bring the other jurors with him. You gotta love jurors with guts. Thank you, Mr. Callahan!

Withdrawal

The guilty verdicts against Hernandez and Cruz, and the hung jury for Buckley, occurred on a Friday. I spent most of the weekend debating with myself on the issue of whether I should continue representing

Steve. There were several very good and valid reasons to withdraw from the case. The time commitment for the retrial would be huge, without anything in the way of financial remuneration. And there was no guarantee that the next trial wouldn't end in another hung jury. My bosses at Clancy, McGuirk and Hulce were ready to back me on any decision I made, but I knew it would be asking a lot to expect them to support another trial. Plus, I had neglected other clients' cases that now needed attention.

I talked it over with Steve—he wanted me to stay on. Cliff thought he and I should remain on the case as well, but said he understood the dilemma. If I withdrew, he would follow suit. I felt a little better after talking to Frank Wesolowski. As Public Defender, his office would be appointed to handle Steve's case since neither Steve nor his family could afford private counsel. He told me he would assign one of his more experienced lawyers, Carol Anfinson, to represent Steve. He assured me Steve would be in good hands.

In the end, the overriding factor was that I was exhausted and completely burnt out. I wasn't sure I could bring the necessary energy or focus to the case. Maybe, I thought, a fresh approach from a different lawyer would help. So on February 29, 1985, one week after the hung jury, Cliff and I requested and were granted leave to withdraw as Steve's lawyers.

Looking back, I have to say this wasn't one of my finer professional moments. Nobody knew that case better than Cliff and me, and nobody ever would. The valid reasons to withdraw were all easily trumped by my obligation to my client, whom I *knew* to be innocent, and, at the risk of sounding self-important, to justice in general. Moreover, I could have solved all of the work-related problems I would have encountered as a result of the retrial. As far as the fatigue and burnout, I was only 32 years old. I could have and would have bounced back. Instead, I let down Steve and his family. And I was left with a guilty feeling that I wouldn't be able to shake.

Death Penalty

Cruz and Hernandez ended up waiving their right to a jury at the sentencing stage after all. I guess they didn't feel confident that our jury would spare their lives. We'll never know for sure if we could have picked a better jury, or if it would have changed the outcome, had they waived prior to jury selection and thereby avoided the death-qualification process.

The decision on life or death was left to Judge Kowal, who, on March 15, sentenced Cruz and Hernandez to death. They both appealed to the Illinois Supreme Court.

Trial—Sidebar

After Steve got a hung jury, with the assistance of private counsel, and Hernandez and Cruz were convicted using public defenders, there were some rumblings about the adequacy of their defense and of appointed counsel in general. After all, people were thinking, sometimes out loud, the only defendant who could figure out a way to pay for private lawyers is the only one who didn't get convicted.

Occasionally, I would hear that kind of talk. There was so much to say in response to that nonsense that I wouldn't know where to begin. But I would always defend the public defenders, and I will again now.

Let's start with Frank Wesolowski and Tom Laz, Hernandez's and Cruz's lawyers. I watched them pour their hearts and souls into the defense of their clients. They fought many of the same battles Cliff and I fought, especially in their attempts to sever their trials. Like Cliff and me, they had to deal with evolving evidence of suspicious origins. When the case began, most people thought Steve's case, with physical evidence in the form of the shoeprint, was the most difficult to defend of the three. But in the end, I believe that it was that very physical evidence that made our case easier and caused the hung jury. We had shoeprint evidence that implanted reasonable doubt in at least four jurors. Hernandez and Cruz, on the other hand, had to deal with a number of alleged admissions that, due to the lack of visuals, presented a more challenging situation.

There were other differences as well. Steve was the only non-Hispanic defendant in front of an all-white jury. Did race play a role? At a minimum, it's a fair question. And Steve had two lawyers working for him. I'm not certain if Cliff or I could have obtained a hung jury had we gone it alone, like Frank and Tom did. Cliff and I were constantly talking, deciding on strategies, and sharing work. Frank and Tom didn't have that luxury. I can also tell you this: Frank Wesolowski and Tom Laz each had more criminal defense experience than Cliff and I had. Whenever we needed advice, they were there to provide it—both prior to and during the trial.

But this does lead me to the only criticism I can muster up for the DuPage County Public Defender in the Nicarico case, and it's this: both Frank and Tom should have had a second chair. I don't know what the workload situation was back then for that office, but the case was way too serious and complicated for there to be just one lawyer for each defendant. I know these days public defenders will make arrangements for co-counsel for the more serious cases that go to trial.

To further emphasize the need for multiple defense counsel in capital cases, consider what occurred in Illinois in the early 2000s after the death penalty began to be put under a microscope, largely as a result of the Nicarico prosecution. The State developed a Capital Litigation Trust Fund to pay lawyers and provide for investigators, experts, mitigation specialists (experts who delve into all aspects of the defendant's life to prepare mitigation evidence for the sentencing hearing), along with other forms of support.

Strict rules were developed to improve the quality of capital defenses. Lawyers had to have sufficient trial experience to be either a first chair lawyer (lead counsel) or a second chair lawyer in the newly created Capital Defense Bar. Mandatory continuing legal education in death penalty relevant areas was instituted. A minimum of two lawyers was a requirement for every case. Usually, if those lawyers were smart, they would take advantage of an additional lawyer provided by the Capital Litigation Division of the State Appellate Defender's Office. That lawyer would assist with the litigation of death-penalty-related motions, but would also stay on for the overall defense.

Lastly, discovery rules were expanded. It's difficult to believe, but Illinois provided for more expansive discovery in civil lawsuits (except small claims cases) than in capital murder prosecutions. The new rules included, among other things, discovery depositions for certain witnesses.

Frank and Tom weren't perfect. They made some mistakes and there were times when Cliff and I might have done some things differently. Then again, they had to stand by helplessly and watch in horror while I allowed Ed German to forensically assault me during my cross-examination of him. It probably affected their cases as well. No, Frank and Tom did just fine—better than fine.

One more thing. Hernandez and Cruz would each get convicted one more time after this trial. And they would do so with teams of some of the very best private criminal defense lawyers in the state.

Now for public defenders in general. Boy, does that group get a bum rap! Occasionally I'll get a call from a prospective client who clearly doesn't have the funds to hire private counsel. The conversation usually goes something like this:

"Do you have a lawyer now?" I ask.

"No, I have the public defender."

"But the public defender, and all of her assistants, are real lawyers. They passed the same bar exam all of us had to pass."

"But I hear they're not as good as private lawyers," they complain.

"Not true," I say. "Some of the best criminal lawyers I know are PDs. They're specialists, most of whom are very committed to their clients and their profession. Let me put it to you this way. You've got about as good a chance of getting a great, good or mediocre lawyer going through the PD's office as you do when searching for a private criminal lawyer. Have any private lawyers agreed to take your case for the money that you have?"

"A couple." Then they proceed to name names. If the lawyer they mention is good, I have no hesitancy telling them so. If not, I'll say nothing. But I will think to myself, *they could have the PD for free, and they're about to spend good money for this bargain basement lawyer! Don't do it!*

"Don't hire a private lawyer just for the sake of hiring a private lawyer," is my final word. "Trust me, you'll be in good hands with the public defender."

Even with this defense of the public defenders, I'm still not being completely forthcoming with those who ask. What I don't tell them is that I rely on the Public Defender's Office. Often, when I have a question about a point of law, a judge, an expert witness, anything, you can find me on the phone seeking out advice from the PD's office. I almost always find that someone over there has the information I need, and they're more than willing to provide it. Our local PD also has continuing legal education courses that are open to the private bar, free of charge. When I travel to a county where I'm unfamiliar with the judges, prosecutors and procedures, who do I call? You guessed it—that county's public defender's office.

You won't ever catch me criticizing public defenders. On the contrary, I will sing their praises. They're committed public servants who, relatively speaking, don't get paid enough and who provide a crucial function.

I've already told you what Bob Lee did for me, and in upcoming chapters you will hear about what Tom McCulloch did in the pursuit of justice in the Nicarico case. Both were public defenders, and it's lawyers like them who I think of when I think about appointed counsel.

****

Every judge who has donned a black robe will tell you that they don't like cases they preside over being reversed by an appellate court. It means that significant error or errors occurred at the trial court level, and it's considered a black mark on that judge's record. Judge Kowal would be reversed twice in the Nicarico case.

I've been pretty critical of Judge Kowal's handling of the joint trial of Buckley, Hernandez, and Cruz, and you probably got the impression that I didn't respect him as a judge. Well, that's not the case. By all accounts, Kowal was a very good judge who throughout his career worked at treating parties who appeared before him fairly. I had him on one or two cases after the Nicarico trial, and was glad of it. One day, a few years after our trial was over, we even had a brief friendly chat while walking down the hall of the Wheaton courthouse. I can say without reservation that he is a truly decent person.

So what went wrong?

It would be easy to say that Kowal was just a good judge who was in over his head in a mega-case like Nicarico. Who knows? There may be some truth to that. Then again, I think the case overwhelmed everyone who dealt with it, including me. I think the bigger problem was that he trusted the State to put on a straight case, and when the evidence started coming out showing that wasn't happening, he didn't have the gumption to really sit on them. Tom Knight took advantage of that. From the Gorajczyk situation, to the alleged vision statement, to Louise Robbins, and to the severance-related issues, Kowal simply got rolled. And the public pressure to put these three guys away didn't help, either.

But I was there when Judge Kowal found out about the Ed German notes, and I saw how upset he was by that. That may have been the beginning of a bit of a turn-around in the case for him—I don't know. Later, in Cruz's second trial, he would allow the defense to put on an important piece of evidence that the judge for Buckley's retrial would refuse to admit, and that the State in both instances fought like hell to keep out—evidence that someone else had admitted to committing this crime alone. Under the circumstances, it took guts.

Don't get me wrong. I'm not letting Judge Kowal off the hook here. There were too many times when it was incredibly frustrating doing that case in front of him. I'm just painting a bigger picture.

Chapter 10
Hiatus

Changes

Fortunately, the other lawyers at Clancy, McGuirk and Hulce had picked up the slack regarding my civil cases during the Nicarico trial, so there wasn't much of a backlog there. The problem was with the criminal cases I had been appointed to as conflict counsel for Kane County. As conflict counsel, I was representing indigent defendants with whom the public defender had a conflict, mostly because that office represented a co-defendant in the same case. Since I hadn't paid much attention to these people during the trial, I had a growing number of antsy clients, many of whom were locked up in jail, justifiably demanding some attention.

Most of the cases I handled in the conflict position were felonies, and some were pretty serious. But after the initiation into the criminal defense world I had received in the Nicarico case, it felt like my conflict cases were a breeze. That's not to say I didn't take them seriously. I did. But in terms of complexity, pressure and the expectation of fairness from my opponents, they were a joy to work up.

During the 10 months of 1985 following the Nicarico trial, I completed six additional felony trials. When you add that to my other conflict counsel work, the civil cases I was doing at the firm, and helping Carol whenever I could, I was working long hours. Added to that, Amy and I were raising a one-year-old daughter in a house we purchased immediately after the Nicarico trial was completed.

They were good times for me, except for one small thing. I felt a nagging sort of guilt and concern over Steve's case.

When Frank Wesolowski appointed Carol Anfinson to handle Steve's case, he didn't provide her with a second chair. Shortly after Carol took over the case, Frank retired as the DuPage County Public Defender and was replaced by Peter Dockery. Carol still didn't have a second chair. Beyond that, Carol was up to her neck with clients from her regular caseload. I was worried that she wouldn't be able to put in the time necessary to defend Steve.

On the flip side of that, the DuPage County State's Attorney also initiated a big change. Since Carol would need a substantial period of time to prepare, the retrial was put off indefinitely. That resulted in Tom Knight leaving the office, and the prosecution team, to work for the U.S. Attorney's Office in Chicago. I didn't know the factors behind Knight's leaving—whether Jim Ryan wanted him gone or whether Knight wanted or had to leave—but I didn't care. Good riddance, was my feeling.

Knight was replaced as first chair by Ryan's First Assistant, Robert Kilander. Based on the reports I got from Carol, and from what I personally learned later, Kilander was entirely more friendly and approachable than Knight. Even Pat King, who stayed on as second chair and who had been chilly and standoffish during the first trial, lightened up considerably. And while approachability and friendliness may appear to be superficial qualities in the mechanics of criminal litigation, trust me, they make a big difference.

Lastly, we learned Steve would get a new judge—Robert Nolan—for his retrial. Much more on him later.

Brian Dugan

The Clancy, McGuirk and Hulce law offices were located in an old and small, renovated vaudeville/movie theater. My office, which overlooked 2nd Avenue in St. Charles, was upstairs in the area that used to be the projection room. My assistant worked in the balcony just a few steps beneath my office. Other offices were spread throughout the building. Three conference rooms were located on what used to be the stage. It was a unique and beautiful setup.

In early December of 1985, at about mid-afternoon, I was in my office when I received a call from a newspaper reporter in DeKalb County. She introduced herself and then asked me if I had heard the news about Brian Dugan. I knew that in November, Dugan had pled guilty to the abduction, rape and murder of seven-year-old Melissa Ackerman (sound familiar?), a crime that had occurred in nearby LaSalle and DeKalb counties.

The Ackerman case had many similarities to Nicarico. There were so many similarities, in fact, that well before the public knew about the Brian Dugan/Jeanine Nicarico connection described below, Steve called me from the DuPage County Jail to say that whoever committed that crime should be looked at seriously as a suspect for Jeanine Nicarico's murder.[28] Anyhow, at the same time Dugan had pled to the Ackerman case, he also pled to the sexual assault and murder of 27-year-old Donna

Schnorr. He was sentenced to two life terms in prison.

"What news?" I asked.

"We're hearing that Brian Dugan has confessed to murdering Jeanine Nicarico."

My heart began to pound. "Are you kidding me? Tell me everything you know."

"Not much yet, just that he says he committed the crime. Some people are claiming it's a defense ploy that you guys [defense lawyers] made up to take the spotlight off your clients."

"What? They think we're, or I'm, making this up for some reason?"

"Yes, that's what's being said."

I was pissed at the accusation, but since I knew it was total bullshit, I didn't let it interfere with the excitement of the news that the real killer of Jeanine may have just confessed.

"That'd be about the dumbest damn thing we could do. How easy would it be to expose that kind of nonsense? Then we'd look like idiots."

"I'm just telling you what they're saying," she responded. "Do you have any further comment?"

"Not yet—not 'til I learn more. But call me later."

When the call ended, I paced about in the office. I was so amped up, my mind was racing and I couldn't think clearly. *Could it be true? Did Dugan kill Jeanine? Where can I find out what's going on? Who can I call? I better let Carol know right away.* Tom McCulloch and Judy Brawka from the Kane County Public Defender's Office had represented Dugan in the Schnorr case, which had occurred in Kane County. *Contact one of them*, I suggested to myself.

I called Judy. She played it pretty close to the vest, but I did learn two things from her. First, it was true—Dugan had confessed to the crimes committed against Jeanine. Second, his confession was being investigated by detectives from the Illinois State Police. I spoke to Tom McCulloch as well. He also confirmed the confession, but all he would tell me was that he was working with Dugan on the matter, the State Police were investigating, and the lead investigator was Ed Cisowski. He suggested I call him.

Ed Cisowski was a heavyweight detective for the ISP. Whenever there was a difficult investigation, he seemed to get the call. In the early 1980s, he had led the ISP investigation into the Tylenol murders—dealing with lethally spiked Tylenol being sold in the Chicago-area and resulting in today needing the skills of Harry Houdini to get into a medicine bottle. Now he was undertaking the task of looking into Dugan's confession.

I called Cisowski to offer whatever information I could. He thanked me and said he would call if he needed anything. I gingerly asked him for information, but he, too, was tight-lipped.

Cisowski did, however, confirm that he was dealing with Tom Mc-Culloch, and Tom had made it clear that any statements Dugan made were part of a plea negotiating process. Also, they were being made in "hypothetical" terms—where the defense lawyer offering the statements of his client says "hypothetically, my client says 'I committed this or that criminal act.' "

The reason McCulloch couched his statements in these terms is simple. His goal was to prevent the admissions Dugan made from being used against him. Statements made during plea negotiations are not admissible against the maker of those statements in the event the negotiations fall apart. It's a good rule that allows for a free and open negotiating process among the parties. And relaying statements in a hypothetical form, a technique often used by defense lawyers in these types of situations, was an additional layer of protection.

All of this is not to say that Dugan's statements weren't exposing him legally to future charges, for they most certainly were. First, there was no guarantee the protections McCulloch set up would be effective. A judge might rule that Dugan's statements were not actually made in the process of plea negotiating and that some of the statements were not sufficiently "hypothetical" to be inadmissible against Dugan. And second, even if the admissions weren't usable against Dugan, they surely shined a light on him—one that didn't exist before. A smart prosecutor would have attempted to investigate to see if there was other information against Dugan for use at a trial. If the State was able to develop its own evidence, that evidence could be admissible against Dugan, exposing him to prosecution. Dugan, and McCulloch, were taking a huge risk.

Eventually, I began to get police reports from Carol, who had received them from the State during the discovery process. Though I would get many more reports later, revealing even more details of the investigation, the first batch I got was enough to paint a clear picture. The details of Dugan's confessions—there were a number of them, including one while he was under hypnosis and another to a polygraph examiner—fit extremely well with the previously known evidence. For the very first time, without having to use my imagination, I was able to accurately visualize in vivid and horrifying detail what had happened to Jeanine.

My heart raced as I read how Dugan decided to take Friday, February 25, 1983 off work at Art Tape & Label. As he drove around smoking pot in his 1980 green Plymouth Volare, his car engine began to act up when he was in Naperville. He stopped at a house to borrow a screwdriver to fix the problem, but the engine continued to be an issue. So he stopped at another house and knocked on the door. A little girl answered, saying she was alone, was not allowed to open the door, and would not get him a screwdriver. "She did what she was supposed to," Dugan said.

He watched through the door window as she walked downstairs. Then he kicked in the door with his right foot. He chased her down, brought her to the upper level of the house, and tied up her hands. He left her on the bed while he went out to his car to get some tape. When he returned, he blindfolded her by taping a cloth or towel over her eyes. Then he wrapped her in a sheet, took her out to his car, and drove off. In search of a "lonely" location, he wound up at the Illinois Prairie Path.

The Dugan reports were a little fuzzy on certain aspects of the rape. After reading all the initial statements, however, it became apparent that he recalled having the girl perform oral sex on him and that he unsuccessfully attempted vaginal sex. And it was absolutely clear he remembered ejaculating while having anal sex in the back seat.

After telling her he was going to take her home, he removed her from the back seat and took her to the rear of his car. He struck her twice in in the back of her head with a tire iron, causing her to hit her head on the bumper as she collapsed. He dragged her body off the path area and struck her in the head again with a thick branch. He drove off, found a place to turn around, and got stuck in the mud, forcing him to rock his car back and forth to get out. He then left the Prairie Path and threw the sheet into a dumpster.

When I was done, I experienced a bundle of mixed emotions. I shuddered at the terror Jeanine must have experienced. I wondered how the Nicaricos felt now that they finally knew how their daughter/sister had died. I hated Brian Dugan. I was grateful to Brian Dugan. I was happy for Hernandez and Cruz, sitting on death row, imagining their newfound feeling of hope. And, I have to admit, I felt vindicated. As the Dugan information became more and more public, I can't tell you how many people I knew approached me to say things like "Jeez, Gary, looks like you were right!" And I wondered if the Dugan information managed to put a dent in Tom Knight's arrogant sense of confidence.

But most of all, I was elated for Steve. Absolution and exoneration had to be just around the corner. Helping to get him the hell out of the DuPage County Jail was foremost on my mind.

Gag Order

When Carol had initially taken over the case, I was encouraged to

144 / GARY V. JOHNSON

hear from a number of sources, including Carol herself, how well she got along with Judge Nolan. That point was fortified when I saw them sitting at the same table at a dinner function in DuPage County. They were socializing and getting on like old friends.

I don't know what happened—and I have to hold out for the possibility that I was misinformed as to Nolan's original attitude toward Carol—but he turned on her pretty quickly. This resulted in a discernable bias against Steve and his defense.

After the initial Dugan revelations, the local press perked up and started asking serious questions. Up to that point Buckley, Hernandez and Cruz had been forced to endure endless negative publicity. From their arrests, to the convictions of Hernandez and Cruz, along with their death sentences and beyond, the public heard nothing but horrible things about the three of them. Then the press managed to learn some of the Dugan information, and they wanted more. Now the public was hearing, in general terms, that Brian Dugan was confessing to these crimes.

But Judge Nolan would have none of that. Claiming its purpose was to ensure both sides getting a fair trial, on his own—or "sua sponte," as we refer to it in the legal business—Nolan issued what he called a "protective order." In reality, it was a gag order, prohibiting the Nicarico lawyers, current and former, from discussing or otherwise publicly disseminating information about the case (read: Brian Dugan).

The gag order, a term I heard Nolan hated, would allow for contempt sanctions in the event it was violated by a lawyer. On top of that, the Illinois Attorney Registration and Disciplinary Commission (ARDC), the arm of the Illinois Supreme Court that disciplines attorneys for violating ethics rules, might also have a say. Any Illinois lawyer will tell you that those folks don't mess around. If you violate any of the disciplinary rules, including the one that regulates lawyers regarding the public dissemination of information about a pending case, they'll come a knockin' at your door. Sanctions run from a mere reprimand to disbarment, along with plenty in between.

William Bodziak

It didn't take DuPage prosecutors long to claim they were unimpressed with the Dugan confessions. Later, during court proceedings, they called him and his statements unreliable. They refused to apply for a grant of immunity for Dugan—something in Illinois only prosecutors can do—and they refused to negotiate a plea with him. A plea of guilty in return for another life sentence, something Tom McCulloch said Dugan would agree to, would have freed him up to testify at Steve's trial—double jeopardy would not have permitted him to be prosecuted for what he would say. A grant of immunity would similarly allow Dugan to testify without fear of his words being used against him.

All of this accomplished an important goal for the State. Without a negotiated plea or a grant of immunity, Dugan wouldn't risk making any unprotected statements that would result in his getting prosecuted and sentenced to death. In other words, he wouldn't testify at any future trials, including Steve's.

As a result, from where I sat, outside the case, Bob Kilander wasn't exactly a day at the beach as a Nicarico prosecutor, either.

My opinion of Kilander would deteriorate further as time passed. That said, I have to give him credit for one huge development that was critical for Steve. At my suggestion, Carol began bugging Kilander to send the shoeprint evidence to William Bodziak at the FBI. At first she got the same response I had received after making an earlier identical request of Tom Knight—the FBI had a policy of declining to reexamine evidence after another lab had given an opinion on the same subject. I don't know if it was because of Carol's urging, or if Kilander was motivated to do so on his own, but he did make the request of Bodziak. And by all accounts, including from Bodziak himself, he was pretty aggressive about it. So in the spring of 1986—maybe as a result of Kilander's persistence, or maybe due to the gravity of and questions surrounding the case, or both—Bodziak, who had the authority to make exceptions to the FBI policy, relented. He would analyze the shoeprint evidence and give an opinion.

Carol and I were ecstatic over the news. The shoeprint evidence was going to the person whom we, and from what I could tell, most of the forensic community, believed to be the world's premier shoeprint examiner. I even heard that Kilander himself—and this is supported by the written report Bodziak later prepared—transported some of the shoeprint evidence to Washington, D.C. So we waited.

It took a couple of months before we heard about the results. If you think that during that time I was nervous about the results, you would be wrong. To me, it was a no-brainer. Just ask my family and friends—I would often carry around photos of the shoeprint evidence and see how fast I could convince them that Steve's shoe was not a match to the door print. I knew that if Bodziak was the straight-shooter that Owen Lovejoy said he was, this would turn out well for Steve.

"That's the kind of decision lawsuits are made of."

Bodziak's report came out on June 16, 1986 and Carol sent me a
copy as soon as she received it. He initially opined that due to the many
dissimilarities between Steve's shoe and the door print, Steve's shoe
probably did not make the print. Not long after the written report came
out, Bodziak orally amended his findings to conclude, without qualification, that Steve's shoe did not make the door print. Even though I was not
surprised, I was still elated. It not only helped discredit the case against
Steve, but also, indirectly, against Hernandez and Cruz as well.

By this time, Ed Cisowski had come to the conclusion that Brian Dugan alone was guilty of the crimes against Jeanine. From time to time, I
would discuss the case with him, and his feelings regarding Dugan's guilt
were strong.

"I started out with the goal of blowing Brian Dugan out of the water
as quickly as possible," Ed explained. "I was searching for the one or two
things—like he was working on the day in question, or he drove a different kind of car—that would show he's full of shit. But as I got into the
meat of the case, the things he was saying started to add up. He got too
many facts right. And when we couldn't find anyone to connect Dugan
up with the other three, I knew he had done this alone.

"I don't think Kilander or the Nicaricos are very happy with me," he
continued. "Especially Pat Nicarico," (Jeanine's mother).

Carol called me to discuss the Bodziak report and an impending
meeting between her, Kilander and King. "Gary, I think they're seriously
considering dropping the case. They're going to meet soon with the Nicaricos, then I'll see them."

"This is a good opening for Ryan [Jim Ryan, the elected DuPage
County State's Attorney] to drop these charges, what with the Dugan
statements and the Bodziak opinion," I responded. "If I'm doing that
press conference, I would have Cisowski on one side of me and Bodziak
on the other. There's plenty of cover there if he needs it."

Preparing for what we believed to be the inevitable dismissal of
Steve's case, Carol and I planned what our response would be. We agreed
to keep it low-key. There would be no angry comments or end zone
dances. We would applaud Ryan's decision, compliment his courage, and
provide as much support as defense lawyers can under those conditions.
We would get Steve on board to follow suit.

All that strategizing proved to be a waste of energy. Carol called a
couple of days later with the bad news. "They're going ahead with the
prosecution," said a clearly frustrated and angry Carol. "I was sitting

outside their office before our meeting. I saw the Nicaricos come out, all smiles. I knew right then what their decision was."

"What did you say, Carol, when Kilander told you they were going ahead?"

"I said that's the kind of decision lawsuits are made of."

Violating the Gag Order
Middle of 1987 (approximately one year later)

Rick Schwind was a lawyer with the Illinois Attorney General's Office, and I had heard through the grapevine that he didn't care too much for me. His office would sometimes prosecute or investigate cases when the local authorities had a conflict of interest. Schwind had been assigned the task of, among other things, investigating who had violated Judge Nolan's gag order, and he wanted to talk to me. Criminal contempt of court was the possible end result. The ARDC would be interested, too.

I frequently counsel clients who are suspected of committing all kinds of crimes. They are nervous, because the police want them to give a statement. They tell me what they're suspected of doing and I ask what evidence they are aware of that the police have. Sometimes they tell me their side of the story. At some point, we get to the issue that needs to be resolved: Should they cooperate? My answer is always—with only a precious few exceptions that I can recall in my entire career and that are too complicated to go into here—no. I don't care whether they've just admitted to me they've committed a crime, denied it, or said nothing at all. I also don't care whether my first impression of their story was that it was bullshit or not—the answer is always no.

"But won't I look bad if I don't talk?" they often ask. "And the officer said it would look good if I cooperate."

"I don't care whether you look bad or not. And you won't get as much as an 'atta boy' for your trouble," is my response.

"Don't say a damn word," I tell them. "I know you want to talk to them. I know you think you're smarter than the cops, and that you can talk your way out of this. You're not, and you can't. The first syllable that spills from your lips will be like a noose that begins to tighten around your neck—sometimes even when you're innocent. I will inform the police that you are not going to meet with them. But, if for whatever reason I don't get hold of them, or they ignore me, when they ask you to answer a few of their questions, tell them you don't want to talk to them and that you want to talk to your lawyer." I finish by having them repeat back to me what I just told them to say.

My clients don't always follow my advice. But they always regret it when they don't.

So when Schwind asked me for a statement, surprisingly, I wasn't sure what to do. From where I sat, the identity of the person who violated the order had been a poorly kept secret. But no one knew for sure. Moreover, it had been roughly a year since the alleged violation. That, and a variety of other factors, resulted in nobody seemingly caring much anymore. So I wasn't entirely certain how serious this investigation was. But there I was anyhow, sitting in an office with a prosecutor, answering all of his non-gag-order-related questions. Finally, Schwind brought up the topic of the gag order.

I wanted to talk to him. *You can go to hell, Schwind, and the same with all your buddies at the A.G.'s Office who kiss the asses of the prosecutors in DuPage County and who hate my guts*, I wanted to say. *Yeah, I violated the court order. I'd do it again. Go ahead and see if you can get a contempt citation issued against me*, is what I was dying to say. But when he asked me if I had any knowledge of who had provided the Illinois State Police investigative reports regarding the Dugan statements to the *Chicago Tribune*, without hesitation or regret, I answered, "Rick, I'm not going to answer any gag order questions. You're going to have to get that information without me."

Back to July 1986

The news media had obtained some of the information from the investigation into the Dugan confessions, but not much in the way of details. Some reporters made it clear to me they wanted what they knew I had—the "Dugan reports." I suppose I was a logical target. I had the reports and I wasn't one of the lawyers currently involved in the defense of Steve. Plus, I had been vocal about my feelings about the case. At the same time, from the outside looking in (sort of), I watched as the DuPage prosecutors disregarded Bodziak's opinion, and also turned their backs on what the investigators were learning about Dugan.

To make matters worse, Judge Nolan was on his way down the path of outright hostility toward counsel for the defense. I didn't like what I was seeing.

Despite that, my first response to the overtures from the press was a firm "no." I wasn't going to expose myself to a contempt charge from Judge Nolan and whatever the ARDC might want to do. But over time, I began to soften my position and I started thinking about what I should do. I hung on to my initial reluctance, but after a long hand-wringing process, I decided to take matters into my own hands.

I don't recall Barb Mahany, the reporter from the *Chicago Tribune* who had been covering the case, being as aggressive as some other reporters wanting the Dugan reports. She had expressed an interest, but never took it much further than that. I decided to offer her an exclusive look at the reports for two reasons. First, of all the reporters who had covered the joint trial, she seemed the most open-minded. The bar was pretty low for that trait, but she was approachable and willing to listen. I remember after John Gorajczyk testified at the trial, she looked genuinely stunned, asking me, "What the hell was that?" Second, it was the *Chicago Tribune*, for Pete's sake, the biggest kid on the block. The *Tribune* was a conservative publication, for sure, but DuPage County was a conservative audience, and loaded with *Tribune* readers.

When I called Barb, she jumped at the chance to read the Dugan reports. I told her I wouldn't give them to her, but she could look at them in my office. So for several hours on a warm night in late July 1986, in a Clancy, McGuirk and Hulce conference room that used to be part of a vaudeville stage, Barb read the thick stack of reports prepared by the Illinois State Police and took notes. For most of the time, except when Barb had questions or when I was offering her a soda, I worked in my office. But I didn't get much done—my anxiety level was way too high.

The July 27, 1986 Sunday edition of the *Chicago Tribune* featured the headline "Fitting Pieces of a Murder Puzzle." The story, written by Mahany and John Kass, was detailed and lengthy. It told in convincing detail of the information provided by Brian Dugan to the Illinois State Police regarding the abduction, rape and murder of Jeanine. Afterward, I received calls from friends, not all of them lawyers, asking if I had seen the article. The comments they provided shared a similar theme—Buckley, Hernandez and Cruz had taken the rap for a crime that Brian Dugan alone had committed. Several days later, a *Tribune* editorial questioned the convictions of Hernandez and Cruz, and the retrial of Steve.

Maybe now, I thought—as I had done several times before—the prosecutors will fold their cards.

Wrong, again.

****

I meant what I said when, in 1987, I wanted to tell Rick Schwind that I would have violated the gag order again given the chance. That was only about a year after it occurred. Today, more than 30 years later, I feel differently. And that's despite the fact that I firmly believe the reason for

Judge Nolan issuing the order was not, as he claimed, to ensure a fair trial to both sides. It was, in my opinion, his attempt to keep the original three defendants from leveling the playing field in the eyes of the media and the public.

There are a couple of reasons for my change of heart. My conduct was an intentional violation of a court order and a violation of the canons of ethics—something I'm not proud of. That's not the kind of lawyer I picture myself as. It's understandable that the conduct of others in the case infuriated me, but that excuse falls short for obvious reasons.

Moreover, though it's impossible to tell, I think the plan backfired. The goal was to affect the court of public opinion to the extent that the DuPage County State's Attorney's Office would be forced to dismiss the charges against Steve, and similarly reverse course on Hernandez and Cruz. The naiveté of that kind of thinking is clear in hindsight. DuPage prosecutors were never going to admit they were wrong. They would do whatever they could to secure a conviction against Steve and make sure all three defendants received the death penalty.

Before my meeting with Barb Mahany, Carol filed a "motion in limine"—which is a motion requesting a judge to rule, in advance of trial, to exclude or admit certain evidence—asking Judge Nolan to admit the Dugan statements at trial. Dugan's statements were hearsay, meaning they were out-of-court statements being offered for their truth. The general rule is that hearsay is not admissible. The reason for this is that a party has a right to test the credibility and reliability of a witness by cross-examining him or her. With hearsay statements, that's impossible.

It can get pretty complicated, and law school students tear their hair out over this stuff, so a simple example that scratches the surface might help. A classic courtroom hearsay statement would be if I testified as follows: "John Doe told me he saw Bob Smith rob the convenience store clerk." It's me telling the court what John Doe told me, and it's being offered to prove the truth of the statement—that Bob Smith robbed the convenience store clerk. In this example, the party this is being used against, Bob Smith, can't cross-examine John Doe, the person who actually says he witnessed the crime. On the other hand, John Doe testifying in court to what he saw is not hearsay.

Regarding the Dugan statements, it would involve witnesses testifying to what Dugan told them to prove their truth—that Dugan alone raped and murdered Jeanine. So for them to be admitted, they had to fall within an exception to the hearsay rule.

There are many exceptions to hearsay, and the rationale for them is they normally carry sufficient trustworthiness and reliability to qualify as an exception. They include statements made to medical professionals for treatment and diagnosis, certain statements showing then-existing state of mind, emotion or physical condition, most business and public records, excited utterances made after a startling event, and more.

Admissions or confessions *made by a party* are also admissible against that party either as a hearsay exception or because they're considered admissible non-hearsay (don't ask me to explain), depending on the jurisdiction. But since Dugan wasn't a party to our case, this exception didn't apply to him.

The applicable hearsay exception in Dugan's case was that the statements were declarations against penal interests—meaning they were statements that could subject him to criminal liability. But these statements were admissible under this exception, pursuant to the U.S. and Illinois supreme courts, only if the trial court first determined that they were made "under circumstances that provide considerable assurance of [their] reliability by objective indicia of trustworthiness."[29] In other words, were Dugan's statements reliable?

Below are some examples of the consistencies and inconsistencies ISP investigators found in the Dugan statements as they related to the known facts of the case. Much of this information was presented at the hearing on Carol's motion in limine to determine if the overall reliability of those statements would allow them to be admitted at trial.

That hearing was held in August 1986, a month or so after the Mahany/Kass article appeared in the *Tribune*. In front of a fair judge, and with prosecutors doing their jobs properly, the evidence would have been admitted at trial—as it would be in the subsequent retrials of Cruz and Hernandez. Brian Dugan was right on the money on so many important details, many of which were corroborated by irrefutable independent evidence, that it should have been an easy call.

- He admitted to committing the crimes against Jeanine Nicarico without any accomplices—crimes that were very similar to the ones he committed against Melissa Ackerman and Donna Schnorr—also without accomplices.

- On a drive-around with ISP investigators, Dugan was able to locate the Nicarico house.

- Business records from Art Tape & Label showed that he took February 25, 1983 off from work.

• He drove a 1980 green Plymouth Volare—a car almost identical to the green Ford Granada that tollway worker Frank Kochanny testified he saw on the Prairie Path.[30]

• Though he was off on the description of the truck, Dugan recalled seeing the tollway workers' truck when he was on the Prairie Path.

• Kochanny said that the Granada he saw was missing a hubcap. A worker repairing the Volare after it had been repossessed from Dugan recalled all four wheel covers missing.
Also, one of the purchasers of the Volare from the bank that had repossessed it told ISP investigators that one hubcap was missing.

• Dugan told investigators he got rid of the tire iron he had used to murder Jeanine. When the bank repossessed Dugan's Volare, it was missing its tire iron.

• Dugan gave a fairly accurate description of the cloth/towel-like blindfold he taped over Jeanine's eyes.[31]

• Dugan said he taped the cloth blindfold around Jeanine's head with jagged edged tape he had purchased from a pharmacy located at a shopping plaza containing an Eagle grocery store on Farnsworth Avenue in Aurora. Serrated edged tape was found on Jeanine's blindfold and had been sold at the time by B & R Pharmacy, which was the pharmacy Dugan had described.

• Dugan accurately described the color of the nightshirt Jeanine was wearing, contradicting some inaccurate descriptions of the nightshirt that had been published in at least one newspaper.

• A secretary for an Episcopal church just blocks from the Nicarico home recalled seeing and talking to Brian Dugan on the day of the crime—he was applying for a job there.

• Dugan said he bought his shoes from an Aurora Fayva shoe store. As it turned out, that was the exact same store where, prior to the first trial, we obtained shoes with New Silver Cloud soles with the design that looked most like the print on the Nicarico door, particularly in the heel.

• Dugan said he threw out the shoes in a farmer's field, and located that field for the police. Though the police never found the shoes, the man who farmed that field said he saw a boot in the field as he plowed it in the spring of 1983.

• Dugan's shoe size generally fit the print on the Nicarico door.

• Dugan informed the state police that he had wiped the inside and outside doorknobs, and the surrounding areas, of the Nicarico front door. Ed Cisowski observed little or no evidence of fingerprints on those areas of the door.

• Dugan described much of the interior and exterior of the Nicarico house very accurately, although not perfectly.

• Investigators were not able to connect Dugan with Buckley, Hernandez or Cruz, despite aggressive efforts to do so. Although they were all from Aurora, Dugan was 27 years old at the time of the crime—seven years older, give or take, than the three original defendants.

But the hearing was not held in front of a fair judge, and was prosecuted by lawyers more concerned with preserving their prior convictions than seeking justice. And the press, particularly the *Tribune*, again turned against the defense when it heard the following minor errors and explainable inconsistencies in Dugan's statements that seemed to visibly impress a biased Judge Nolan:

> • Dugan did not remember the 22-foot sailboat in the Nicarico driveway (the only inconsistency that came close to impressing me).

> • He incorrectly recalled that Jeanine had toenail polish on.

> • Upon entry into the Nicarico home, to the left was a set of stairs leading to the upper level, immediately followed by a set of stairs going down. Dugan incorrectly reversed their order. He was also mistaken as to some other details of the Nicarico house interior and exterior.

• Dugan said he left Jeanine face-up at the Prairie Path, but the young men who found her said she was facing down.

• Dugan said that prior to going into the Nicarico home he stopped at a nearby house and borrowed a screwdriver to fix a carburetor problem, but the police were unable to locate the person who loaned him the screwdriver.

• The prosecution put on testimony from the case's original forensic pathologist who stated, contrary to the State's theory at the first trial, that there wasn't enough blood at the Prairie Path for the brutal beating to have occurred there, as Dugan said. The same pathologist also claimed that an automobile tire iron was not large enough in diameter to have caused Jeanine's cranial injuries. (Several years later, during subsequent litigation for the retrials of Hernandez and Cruz, defense pathologists would rebut both of those points).[32]

• The State also argued that Dugan could have learned details of the case from press accounts.

• Although not a factual inconsistency, the State argued that since Dugan's statements were not usable against him, they were not actually against his penal interest. This argument fails because, even if the statements were not admissible against Dugan, the very fact that he made them exposed him to criminal consequences.

There were other consistencies and inconsistencies, but you get the idea. And for what it's worth (I think everyone knows, in general terms, the limitations of lie detector tests and their inadmissibility in court), in the qualified opinion of an Illinois State Police polygraph examiner, Dugan told the truth when he subjected himself to a "lie box" and said he alone killed Jeanine Nicarico. The examiner qualified his opinion because, as a result of Dugan already spending the rest of his life in prison for two other homicides (Donna Schnorr and Melissa Ackerman), he might not have the necessary fear of detection if he lied in admitting to a third homicide.[33]

One additional consistency between the Dugan statements and the facts discovered during the original investigation bears noting here, and would play a pivotal role in the future. Dugan specifically recalled ejaculating when he anally raped Jeanine—something substantiated by the fact that semen was found in her rectum.

Even though it would take several years for DNA to link Dugan to the semen found inside Jeanine, and exclude the other three, from my admittedly biased point of view, the evidence against Dugan was already overwhelming. Prior to indicting Buckley, Hernandez and Cruz, the DuPage County State's Attorney's Office and the police task force had spent over a year investigating the Jeanine Nicarico homicide, and they came up with garbage. If they had not prosecuted the original three defendants with the flimsy and questionable evidence they developed, and instead waited and obtained the Dugan confessions when they did, they rightfully would have gone after Dugan with confidence and zeal, and ignored Buckley, Hernandez and Cruz. They would have sneered at the inconsistencies in the Dugan confessions that they so vigorously utilized to discredit him at the hearing on Carol's motion in limine. "He confessed, plus he got every major detail right," they would have argued. "How could you possibly expect him to recall every single precise detail from a crime he had committed so quickly and furiously, while his brain was foggy from smoking pot, nearly three years before he made his statements?" they justifiably would have asked.

After the hearing, Barb Mahany, writing for the *Tribune*, seemed to damn near apologize in print for the articles she had written after I showed her the Dugan police reports. Overall, the press was critical of the Dugan statements. I was beyond disappointed. But playing amateur psychologist and engaging in rank speculation, I think that had the press heard all of the evidence at one time at the hearing, without the prior leak by me, they might have weighed that evidence more fairly. Both the consistencies and the inconsistencies would have been new news. As it worked out, only the inconsistencies were fresh, and that got most of the attention.

Fortunately, not all the press was bad. Tom Frisbie, writing for the *Chicago Sun-Times*, and who would later co-author, with Randy Garrett, the definitive works on the Nicarico case, *Victims of Justice* and *Victims of Justice Revisited*, displayed an even-handed approach to the Dugan statements. Eric Zorn, a *Tribune* columnist, wrote numerous pieces casting doubt on and criticizing the State's case in general and their refusal to acknowledge the accuracy of the Dugan confessions. And Rob Warden, editor and writer for the *Chicago Lawyer*, was very critical of the conduct of the DuPage County State's Attorney's and Sheriff's offices, and banged the drum for the immediate release of Buckley, Hernandez and

Cruz. So there was hope.

I don't know exactly how Carol let this happen, but at the end of the last day of the Dugan hearing, she had to catch a plane for a European vacation she and her husband had planned for some time. The conclusion of the hearing ran long, and Carol was worried about missing her plane. There was quite a commotion as she rushed from the courthouse to get to the airport. The press was chasing her, asking about what had occurred at the hearing. She wasn't scheduled to return until just before the beginning of Steve's retrial on September 19.

The Buckley family wasn't happy about that, and it made me nervous, too.

Judge Nolan took the issue as to whether to admit the Dugan statements under advisement. I don't doubt he was giving the matter serious thought, but I'm certain the time was spent thinking how he could most effectively deny the motion, while at the same time demolish the veracity of the Brian Dugan statements. He came through with flying colors in a written opinion dated September 5, 1986. And for those who might still hold out for the possibility that Dugan was telling the truth, Nolan determined that the evidence established multiple assailants. Then, concluding that Dugan's statements were unreliable and, therefore inadmissible hearsay, he wrote the following:

"Mr. Dugan had absolutely no risk of any kind regardless of what he said. I think he took full advantage of that. For awhile, he has been Mr. Big. Maybe that's why he did what he did. He certainly has been the center of attention. Maybe if he could throw a monkey wrench into this case he would be an even bigger Mr. Big.

"Whatever Mr. Dugan's involvement, if any; whatever his motives; it is clear he was fabricating. I'm not convinced he was in such a hypnotic state [referring to the most detailed statement Dugan gave, which was while he was under hypnosis] as that which, in my opinion, he pretended. He slipped in and out of his role like a bad actor on a stage. Perhaps he was gratifying some impulse or need he had. Perhaps it was his idea of fun. He has been convicted of offenses which coupled with the facts brought to light in this case indicate a capability of weirdness, deceipt (sic) and acting. I have no evidence to indicate to what degree, if any, he might have been fantacizing (sic). His statements are totally unreliable."

What kind of a judge says shit like that in a court ruling? So much for judicial restraint! The one good thing that came from such a bizarre holding was that, to anyone in the legal business not used to that kind of language in an opinion, Judge Nolan's bias was apparent.

****

Carol and others kept me informed as to what was occurring during the course of the Dugan hearing. From very early on, it was apparent how Nolan would rule and that Brian Dugan's confessions would play no formal role in Steve's retrial.

Also during that time, since it was clear that Carol would not be getting a second chair, I began to talk to her about joining the defense "team." Even though my earlier withdrawal from the case—which caused a significant delay in the retrial and allowed for the Dugan information to come to light prior to retrial—turned out to be, I think, helpful to Steve, I was still feeling guilty about it. Both Carol and her boss, Pete Dockery, approved of the idea. It would be pro bono, of course, so that brought Clancy, McGuirk and Hulce into play.

I couldn't ask them to put me out on loan for the duration of another trial and whatever aftermath might take place, so after consulting with the final major player in the decision-making process, Amy, I left the law firm to go into practice for myself.

I set up my new solo law firm, rent free, in a room at my dad's real estate office, thanks to the generosity of the managing Realtor, Phyllis Jeske. And my family and I were able to survive until I got my feet on the ground as a result of a nice "retirement" package from Clancy, McGuirk, and Hulce. So on a status date for the formal entry of the order denying the use of the Dugan statements, a court date which I could not attend, Pete Dockery entered my appearance as co-counsel for the retrial of Steve Buckley.

The hiatus was over.

Hiatus—Sidebar

Tom McCulloch walked into the Firehouse, a bar near the old Kane County Courthouse in Geneva, after work one day after the Dugan statements had become public. Inside he saw his old friend, Van Richards, seated at a table. "Hey, McCulloch," Richards shouted out. "I don't think there's much of a market these days for criminal defense lawyers who cough their clients up for murder confessions."

"Is that what people think I did?" Tom wondered. "Do people really think I did that?"

****

Tom McCulloch,[†] and to an extent, George Mueller before him, took a huge gamble. The name "Brian Dugan" hadn't been uttered a single time in the years of the Nicarico pretrial investigation, the first trial and its immediate aftermath. Mueller started the ball rolling, but after a short while, Tom took over, and really pushed it. McCulloch never denied that one of the goals of making the statements was to pave the way for Dugan to plead out for a life sentence and eliminate any further possibility of prosecution and the death penalty for the abduction, rape and murder of Jeanine. But the goal of freeing three innocent men incarcerated for Dugan's criminal behavior was equally important. And when the Dugan/McCulloch team continued to cooperate after the DuPage County prosecutors refused to enter into a plea, the motive of justice for three innocent men became paramount.

Trust me, I'm not trying to put a halo over Brian Dugan's head here. He doesn't deserve it. I'm a believer in redemption, and whatever of that he gets, he gets, and I'm glad for that. It's Tom McCulloch who deserves to be acknowledged, right along with the previously noted John Sam, and Ed Cisowski and Mary Brigid Kenney, people whose virtues I will extol later. Many lawyers would have shut Dugan down, telling him not to expose himself to potential prosecution after not even being on the Nicarico radar screen. But McCulloch continued to push, which resulted in more than a few sleepless nights for him. It brought out cries for the prosecution of Dugan from some of the defense teams of the original defendants and eventually resulted in his being charged, convicted and sentenced to death for the crimes against Jeanine. It was a sentence that would never be carried out.

---

† In the late 1990s, Tom McCulloch became a partner of mine in the law firm of Camic, Johnson, Wilson and McCulloch, and in another partnership with Camic and me regarding the ownership of several pieces of real estate. Since then, Tom has left the law firm, which is now called Camic Johnson, Ltd. He is currently the DeKalb County, Illinois, Public Defender. Tom continues to be a friend, and a partner with David Camic and me in the ownership of real estate.

Chapter 11

Preparing for Retrial

Carol returned from her trip just before the September 19, 1986 start date for Steve's second trial. I don't know how she could possibly have enjoyed that vacation, but she was focused and in trial mode after she returned. Before Carol left, she lined up witnesses and got out the necessary subpoenas. While Carol was gone, I caught up on the newer aspects of the case. I felt ready.

On day one of jury selection, the courtroom was crammed with prospective jurors. Judge Nolan already had made some opening remarks to them when Kilander informed us of a new witness named James Byrnes, who was claiming that Steve had made incriminating statements to him while they were both in the DuPage County Jail. Since Byrnes would be testifying within the next week or so, Carol and I quickly asked for and received a continuance to investigate Mr. Byrnes and his statement.

Although we told Judge Nolan this would take a significant amount of time, surprisingly, it didn't take us long at all to determine the State's new evidence was worthless. After interviewing Mr. Byrnes in an Indiana prison, we learned the statements he claimed to have overheard were not incriminating, and someone other than Steve had made them. So, on October 30, 1986, Carol and I announced we were prepared to schedule a trial date. We thought the judge would be glad to hear it. Instead, it led to our several-hour stint in the DuPage County Jail.

Contempt of Court (Continued from Chapter 1)

Judge Nolan didn't want a trial of this magnitude to be held over the holidays, so he tentatively scheduled jury selection to begin on January 14, 1987. But he had a concern—the speedy-trial statute. According to Illinois law, an incarcerated defendant must be brought to trial within 120 days of being taken into custody. Failure to do so will cause a case to be dismissed if a motion is filed by the defendant. What complicates the counting process is that continuances asked for or agreed to by the defendant are not included in the 120 days. Counting days is a little trickier than it sounds, and dismissals resulting from violating the statute don't occur often.

On November 5th, I want a calculation by the People and a calculation by the Defendant as to the term [speedy trial] **time,** ordered the judge. Carol and I were surprised that Nolan would order us to proceed with such a calculation, since we had not filed a motion to dismiss based on the speedy-trial statute. As a matter of fact, since most of the continuances were either agreed to or even requested by us, up to that point we hadn't even thought about that issue.

There was a principle involved here. Since I felt it was the State's responsibility to get the matter to trial within the prescribed period, not the defendant's, I didn't think we should be required to comply with the judge's order. Carol agreed, but since we knew that our refusal to comply might lead to contempt-of-court problems, I contacted Van Richards, a defense lawyer I knew and respected. Van had an encyclopedic knowledge of criminal law, and also could cite sports statistics and quote Shakespeare until you cried uncle. He, in turn, got hold of Mary Robinson, another highly regarded defense lawyer who specialized in appeals. She later would become the head of the Illinois Attorney Registration and Disciplinary Commission (ARDC). They both agreed with us. Beyond the principle, Van warned of another problem if we shared our math with the court. If our calculations revealed a speedy-trial issue in the future, we might be forewarning the State of the problem, and giving them time to correct it. On the other hand, if our calculations showed otherwise, and we had counted incorrectly, we might be waiving a legitimate issue that could benefit Steve. Either way, Van thought, it could amount to malpractice because we would have provided information against our client's interests.

On November 5, 1986, Kilander informed Nolan that the January 14 date would not present a speedy-trial problem. In a rather edgy give-and-take between the judge and me—Carol had to be in another courtroom that morning—I told Judge Nolan that we were not in a position to comment on the State's opinion, making it clear that we were not going to present a calculation as to how many days had passed under the statute. After the judge threatened us with contempt of court, he teed us up for such a finding by specifically, and very formally, wording his demand.

Court orders the Defendant within seven days hereof to provide to the court its calculation as to the running of the term time. That is a direct order of the Court, Counsel.

Contempt of court is a tool that judges use to control their courtrooms and enforce their orders. Civil contempt normally involves a person's refusal to obey a court order, while criminal contempt usually involves behavior that is disruptive of or offensive to the court. The penalty for contempt of court can be either a fine, incarceration, or both. In civil contempt, the penalty is imposed to encourage or force the contemnor to comply with the court's order, and is lifted, or "purged," upon compliance with the order. The purpose of criminal contempt is punishment, plain and simple.

Beyond that, criminal contempt can be broken down into two more categories—indirect and direct contempt. Indirect contempt of court is conduct that occurs outside the presence of the judge, thereby requiring a separate hearing for the judge to determine if the contempt occurred. Direct contempt happens in the presence of the judge, eliminating the necessity of such a hearing.

Carol and I discussed our dilemma at length. We figured Nolan would hold us in civil contempt on the next court date if we refused to abide by his order, but we didn't think he would lock us up. That turned out to be a bad read on our part. On November 12, we both appeared before Judge Nolan and started out by requesting that he withdraw his order requiring us to make a speedy-trial calculation. We supplied him with case law that supported our position. I was doing most of the arguing, and I was as obsequious as I could be. But no amount of "with all due respect" and "if it please the court" language would placate Nolan. He refused to withdraw his order, and we refused to comply with it.

Very well, Nolan responded. **The Court then finds both defense counsel in contempt of this Court, and I guess each is hereby remanded to the custody of the Sheriff of DuPage County pending compliance.** The compliance language indicated that it was civil contempt. He then set an appeal bond of $100 each, and warned that he was still considering holding us in criminal contempt as well.

Are you kidding me? We're being arrested?! I have to figure out a way to get $100 over here, and right away, were my first thoughts. The next thing I knew, my hands were cuffed, a guard was jokingly reciting Miranda warnings, I got fingerprinted, my mug shot was taken, and I ended up in a cell where, after a warning from a guard, I worried about lying down on the mattress.

After an hour or two of pacing around and worrying about a variety of things—what to do about a hostile judge, my political career, how my bond would be posted, why Carol got to watch *Jeopardy!* and drink coffee, while I didn't—a guard escorted me from my cell for transport to DuPage County's brand new jail. When I stepped out, he handcuffed me and shackled my ankles.

I shuffled to the van located outside the courthouse's lockup. Wearing only a T-shirt, pants, shoes and socks, I was chilly in the November weather. Carol sat in the heated cab with the driver. I was instructed to get into the back end of the van via the rear door. When I lifted my right leg to step in, the chains weren't long enough to allow my foot to reach the van floor.

"How am I supposed to do this?"

The deputy watching me laughed. "You just have to jump and roll in."

I took a step back, hopped up and managed to finesse my way into the cab. The ride to the jail took only a few minutes, and before I knew it, I was alone in the lockup of a brand new facility. There were no bunks, bars, or mattresses—just white walls with a small door window and a ledge to sit on. I spent my time there pacing and smoldering.

Finally, after about a total of three-and-a-half hours of incarceration, Carol's husband posted bail for us both and we were released. Technically speaking, since it was civil contempt of court and Nolan chose to incarcerate us, the most logical thing for him to do would have been to refuse the appeal bond and keep us in jail until we agreed to complete the speedy-trial calculation. I imagine Nolan didn't want to martyr us. I wasn't going to quibble. I was glad to get out of there.

Motion for Substitution of Judge

It was time to stop being Judge Nolan's punching bag. So even though the law wasn't all that favorable, Carol and I agreed we should file a Motion for Substitution of Judge for Cause, otherwise known as an SOJ motion. A "for cause" SOJ motion is different from and more difficult to obtain than the SOJ motions that are granted as a matter of right when filed during the very early stages of a case soon after a judge has been assigned.

In Illinois murder cases, a defendant is allowed to sub out two judges as a matter of right if that motion is filed within 10 days of the case being placed on the judge's trial call.[34] But at an SOJ hearing for cause, which usually occurs after that 10-day time period has lapsed, we would have to show that Judge Nolan had actual prejudice against us. That's no small task, even with a judge who had just thrown us in jail. We figured the motion would be denied, but we wanted Nolan to know we weren't going to let him roll over us anymore.

The matter was heard before Judge Robert Lucas on November 25, and the evidence dealt with several matters, but mainly the contempt order. Judge Lucas ruled against us, but after he left the bench, and as Carol and I were packing up to leave his courtroom, I saw him in the hallway outside his chambers. He was beckoning us to come over, which we did.

"Listen, I ruled against you because the law just didn't work out for you on this thing," he correctly pointed out. "But I just wanted to tell you that I'm pulling for you guys. I wish you the best of luck."

"Thanks, Judge, for the encouraging words," I responded. "That really means a lot." And it truly did.

I always liked Judge Lucas. He worked mostly in civil courtrooms, and I had a number of cases with him when I was with Clancy, McGuirk and Hulce. A year or two later, I saw him in the hallway of the DuPage Courthouse. He laughed and said, "I see they're allowing you east of the Rio Fox (the Fox River is near the border between Kane and DuPage counties) without a visa!"

Another Continuance

A few months after Steve's hung jury, the State came up with a witness, Eric Hook, who claimed Steve had made incriminating statements to him while they were together in the DuPage County Jail. Unlike the later similar claim of James Byrnes, this was evidence we had plenty of time to look into (some of which I did after getting back into the case), and after a little digging, we thoroughly defused it. We were able to show, largely by way of a guard at the jail, that it was highly unlikely that the circumstances during which Hook claimed the statement was made had occurred. Also, Hook had a lengthy criminal record and a provably terrible reputation for truthfulness. A witness's poor reputation for truthfulness is something that can be presented in court to impeach that witness. Same goes for certain aspects of a witness's criminal record (generally speaking, any conviction or release from prison within the last 10 years for a felony or a crime of dishonesty). And finally, Hook never said a damn thing to authorities about Steve making any admissions until he (Hook) was arrested on other charges and the providing of such "information" could secure him leniency.

As the January 14, 1987 trial date that Nolan had set approached, a couple of important events occurred. First, Eric Hook went missing, saying in a letter that he was afraid of gang retaliation. This was an interesting claim, seeing as Steve had absolutely no gang affiliations. The second, and more important, thing that occurred was that Dr. Robbins, the State's principal shoeprint witness at Steve's first trial, who had previously been diagnosed with brain cancer, experienced a recurrence of that disease. Though she was fit to testify, she wasn't physically able to

164 / GARY V. JOHNSON

travel from her North Carolina home. So in early January, Kilander filed a motion to continue the case. The State needed time to resolve both of those matters. Judge Nolan granted their motion, and the trial was continued to March.

Louise Robbins not being able to travel to DuPage County to testify was not necessarily good news for us. If she couldn't testify at trial, we feared the State would move to use her testimony from the first trial as evidence at the retrial. Under the right circumstances, if a witness is unavailable to testify at trial, her prior trial testimony can be admissible. It would require someone reading her transcript, or having a person actually sit in the witness chair while the prosecutor, the defense lawyer and the "actor" asked and answered questions from the transcript. That normally wouldn't be a big deal, except that in order for the cross-examination of Dr. Robbins to be effective, the jury would need to see the physical evidence and what she was referring to or pointing at while she testified—the parts of shoes, test prints, and images of the print on the door—along with her explanations for the various differences. The verbal descriptions from the first trial, without the concurrent visuals, were not sufficiently clear.

So on January 27, I filed a motion for an evidence deposition of Dr. Robbins, asking that she be allowed to testify on video as to her findings, as if she were at the trial. Since Dr. Robbins was able to testify, but unable to travel, we would have to do the deposition in North Carolina. By doing this, if Dr. Robbins was unable to testify at trial, we would be able to use the videotaped evidence deposition instead, and the jury would still be able to see and hear her testimony and evaluate her analysis.

The rules allowed for the use of evidence depositions for this very reason—to preserve testimony,[35] and in this case, the visual part of her testimony. The process was fair to both sides. Sounds reasonable, right? Well, not to the prosecutors, who objected to the procedure, or Judge Nolan, who agreed with the State and denied our motion.

Death of a Reputation

Deteriorating as quickly as Louise Robbins's health was her professional reputation. Her unproven theories concerning the uniqueness of human shoeprints had been taking a beating in the forensic science and legal communities for a while, but it mainly consisted of experts, scientists and lawyers telephoning, writing letters, and exchanging transcripts and ideas. It was all very unofficial. That was about to change.

In the summer of 1986, the American Academy of Forensic Scientists made plans to convene a panel to review the claims, theories and court-room testimony of Dr. Robbins.[36] The panel met in San Diego on February 20, 1987, and was made up of five forensic anthropologists and crime lab experts. The meeting of the panel was attended by approximately 100 people—lawyers, judges and other forensic anthropologists and criminalists.

The panel concluded that there was no basis for the claims made by Dr. Robbins regarding the uniqueness of shoeprints to an individual wearer. During the session, not a single attendee supported Dr. Robbins. The scientists were encouraged to publish their opinions so that, in the future, courts would see her methods were not considered reliable.[37] These publications could then be used in pretrial hearings, like the one we had requested before Steve's first trial, to show that her theories did not satisfy the *Frye* standard—that they were not generally accepted in the scientific community.

Finally, Dr. Louise Robbins and her shoeprint uniqueness theory had been thoroughly discredited. It left Carol and me wondering whether Kilander was nuts enough to try to use her as a witness again. And if he was, what would be the best strategy for Steve? Should we attempt to keep her off the stand by asking for the *Frye* hearing we didn't get before the first trial? With the results from the San Diego panel, even Judge Nolan might have been forced to go our way on that. Or should we let her testify and absolutely destroy her at trial with as much of the new information as we could get admitted? It would impeach not only Dr. Robbins, but the entire prosecution, by showing they were desperate to sell their case to the jury with any kind of forensic sewage they could tap into. After some debate, we decided to play it conservatively and try to keep Dr. Robbins off the stand altogether.

As it turned out, we never had to have that *Frye* hearing.

Brian Dugan Declines to Testify

"They'll kill me if I testify, Mr. Johnson. My lawyers have worked real hard to keep that from happening, and I don't want to screw it up now," Brian Dugan said to me, calmly but emphatically, in the prison where he was housed.

It was at the same time Brian Dugan had confessed to the abduction, rape and murder of Melissa Ackerman and Donna Schnorr, as well as assaults on three other women—confessions that the various police and prosecutorial authorities accepted and believed as true, leading to guilty pleas and two life sentences—that he also confessed to doing the same thing to Jeanine Nicarico. Unfortunately, the DuPage County authorities already had their convictions and were committed to their incorrect theory of the Nicarico case, so they refused to accept Dugan's confession.

Actually, Dugan made a series of confessions pertaining to Jeanine's murder. I just wanted one more. The problem with my request was that Dugan's prior confessions were made in such a way that they couldn't be used against him if he were ever charged with the crimes against Jeanine, and I was asking him to testify, without those protections, at the retrial of my innocent client indicted for those very crimes.

This interview was a last-ditch effort by Carol and me to get the Dugan story in front of the jury, straight from the killer's mouth. Carol's motion to admit Dugan's statements, through hearsay testimony from those who had heard the confessions, had been denied the summer before.

Beyond that, we asked the State to petition the court for a grant of immunity for Dugan—something Illinois law allows only prosecutors to do. Dugan's lawyer made a similar request. This would have allowed Dugan to testify freely, without his words being used against him. The State rejected our requests. And despite knowing that only prosecutors may request witness immunity, we asked the court to grant it to Dugan anyhow, without a motion from the State. That, too, failed. Dugan himself was our last hope.

So in February of 1987, just weeks before Steve's retrial, Randy Garrett, a private citizen with exhaustive knowledge of the case, and I traveled to the Pontiac Correctional Center to convince Dugan to testify. We were met by Dugan's lawyer, Tom McCulloch, and Illinois State Police investigator Ed Cisowski. The tiny drab and dreary conference room, located in the huge, dank and dour prison, required the others to stand while Dugan and I sat facing each other across a table. McCulloch had spoken to Dugan before we arrived to inform him of the purpose of the meeting and to counsel him not to cooperate. My legal advice would be different.

"I really don't think they'll prosecute you, Mr. Dugan. DuPage County prosecutors have gone out of their way to paint you as a liar and your statements as false. They've committed themselves. There's no way they would change course now and accept your confession as true and prosecute you. They'd look silly."

Naively, I believed what I told him.

Dugan glanced up at McCulloch, and then back at me. "I wish I could help, I really do. If they would give me immunity, I'd talk all day. But without that, no way I'm going to testify. If I do, they'll charge me, try me, find me guilty, and give me the death penalty. I know I would if I was them."

With that, any possibility of Brian Dugan, Jeanine Nicarico's sole kidnapper, rapist and killer, being a factor in the retrial of Steve Buckley, disappeared.

Nolle Prosequi (sometimes "Nolle Pros" or just "Nolle")

On March 5, Carol and I were prepared to proceed on a motion to dismiss the charges against Steve based on our allegations of prosecutorial misconduct. The motion had some legs, and we were anxious to hear the State's response. We almost certainly wouldn't get the dismissal we were seeking, but I was sure some prosecutors and police were about to be embarrassed.

As we entered Judge Nolan's courtroom, I noticed it was more crowded than usual with Nicarico supporters. There was a quiet buzz among them. I sensed something was about to happen—something good. I tried not to indulge the feeling. *Concentrate, Gary,* I told myself. *You have a motion to present. Eyes straight ahead. Don't look around.* But I couldn't help it. Steve's case was still primarily based on the shoeprint, and with the advent of Bodziak's opinion, Robbins's theories falling into disrepute, plus the Gorajczyk information and the discovery of German's notes—not to mention the very visible differences between the door print and Steve's shoe—the State had nothing. *They're going to dump this thing!* I thought, but wouldn't say it out loud, not even to Carol. The case was called, the lawyers stated their names for the record and Kilander took over:

Robert Kilander:

> **Judge, I have a statement I wish to make to the Court.**
> **Dr. Louise Robbins has suffered a relapse necessitating two additional surgeries. Yesterday it was confirmed she is completely unavailable as a witness and that her unavailability is probably permanent.**
> **Eric Hook's whereabouts continue to be a mystery despite our repeated and thorough efforts to locate him. He has violated parole and warrants are outstanding for his arrest.**
> **Because of these and other factors, the case of The**

People of the State of Illinois versus Stephen Buckley is nolle prossed (dismissed).

Despite my sixth sense telling me something like this would happen, I was still stunned. But before we could do anything, Nolan ordered the lawyers into his chambers. *What could he possibly want?* I wondered. *Just sign the nolle order, order Steve's release, and get us the hell outta here!*

In his chambers, Judge Nolan was clearly unhappy. "There were things that happened in this case that should not have happened. I'm going to ask State's Attorney Ryan to arrange for the appointment of a special prosecutor to look into these matters."

Well it's about fuckin' time, I thought. *He's asking for an investigation as to how three innocent people came to be prosecuted for a crime that—especially with recent revelations—anyone with half a brain could see they had nothing to do with. Hallelujah!*

Sadly, my naiveté had once again gotten the better of me, but this time, I wasn't alone. Others were under the same misimpression, including the editorial board of the *Chicago Sun-Times*, who agreed with the call for a special prosecutor to investigate "nagging doubts" concerning the evidence against the three defendants.[38]

Unfortunately, that was not at all the reason for Nolan's request for a special investigation. It would take a while, but I later found out that he had two very different things in mind. First, Nolan somehow got the idea that the Illinois State Police investigators, particularly Ed Cisowski, had either intentionally or inadvertently fed Dugan facts about the case which were later incorporated into his confessions, thereby making them appear more accurate. He wanted that looked into. Second, he wanted the identity of the person who leaked the Dugan statements to the *Chicago Tribune*.

****

It took about an hour for Steve to get released. We were totally unprepared for the process of getting him out and away from the jail and the press. I waited for Steve in the jail lobby, and Carol stayed outside. While waiting, I thought about how we should handle the reporters outside clamoring for access to Steve. One other person, Art Norman from *WMAQ News*, was inside with me. He could tell I was nervous and unsure of myself. The guy couldn't have been nicer, congratulating us and giving me suggestions as to how to deal with the crowd. When

Steve finally got out, Carol and I got on either side of him and we walked briskly to Carol's car, answering reporters' questions on the move. She then drove Steve to the Public Defender's Office, where his sister, Carol Brusatori, and parents scooped him up and drove him to the Brusatori home.

Later that day, Steve and his family gave an exclusive interview to Tom Frisbie of the *Sun-Times*. That evening, Steve was treated to a home-cooked lasagna dinner. Later, he sank into a chair and watched TV—a luxury he had been largely deprived of in jail after he was placed in a sort of solitary confinement for his own protection after he had been injured when a fellow prisoner punched him in the face.

Just like that, for the first time in three years, Steve Buckley was a free man.

****

Meanwhile, Jeanine's parents, Tom and Pat Nicarico, were expressing their displeasure to the press. "We feel that the man that murdered our little girl is back on the streets," Tom Nicarico told Barb Mahany and John Schmeltzer of the *Tribune*. "It's a standard defense tactic," he continued. "Drag it out and the witnesses fall away. Both sides are at fault."[39]

Did Tom Nicarico forget that we had filed a motion, objected to by the State, then denied by Judge Nolan, to preserve Dr. Robbins's testimony on video—forever? I wondered.

****

As for me, I was elated beyond words that Steve had been released from three years of an unjust incarceration. But a cloud hung over the matter that formed the basis for one of two major fears I had which muted my celebrations. Since Steve's trial had ended in a hung jury, which is technically a mistrial, and no retrial occurred, the Double Jeopardy Clause of the 5th Amendment to the U.S. Constitution would not bar a further prosecution. I was sure the Nicaricos, Tom Knight, and maybe others were regularly pressing for Steve to be recharged.

This was especially true when, in mid-April of 1987, Eric Hook was rearrested in Florida, and State's Attorney Ryan was asked if a re-prosecution was being considered. Ryan was noncommittal.[40] I suspect that Jim Ryan and Bob Kilander were cognizant of the dangers of basing a prosecution on the likes of Eric Hook. And with their shoeprint evidence having gone completely south on them, I figure they were just as glad to be done with Steve and were willing to fend off any public criticism that those favoring a re-prosecution might generate. Still, without a statement of exoneration or a public apology, I remained worried.

The second fear I had was that any kind of sex crime against a minor that occurred near where Steve lived could result in his automatically being a suspect. As a matter of fact, almost immediately after he was released, just such a crime occurred in southern Kane County, and I went into a slight panic. Fortunately, Steve's sister had planned a trip to Las Vegas for him, and that's where he was. I contacted Steve and had his sister take a picture of him at his hotel holding a newspaper in such a way so that the date could be seen. Even with that I was a little nervous—at least until the police arrested someone else for the offense.

Neither of my fears ever materialized, but it would take a few years for them to dissipate.

****

One of the reasons the State said they nolled the charges against Steve was their initial inability to find the thoroughly impeachable Eric Hook. Prosecutors claimed they looked high and low, but still couldn't locate him. You'd have thought he was a damn Richard Kimble—the fictional character from the 1960s television series *The Fugitive*—by the way the State complained he had eluded authorities. Later, in a phone call to representatives of the *Chicago Tribune*, Hook claimed he had withheld from prosecutors even more incriminating evidence, this time against Hernandez and Cruz.[41] Hernandez and Cruz would each go through two more trials, and Eric Hook didn't testify in any of them.

****

Dr. Louise Robbins died in late 1987 at the age of 58. It boggles the mind to think what courts allowed her to get away with regarding shoeprint testimony. Between 1976 and 1986, she polluted courtrooms in 10 states and Canada with her later-to-be-discredited theory of the uniqueness of shoeprints.[42]

Two of those instances occurred in DuPage County. The Nicarico case was actually Dr. Robbins's second appearance in Wheaton. About two months before her testimony in Steve's trial, she testified for the State in the prosecution of Dennis Ferguson. In that case, police found shoeprints in white powder and mud at the scene of a murder. When the police searched Ferguson's house and Mr. Ferguson, they didn't find the shoes that had left the prints, but they did find three other pairs of shoes belonging to Mr. Ferguson. Dr. Robbins testified that, based on the wear patterns on the shoe soles found in the Ferguson residence and on Mr. Ferguson, and comparing them to the wear patterns on the crime scene shoeprints, they were made by the same person. Her critics have dubbed such a quantum leap as "Cinderella analysis."[43]

In June 1988, the Ferguson conviction was reversed by the appellate court, and remanded for a new trial. The court ruled that while evidence of shoeprint comparisons between a shoe suspected of making a print and a shoeprint are common and accepted, connecting shoeprints to a suspect by comparing the wear patterns of those prints to the wear patterns of a different pair of shoes worn by a suspect did not comply with the *Frye*'s "general acceptance" standard. The court noted that "Robbins testified that the wear patterns on the soles of shoes are unique to the individual who wore the shoes, and by measuring the wear patterns on the soles of different pairs of shoes, she can determine within a reasonable degree of scientific certainty whether the same person wore both pairs of shoes. By her own testimony Robbins stands alone in the anthropological community regarding the belief that an identification can be made solely by measuring and analyzing the wear patterns on the soles of shoes."[44]

In 1992, the *CBS* show *48 Hours* aired a two-hour episode on questionable scientific/expert testimony that had been used in court. One of the featured segments was on Louise Robbins. A number of lawyers, including Tom Knight and me, appeared on the show arguing both sides of the issue. In it, I called Dr. Robbins the "forensic expert from hell." Which is exactly what she was.

****

It's appropriate to highlight here the courageous conduct of one of the truly good guys. The third person of heroic stature in this case is Ed Cisowski. As his investigation into the Dugan statements led him to the conclusion that Brian Dugan alone was responsible for Jeanine's abduction, rape and murder, he didn't shy away. He let the Nicaricos and the DuPage County State's Attorney's Office know how he felt.

He could have taken the path of least resistance. He knew where the Nicaricos and the prosecutors stood—they wanted to defend and maintain the convictions against Hernandez and Cruz, and obtain a conviction against Steve. To make matters even more uncomfortable, Ed was a Naperville resident who lived near the Nicaricos. They even attended the same church. But getting at the truth trumped all of that for Ed, and that

172 / GARY V. JOHNSON

path was full of all kinds of resistance, including allegations of misconduct.

The Nicaricos went to the press in mid-April of 1987 suggesting that Ed and his fellow police investigators may have either intentionally or inadvertently relayed essential facts to Dugan so that he could make his statements more accurate.[45] This was one of the issues of the investigation Nolan had ordered on the day Steve's charges were dismissed. It came at a time when the Nicaricos and the state's attorney's office were continuing to make it clear they didn't believe Dugan, so discrediting him and the investigation into his statements was critical.

The Nicaricos' claims were provably false. Unfortunately, that proof was in the possession of prosecutors who, for whatever reason, did not part with it for several years. You see, on November 13, 1985, shortly before authorities from the other counties where Dugan had wreaked havoc were accepting his confessions and working out plea agreements to the Schnorr and Ackerman murders, as well as two other sexual assaults and an attempted abduction, but several days before Ed Cisowski and the State Police even began their investigation into the Dugan statements concerning Jeanine Nicarico, Bob Kilander and Pat King got a hypothetical statement from Dugan through his then lawyer, George Mueller. This fact was commonly known, but a record of the statement was not initially provided.

As I noted earlier, a hypothetical statement is a technique used by defense lawyers to give information without it being usable against the person giving the statement. The hypothetical statement Dugan gave, admitting he alone committed the crimes against Jeanine, had been reduced to a few pages of handwritten notes, which were in the possession of the prosecution, but were not turned over to any of the defense attorneys or the state police until August of 1989—nearly four years after the statement—before the retrials of Cruz and Hernandez. Those "pre-Cisowski" notes contained numerous accurate facts (with some mistakes, too) verifying much of the state police investigation, but which could not have been fed to Dugan by the state police.‡

Now I certainly have no standing, for obvious reasons, to complain about the Nicaricos using the press to advance their side of the case.

---

‡ In a related court hearing, Kilander claimed to have previously turned over the notes of the Mueller/Dugan interview to Hernandez's private investigator, Bill Clutter. He also claimed Clutter confirmed this, when asked, with a nod of the head at said hearing. Bill Clutter has consistently denied that Kilander, or any other prosecutor, gave him those notes. He has also denied that any such "head nod" confirmation ever occurred.

More importantly, I think the Nicarico family gets a pass on pretty much anything they say, think or do pertaining to the crimes committed against Jeanine. But the State's Attorney's Office gets no such relief. It's astonishing that they stood silent in April of 1987 when the Nicaricos made these claims, as well as during the investigation ordered by Judge Nolan in March of the same year concerning that very issue. They hung Ed Cisowski and his fellow state police investigators out to dry. I can only imagine how vindicated Ed must have felt when he heard about those notes.

That vindication would be complete years later when DNA, along with other factors, conclusively linked Dugan as the sole perpetrator. And every step of the way, Cisowski took the high road, letting the facts of his investigation do all the talking and never complaining publicly about the treatment he received.

****

There was a resolution of one aspect of Judge Nolan's two-pronged investigation request. After multiple requests by Jeremy Margolis, the head of the Illinois State Police, for a report of the results of the investigation into claims that ISP detectives fed information to Dugan, in January, 1991, the Illinois Attorney General's Office finally released its findings exonerating Ed Cisowski and his fellow investigators of any wrongdoing. It was done without fanfare or publicity. As far as I'm concerned, they all should have received medals and a public apology from a number of sources—but I'll take it.

Regarding the leak to the *Tribune*, the other prong of the Nolan-initiated investigation, after my refusal to discuss the issue with Schwind, except for some grousing that I had "taken five," (criminal lawyer shorthand that I had taken the 5th or refused to talk) that made its way to me, I never heard a thing. I'll take that, too.

Preparing for Retrial—Sidebar

Carol and I appealed Judge Nolan's contempt ruling to the Illinois Second District Appellate Court. The three justices hearing the case were not kind to us. Not only did they affirm the contempt finding, but they accused us of "gamesmanship" in our refusal to calculate days under the speedy-trial statute. While conceding that it's the State's burden to bring a defendant to trial within the prescribed time period, the appellate court held that the defendant must assist the State with that burden if asked to do so by the court.[46] When it comes to this issue, apparently, our duty as defense counsel to our client is trumped by our duty as officers of the court.

Since the Illinois Supreme Court refused to review the appellate court's decision, and no other Illinois appellate court has ruled to the contrary, the Second District Court's opinion in our contempt case is technically the law in Illinois. While this ruling may seem appealing to non-lawyers—perhaps understandably so—it didn't sit well with defense lawyers. There was a fear that because of this decision, judges and prosecutors would habitually begin to request the defense to assist in the calculation of speedy-trial time.

Mary Robinson, who represented me on appeal, told me that after the appellate court ruled, some defense lawyers in Cook County were thinking about attempting to set up a similar situation there with hopes of getting a trial court judge to hold a defense lawyer in contempt of court for the same reason. The goal would be to convince their appellate court in the First District to rule contrary to the Second District. Then, as a result of the conflict among appellate court districts, the Illinois Supreme Court would be much more likely to hear and resolve the issue. Unfortunately, that never occurred.

There really was a larger principle involved here. When the threat of contempt was looming for Carol and me, I did some research. As it turned out, there was Illinois case law holding that after a defendant has been brought to trial once within the statutory speedy-trial time, with said trial resulting in a mistrial—which is what a hung jury technically is—the statutory speedy-trial requirements are satisfied. There are separate and concurrent state and federal constitutional (as opposed to statutory) speedy-trial requirements that still exist for the retrial, but they only require that the defendant be retried within a reasonable time—a vague requirement that isn't nearly as strict. Due to the number of continuances that we had either requested or agreed to, the State had easily brought Steve to trial within the time required by statute. So for the second trial all they had to do was get Steve retried within a reasonable period of time, thus satisfying the constitutional speedy-trial provisions, and there would have been no problems. I was surprised when neither the State nor the judge cited that case law.

In the end, though, Judge Nolan killed off the contempt issue by saying that, after he did his own calculations, he no longer needed ours. He agreed with the State that the speedy-trial statute had not been violated.

****

The Nicarico case wouldn't be the last time I would be held in contempt of court. In mid-December of 1991, when I was the elected state's attorney for Kane County, I prosecuted a man named David Strand for the alleged sexual assault of two nine-year-old girls, DeShondra Keane and Adriana Vela. (The real names of the defendant and the girls have been changed for privacy purposes). Even though the cases were factually connected—they were both assaulted while they were staying at DeShondra's house when her mother was at work—the cases were being tried separately. And despite the fact that Strand was a father figure of sorts for DeShondra, she made the more compelling witness against him and I chose her case to go first.

Strand's lawyer was Tom McCulloch—the very same Tom McCulloch who had represented Brian Dugan. Tom and I had done a number of trials against each other, with mixed results. He was one of the very best in the business. Tom had been a U.S. Navy fighter pilot, and he fit the mold perfectly. He was smart, but more importantly, he was unflappable in the midst of confusion. As it turned out, it was that latter attribute that would save me from going to jail—again.

Day one of the trial was consumed with the arduous process of picking the jury, then giving opening statements. First thing the next day, I called DeShondra to the stand. Due to her age, the presiding judge, Barry Puklin, cleared the courtroom of all non-essential persons, including DeShondra's grandmother, whom I had asked to remain in court for moral support. Things did not start well when, prior to being sworn in and as she was approaching the witness stand, DeShondra declared, "Guess what, I'm not testifying."

I didn't panic. I had spoken to her before, and while she had expressed a reluctance to testify, she indicated that she would. After DeShondra was sworn in, I asked her a few introductory questions.

"DeShondra will you tell the members of the jury who you are?"

"You just said my name."

"All right," I responded. "Would you tell 'em your whole name?"

Things obviously had not started well, and after she answered a few more warm-up questions, which included DeShondra referring to Strand as her dad on several occasions, things really started to go south. When we got to the point that I began asking the meaty questions about the charges, she dug her heels in.

"I don't remember nothing. Where my grandma at?"

"Would it help to have your grandmother in the courtroom?" I asked.

"No, 'cause I'm not testifying. I want to go home right now."

Not only was DeShondra refusing to answer questions, but she was overtly hostile. According to her, what had occurred was none of our business. This continued for a while, so I asked Judge Puklin to instruct DeShondra to answer my questions, and also to allow her grandmother in the room for support. Puklin agreed to let the grandmother in before making any demands of the witness, hoping that would be sufficient.

DeShondra's response was to stop speaking altogether. She wouldn't utter a syllable.

Puklin sent the jury back to the jury room for the second time—the first had been when he decided to allow DeShondra's grandmother into the courtroom—to have his first direct words with DeShondra. After explaining the importance of following the rules, and that there were consequences for not doing so, Puklin told her, firmly, that she had to answer the lawyers' questions.

"Maybe you don't like this man over here, Mr. Johnson, right, do you like him or not?"

"No," was her curt reply. That was news to me.

"You don't like him?"

"No."

"All right. See, even if you don't like him, you still have to answer his questions. That's the rule, is that okay?"

"No."

"Well, what do we have to do to get you to follow the rules?"

"Nothing."

Judge Puklin continued. "You told other people, haven't you?"

"So?"

"Told your mother?"

"Yeah, so?"

"Told the policemen?"

"Yeah, so?"

"Told the person from DCFS, didn't you?" [Illinois Department of Children and Family Services].

"So?"

"What I'm saying is you have told people. Now, all we're doing is asking you to tell us what happened. It's our turn to hear what happened, so will you tell us?"

"No."

An exasperated Judge Puklin temporarily excused DeShondra while we figured out what to do next. We had a legal discussion concerning whether there was a case left if she continued to refuse to cooperate. I'll spare you the technical and boring legal explanation, but the simple answer was no. While noting that an adult refusing to testify would result in a jail sentence for contempt of court, Judge Puklin's initial position was that he would place her in foster care through DCFS until she changed her mind. But no matter how you looked at it, that would be civil contempt of court. DeShondra could purge that contempt only by testifying.

At this point, much to my surprise, Tom offered, after conferring with his client, to have Strand either talk to DeShondra to try to convince her to testify, or to leave the courtroom while she testified, or both. Apparently, these were suggestions made by Mr. Strand himself, with Tom going along reluctantly. I had never heard of a defendant attempting to convince a victim to testify before, particularly in open court, but we all agreed it would be worth a try. So DeShondra was brought back into the courtroom, and Strand earnestly appealed to her.

"DeShondra, I know whether you want to answer the question or not, okay, when he asks you a question, whether you say yes or no, I want you to answer the question, okay, okay, baby? 'Cause you went through enough. I don't want them to prolong this and I don't want you to go through no more. So whether you say yes or no, I want you to get up here and answer your question. Like I say, whether you say yes or no, answer the question, okay?"

"What do you say, DeShondra?" Puklin asked.

"No."

My case was flatlining, and I had a pretty good idea where we would end up. I wasn't sure if Puklin would follow through with his threat to put DeShondra in foster care until she agreed to testify, but I told him and McCulloch I would end the case before we got there. Puklin seemed fine with that.

I knew my choices were limited and a number of things were going through my mind. First, by the way she was acting, there was no way of knowing how long DeShondra would continue to balk. Second, how long would Judge Puklin be willing to put an already selected and sworn jury on hold while we waited? And lastly, DeShondra had gone through enough—Strand and I agreed on at least that point—and I didn't want to make her life any more miserable than it already had been.

I was using Judge Puklin—I was more than willing to let him be the hammer—and he knew that. But I didn't want the hammer to actually fall. I'm sure Puklin didn't either.

I wasn't ready to give up just yet. DeShondra had a lawyer, Carole Grahn, in a related juvenile matter, and she happened to be in the courthouse. Judge Puklin had her brought to the courtroom, and in an off-the-record conversation, Puklin informed us that if DeShondra continued to refuse to testify, she would be held in contempt of court and sent to the youth home. The youth home was a juvenile detention center, and far worse than the foster care, family-type, setting originally threatened by Puklin. So we waited as Carole spent the next 45 minutes advising De-Shondra about her legal situation and the looming prospect of her going to the youth home.

When they were through, Carole pulled me aside and informed me that she wasn't getting anywhere with her, and that it would be horrible if she were sent to the youth home. I assured Carole that I wouldn't let that happen. Then Judge Puklin re-convened everyone but the jury and questioned DeShondra.

"DeShondra, do you understand what I'm saying? Are you going to testify?" Puklin asked.

"No."

"You refuse to testify?"

"Yes, I do." DeShondra crossed her arms in a gesture of finality. "You gonna put me in the youth home, oh, boy."

"I'm gonna put you in the youth home," Puklin confirmed.

"I don't care."

"First, I have to directly order you to testify. You must testify or you will be in contempt of court."

"I don't care."

"Will you testify?" Puklin asked one final time.

"No."

"I hereby ..." Puklin began to declare DeShondra in contempt of court.

It was now over, and I knew it. "Your Honor," I jumped in, "may I approach the bench ..."

I requested that DeShondra be excused from the courtroom, which was granted. Rather than dismiss the case, I simply rested, knowing that there was no evidence establishing the allegations against Strand. Either way, since jeopardy had attached, meaning that double jeopardy would prevent me from retrying the case regarding DeShondra, the case was over.

Tom moved for a directed verdict of not guilty, which was granted, and the jury was given a thorough explanation and excused. The prosecution of David Strand would now rest on the shoulders of Adriana Vela at the next trial.

It was late in the morning, and with one of Strand's cases out of the way, Tom made an oral motion to reduce his bond. Strand had been in the Kane County Jail waiting to be tried, and he wanted out. The judge agreed to hear that motion, along with the scheduling of the trial with Adriana, after lunch.

The hearing that afternoon was brief. Tom requested that Strand be released on a personal recognizance bond. Otherwise known as a "recog," it amounted to nothing more than Strand signing his name, without the need to post money, and promising to make his court appearances. I argued that he still had a serious charge pending, and that he should be required to post some kind of monetary bond.

Then Barry Puklin did what he loved to do. He tweaked the nose of the prosecution—which in this case, was me. He started by commenting on the relative weakness of the next case, stating that Adriana was not as strong a witness as DeShondra—knowledge he had gained from pretrial motions. Then he predicted we were going to lose that case as well.

"He's done eight, ten months—ten months waiting trial on the case that got dismissed today. That's enough state's attorney's time. He'll be released on his signature," Puklin concluded.

"State's Attorney's Time" in the vernacular of criminal lawyers means that the prosecutor has charged a defendant knowing that he couldn't prove the case, but also knowing that the defendant wouldn't have sufficient funds to make bail, thereby keeping the defendant in jail until the trial is inevitably lost. It's an insult to the integrity of the prosecutor.

Normally a shot like that would have been water off a duck's ass for me. Maybe it was the long morning, or the refusal of DeShondra to testify, or the derailing of the case. Or maybe it was the charade of having the judge threaten a nine-year-old alleged sexual assault victim with incarceration. I'm not sure. But I snapped. I could feel my face go purple and my heart pound. I rose to my feet and pointed at Judge Puklin.

"Your Honor, for the record, for the record," I stumbled and raised my voice, poking my finger in the direction of the judge. "For the record, I object to the Court's comments about state's attorney's time."

"That's ..." Puklin began.

"No, sir," I interrupted.

"... an expression we use on every ..." Puklin continued.

I probably should have let Puklin go on, but I was in no mood. As far as I was concerned, there was no satisfactory explanation. So I cut in again.

"Yes, sir, and, for the record, in case anybody in the appellate court doesn't know it, that means we're keeping him knowing we have weak cases. I—for the record, I resent that remark. It is untrue. I do not appreciate nor agree with the Court's characterization of the second case as a weak case. I want that on the record. Those are—that's all I have to say."

It wasn't as much what I said, which was provocative enough, and deservedly so. It was the way I said it—raising my voice and poking my finger at him—that brought out the wrath of Puklin.

"I'm not sure that was an appropriate outburst, Mr. Johnson. Where in the rules do you have the right to criticize what I say?"

"I'm just saying, for the record …"

"Nowhere do you have the rules. Where do you have the right to make that criticism?"

"Where do I not have the right?" was my retort.

"I'm going to hold you in direct contempt, and give you five days in the county jail. Take him away," Puklin said to the deputy in charge of court security. "Merry Christmas." And with that, Judge Puklin stormed off the bench.

I sat down and just stared ahead. Everyone in the courtroom was stunned. The elected Kane County State's Attorney had just been sentenced to jail. Then Tom jumped out of his chair and nearly leaped over the defense table to get to me. "You have to get in there and apologize to him. You can't spend five days in jail. Swallow your pride."

"Fuck him, fuck you, too! And fuck me." That was all I could come up with. Tom laughed and continued to encourage me to settle things with Puklin. I looked at the deputy whose job it was to take me in. He shrugged his shoulders. We all sat there waiting for me to cool off. It took a few minutes.

"Look," Tom said, "I'm going to talk to Puklin and set things right between you and him. But you're going to have to apologize." I was still livid, but I knew it was what I had to do. So I didn't stop Tom as he entered Puklin's chambers for a chat.

When Puklin returned to the bench, we set a court date for the next case, and then I brought up the subject of my jail sentence. Still finding it difficult to apologize, I requested an appellate bond, using the same strategy that abbreviated my jail time in DuPage County years earlier. This time it didn't work. Then, tail between my legs, I gave a brief, but complete, apology. Puklin immediately vacated my jail sentence.

I practiced many more years in front of Barry Puklin, as a prosecutor and defense lawyer, and neither of us let what had occurred affect our professional or personal relationship. I guess neither of us was very good at holding a grudge. And several months later, contrary to the judge's prediction, Adriana Vela came through with flying colors at Strand's second trial, resulting in a lengthy prison sentence.

One person did receive a benefit from the day's events. I was with Tom at a social event some time later. There were a number of lawyers present as he regaled them, with only slight exaggeration, with the events that led up to my contempt finding.

"Can a defense lawyer have a better day than I did?" he laughed. Victim—jail. Prosecutor—jail. Defendant—set free!"

Tough to argue with that.

You may not believe this, mostly because it doesn't fit the narrative of how the public feels about the legal profession, but there are plenty of lawyers who, without fanfare and unnoticed, do great things for their clients without hope of financial remuneration. Carole Grahn, DeShondra Keane's lawyer, is a shining example of that. Carole works a lot in family court and DCFS-related cases, mostly representing the interests of children in family-related litigation. There aren't many press accounts about that kind of thing, and Carole's name will never be mentioned by any of those groups that extol the virtues of the best lawyers in the various specialties. She flies too far under the radar for that sort of thing. But DeShondra was one lucky girl when Carole was appointed to represent her in juvenile court.

DeShondra's troubles didn't end with the David Strand case. In fact, she had a lifetime full of unimaginable difficulties, and she struggled emotionally and physically every day until her death, just before her 35th birthday, in early 2016. Through it all, counseling and comforting her on an almost daily basis, was her lawyer and dear friend, Carole Grahn.

Chapter 12

Reversal

"Hey, Hanlon. How'd you like to do a death penalty case?" Dan Yuhas was the Deputy Appellate Defender for the 4th Judicial Circuit in central Illinois, and he wanted to know if one of his assistants would be willing to accept his first capital case.

The request was somewhat unique for a couple of reasons. First, capital cases in Illinois skipped the initial level of the appellate process, where John Hanlon normally worked, and went directly to the Illinois Supreme Court. And second, because of that, the Office of the State Appellate Defender (OSAD), the government-run agency that handles appeals for indigent defendants (they're the public defender's office for appeals), had death penalty lawyers in their Supreme Court Unit for that very purpose.

Out of law school less than two years, and on the job about 17 months, Hanlon was too eager and green to be intimidated. "Sure, I'll take it," was his instant response.

Roughly 11,000 pages of transcript relating to the Cruz conviction later, the 27-year-old Hanlon realized that maybe he should have been a little more circumspect. His appellate co-counsel representing Cruz, Tim Gabrielsen, was even less experienced. But since Larry Essig from OSAD's Supreme Court Unit—a "grizzled veteran" with about one more year of appellate work under his belt than Hanlon and Gabrielsen—had been assigned the Hernandez appeal, and there was fear of a possible conflict of interest, the job of representing Cruz on appeal fell to two lawyers with a total of about two-and-a-half years of experience.

The three appellate lawyers got to work digesting the trial court record. Upon completion, Hanlon, for his part, wondered how Cruz got convicted. "There's got to be something else here," he thought. "Maybe I'm missing a volume of the transcript."

After confirming that he had, in fact, read the entire trial court record, Hanlon, along with Gabrielsen and Essig, plotted a strategy that involved not just the Illinois Supreme Court, but also the trial court. So, in DuPage County, they filed 2-1401[47] motions—a post-conviction procedure nor-

mally used in civil cases, but applicable to criminal convictions as well—
for Hernandez and Cruz, asking the trial court to vacate their convictions.

The main basis for the motions was the Dugan information that had
been unknown at the time of their trials. These motions would require
an extensive hearing, much like the one Carol Anfinson did for Buckley,
but with the advantage of knowing how the State would attack the Dugan
statements. Along with that, though, the primary focus was still on the
two appeals at the Illinois Supreme Court dealing with a variety of issues, particularly severance.

Hanlon didn't necessarily think they would win with the 2-1401
motions in DuPage, but he knew they would shine a bright light on the
case—a light the Illinois Supreme Court couldn't help but notice. "We
were relatively confident on the severance issue," Hanlon noted. "And
with the Dugan stuff getting the case more attention, we thought we'd get
a new trial."

Hanlon was right. Before DuPage County could complete the 2-1401
hearings, the Illinois Supreme Court issued two decisions. Both cases
were reversed and remanded for retrial.

****

Following are portions of those two opinions. I have omitted the case
citations and used a bold font for the quoted parts of the opinions.

****

The People of the State of Illinois v. Alejandro Hernandez[48]
Illinois Supreme Court
Decided January 19, 1988

The Illinois Supreme Court took note, as shown from the quotes
below, of certain admissions that Hernandez's non-testifying co-
defendant (Cruz) allegedly made that resulted in also implicating
Hernandez.

**Daniel Fowler, who knew Cruz and said he disliked him,
testified that he was alone with Cruz one day in the spring of
1983 when Cruz brought up the topic of the Nicarico killing
and said he knew who had done it. During examination by
the State, Fowler testified:**

Answer:
> He [Cruz] just said that they [the people who com-
> mitted the crimes] were friends of his.

Question:
> Did he say where they were from?

Answer:
> Aurora.

Defense counsel's objection was overruled.

A second instance of allegedly improper redaction occurred
in the testimony of Ramon Mares, a distant cousin of Cruz.
During his examination by the State there was the following
colloquy:

Question:
> Just without mentioning any names of anybody, just
> mentioning whether he [Cruz] said anything else
> about she was molested (sic) other than the fact that
> he didn't rape her?

Mr. Johnson [Buckley's counsel]:
> Your Honor, I am going to ask to be heard, not at this
> time.

The Court [Judge Kowal]:
> All right.

By the witness:
> A: That a friend was there and that he knew—he
> knew also.

Mr. Johnson:
> Objection, your Honor. Now I ask to be heard, right
> now.

The Court:
> Objection sustained and the last answer will be

stricken. The jury is instructed to disregard it.

Mr. Knight [Prosecutor]:
   I believe that is all I have of the witness.

The final instance allegedly prejudicing the defendant's
rights occurred during Lt. Winkler's testimony of a statement Cruz made to him while incarcerated in the DuPage
County Jail.

> He [Cruz] stated that on the day—he was approached
> one day in February of '83, and that some of his friends
> asked him if he wanted to be involved in a burglary, be
> involved in it. And he said no, he didn't want to.
>
> And they told him that they had a problem. They didn't
> have a vehicle, and they would like to know if they could
> borrow his vehicle to use in the commission of this felony.
>
> And he stated, no. However he would then assist them in
> how to hot-wire a vehicle. Then they could gain posses-
> sion of a vehicle to use.
>
> The named individuals then approached him, as he
> stated, two days later and asked him if he wanted to have
> sex with a little girl.
>
> He stated that the little girl was at the residence of the
> named individuals.

The Illinois Supreme Court reviewed the relevant case law pertaining to severance and the sufficiency of redactions when cases weren't
severed, and made a number of conclusions:

> The defendant here was plainly incriminated by the refer-
> ence to "friends" not only because of the State's repetitive
> attempts to establish friendship but also by the prosecutor's
> closing argument, in which he linked the "friends" evidence
> to admissions made by Cruz and the defendant: (The Court
> then quoted much of that portion of Knight's closing argument
> which is set forth on pages 129-130 in Chapter 9—Trial, which I

will not reprint here).

Use of "friends" in redacted statements was not limited to those three circumstances previously quoted, notwithstanding the trial court's directions that "friends" was not to be used in redacting the admissions. Statements made by the defendant and properly admissible against him were also edited, and references to the co-defendants were replaced with "some friends" in the testimony of Sgt. Roberson and "two other named individuals" in Lt. Winkler's. No imagination was required for the jurors to conclude that when Lt. Winkler referred to "two other *named* individuals" in recounting the defendant's statement, the "two other *named* individuals" were the two co-defendants seated next to the declarant. It was equally obvious that when Lt. Winkler testified that Cruz told him he was approached by "(t)he *named* individuals" and asked "if he wanted to have sex with a little girl," Cruz had referred to the defendant.

Aggravating the effect of those improper redactions was the State's disclosure to the jury that they were not hearing the full story. Twice the jury was informed during direct examination of the State's witnesses that the admissions being testified to had been redacted. As quoted above, the prosecutor asked Ramon Mares to continue his testimony "without mentioning any names of anybody." Also in the jury's presence the prosecutor told his witness Jackie Estremera that "I am going to ask you a series of questions about that conversation, but as I ask you those questions *** do not mention the name of any other person to whom he [the defendant] referred.

On notice that the defendants' admissions were being edited, it was not difficult for the jurors to recognize the connection between the prosecutors' repeated elicitation of testimony that the three defendants were friends, and the use of "friends" in testimony regarding statements made by Cruz and the defendant. Furthermore, during the questioning of Daniel Fowler, the State purposefully inquired whether the "friends" Cruz spoke of were from Aurora. As the jury was informed, all the defendants were from Aurora, and it is difficult to attach any intention to the prosecutor's inquiry other than to establish in the jurors' minds that Cruz was referring to the defendant in his statement to Fowler.

We find ... that the defendant did not receive a fair trial in that the statements made by Cruz, and admitted at trial, inculpated the defendant because they were improperly and insufficiently redacted. The defendant was, therefore, implicated by a witness whom he had no opportunity to confront and cross-examine, a violation of this court's precedents and an error of constitutional magnitude. As a consequence, his convictions must be reversed.

****

The People of the State of Illinois v. Rolando Cruz[49]
Illinois Supreme Court
Dated January 19, 1988

Using logic similar to that in the *Hernandez* opinion, the Illinois Supreme Court presented examples of trial testimony of State's witnesses who had testified as to alleged statements made by Hernandez that, in the context of the entire trial, unfairly implicated Cruz:

Cruz complains that testimony by several witnesses improperly linked him to Hernandez's admissions. Lt. Robert Winkler, an officer of the DuPage County Corrections Center, where Cruz and co-defendant Hernandez were held, testified that early in June 1984, co-defendant Hernandez requested to speak with him. Hernandez told him that in February 1983, he had planned a burglary in Naperville "with two other named individuals." He said that they had proceeded to the location but when it came time to carry out the crime, he, Hernandez, lost his nerve and told the "two other named individuals" that he did not want to go through with the burglary, at which point they dropped him off three blocks away. He stated that they returned a short while later to pick him up and when he entered the vehicle, he noticed a little girl, as well as other items that were fruits of the crime. They returned to Aurora, at which point the "two named individu-

als" dropped him off at his home and that was the last he saw
of the little girl. Prior to trial, Winkler had identified as the
"two named individuals" Cruz and co-defendant Buckley.

Deputy Sheriff James Roberson stated prior to trial that
co-defendant Hernandez had told him that Cruz and co-defendant Buckley had abducted the little girl and brought her
to him. At trial, Roberson testified that co-defendant Hernandez told him that he and "some friends" went to the Nicarico
home to burglarize it, and that they had taken the young girl
from the home to try to get money for her. Roberson testified
that Hernandez told him that when he left the place where he
had taken the girl, the girl was still alive.

The Supreme Court listed other examples of inappropriately
redacted statements allegedly made by Hernandez, went over the case
law, and made the following definitive findings:

Defendant argues that Hernandez's statements are both
directly and contextually incriminating. In our opinion, although Hernandez's admissions are not directly inculpatory
of defendant, in that they do not explicitly state to the jury
that Rolando Cruz was his accomplice, the nature of these
redactions in the context of the joint trial and the testimony
linking Cruz with Hernandez rendered it impossible for
the jury to conclude that the persons to whom Hernandez
referred were anyone other than the two men seated next to
him in the courtroom ... In the case before us, the physical
setting of the trial as well as the prosecution's introduction of
acquaintanceship evidence formed an impermissibly incriminating context when they established the terms "friends" and
"two named individuals" as thinly veiled references to Hernandez's co-defendants ... As a result, it would be unrealistic
in the extreme to expect a jury to ignore the clear import of
Hernandez's statements, despite their redaction.

Furthermore, any possibility that the jury would be able to
follow the court's limiting instructions [ordering the jury to
consider Hernandez's statements against Hernandez only] was
removed when the prosecution encouraged the jurors to consider each co-defendant's admission against the other defen-

dants, implying that the defendants' friendship allowed them to do so. In his closing arguments, the prosecutor directly addressed the connections between the defendants' statements. (The Court then quoted that portion of Knight's closing argument that is set forth on pages 129-130 in Chapter 9—Trial, which I, again, will not reprint here).

... In light of the prosecution's evidence relating solely to the friendship of the co-defendants, in the testimony of Claudino Montanez and Benigno Rodriguez, as well as its attempts during closing argument to lead the jury to connect defendant with Hernandez's statements, we find a deliberate and constitutionally unacceptable attempt by the prosecution to circumvent the strictures of *Bruton* [a U.S. Supreme Court case dealing with the issue of severance] and the confrontation clause.

Finally, buttressing our conclusion that defendant was denied a fair trial is the fact that the jury was informed by the prosecution, in the course of the examination of People's [State's] witnesses, that the statements of Hernandez testified to by that witness had been redacted. During the direct examination of witness Jackie Estremera, the prosecutor remarked, "I am going to ask you a series of questions about that conversation, but as I ask you those questions***do not mention the name of any other person to whom he [Hernandez] referred." The People argue that this statement, far from prejudicing defendant, assisted his cause by precluding an inadvertent identification of defendant by the witness. Informing jurors that statements have been redacted can itself be grounds for a mistrial ... and, in this case, put the jurors on notice that the testimony was being edited to protect someone involved in the trial, encouraging them to speculate as to the missing names.

Defendant argues that a severance should have been granted and that the denial of severance by the trial court was an abuse of the court's discretion. As noted in *Richardson*, anticipating the possibility of contextual inculpation presents practical problems for a trial court, when the court would be required to examine the evidence in advance to determine whether or not particular pieces of evidence, harmless individually, could be linked by the prosecution to effectively use one defendant's statement against another ... In the case at bar, however, the prosecution's course was sufficiently clear in advance of trial, during argument on the defendants' motion to sever, as the People had indicated their intention to introduce statements detailing a friendship among the defendants. Given the People's heavy reliance upon the inculpatory statements of the co-defendants, the likelihood of prejudice was predictable enough to require a severance ... While the circuit court ordered the parties to cooperate in redacting the defendants' statements, it apparently never ruled on a final edit. The record reveals that it became increasingly clear in the course of the trial that the redactions were insufficient to safeguard defendant's rights. When the prosecution introduced the acquaintanceship testimony by Rodriguez and Montanez, following the testimony on Hernandez's admission, the prosecution's announced course was completed and the predicted prejudice realized.

****

The reversal of both cases by the Illinois Supreme Court was unanimous (6-0), with one justice declining to participate in the proceedings.

Cruz's and Hernandez's appellate lawyers had hoped for an outright reversal, without a remand to the trial court for a retrial. Such a ruling, barring the extremely doubtful intervention of the U.S. Supreme Court, would have been the equivalent of an acquittal. But the justices of the Illinois Supreme Court did not want to replace a jury's judgment with their own, and sent both cases back for retrial.

Still, it was a win, and a big one. With the dismissal of Steve's case, and the reversal of the Cruz and Hernandez convictions, we all felt that the State's case was beginning to break apart. But the prosecution wasn't going to give up easily and, as it turned out, the Nicarico case was far from over.

Chapter 13

Aftermath

In various forms, criminal and civil litigation related to the Nicarico case would continue until 2011, some 28 years after Jeanine was murdered. A chronicling of most of those events is described in accurate detail in the excellent books *Victims of Justice* and *Victims of Justice Revisited*. As for me, other than the fact that I flirted with representing Rolando Cruz for two of his retrials, my role was reduced to testifying on a couple of occasions and cheerleading from the sidelines.

Before the reversals even came down, John Hanlon asked if I would consider representing Cruz in the event of a retrial. The preliminary plan was that he would get permission to try the case with me. It was logical in that we both knew the case well and believed in his innocence. Plus, I had always liked Cruz—during the trial we would occasionally chat about non-Nicarico related topics. So I met John in Springfield and we both drove farther downstate to the Menard Correctional Center, a maximum security prison, where Cruz was locked up. We had a good conversation, but nobody made any commitments.

As it worked out, by the time the Illinois Supreme Court sent the cases back for retrial, I was running for Kane County State's Attorney, which was one of the reasons our plan never materialized. Both Cruz and Hernandez obtained, pro bono, some of Illinois' most talented criminal lawyers. Springfield attorney Michael Metnick, along with Chicago lawyers Jeff Urdangen and Jane Raley, signed on to represent Hernandez, while Chicago-area lawyers Jed Stone, Isaiah "Skip" Gant and Susan Valentine represented Cruz.

I met with both teams of lawyers on several occasions to help them prepare for trial, with some of those meetings occurring while I was Kane County State's Attorney.

The unprecedented nature of that cooperation between career defense lawyers and an elected prosecutor from a neighboring county was not lost on me. And nobody felt the least bit uncomfortable. I was impressed by how Metnick, Stone and the other lawyers went about their work. They were eager and confident, especially on the day Judge Kowal ruled

192 / GARY V. JOHNSON

the Dugan statements would be admitted at their retrials.

This time, even though I wound up being wrong, I don't believe it was naïve to think that victory was in sight.

****

As the Nicarico case was developing after the first trial, something else was also evolving that would eventually, but not as quickly as you might expect, affect things—DNA technology. A small amount of semen had been found in Jeanine's rectum as a result of the sexual assault,[50] but DNA evidence had yet to be admitted in criminal cases in the United States at the time of her murder and the first trial. That changed, however, very shortly thereafter,[51] and Hernandez's and Cruz's lawyers began asking for DNA testing on the semen as early as January of 1988 during their post-conviction requests for new trials.[52] In early May of 1989 blood was taken for DNA comparison purposes from four people—Brian Dugan, Alex Hernandez, Rolando Cruz and Steve Buckley.[53]

The request for a sample of Steve's blood came through me, as Steve's lawyer, at a time while I was the state's attorney of Kane County. It wouldn't be the only time I would act as his lawyer when I was the state's attorney, even though by statute my job did not allow me to represent private clients. On another occasion, and I can't recall if it came before or after the request for Steve's blood, Bob Kilander called me to see if Steve would be willing to testify against Cruz in return for a plea of guilty to a lesser charge—residential burglary or home invasion—with a sentence of time already served. So I called Steve from my office in Geneva.

"Steve, I got a call from Bob Kilander about the Nicarico case."

"Yeah, what's he want?"

"Listen, I know what the answer to this is already, but ethically I'm required to run all plea offers by you, so hear me out. They want you to testify against Cruz in his upcoming trial. In return, they would allow you to plead guilty to residential burglary or home invasion and receive a prison sentence that, with credit for time you've already served, would not require you to serve any more time. What you get out of this is, as you know, as things stand right now, they can still prosecute you. Once you plead as they request, double jeopardy will not allow them to prosecute you for these crimes ever again. You can, once and for all, turn your back on this case."

"You mean they want me to say I committed this crime with Cruz?"

"That's right."

"But that's a lie."

"I know."

"No way! Tell 'em no."

So I did.

Steve's response to the other request for his cooperation—the taking of a sample of his blood for DNA comparisons—yielded a totally different reaction. After explaining the situation to him, I don't think the Russian army could have kept Steve from giving his blood. And the same was true for Cruz and Hernandez. The only one who had to be forced was Brian Dugan.[54]

The DNA tests were conducted by a very highly regarded expert from California, Dr. Edward Blake. His results came back later that same May. Buckley and Hernandez were excluded as persons who could have left the semen, while Dugan's DNA was consistent with that of the deposited evidence. The problem was that Cruz's DNA could not be definitively excluded.[55] Still, DNA technology was relatively new, and that meant that it was continually being improved upon. By October of 1995, Dr. Blake retested the seminal material and blood using more advanced techniques and excluded Cruz as a possible donor. Only Dugan's DNA matched.[56]

None of this deterred the State and they went on with their prosecutions, even enjoying some early successes with guilty verdicts against Hernandez and Cruz in their retrials. They just changed their strategy. No longer was Dugan just a liar—now he was also an accomplice who had committed these crimes with the original defendants.[57]

****

On February 1, 1990, Cruz was convicted again, and was sentenced to death after his jury recommended the death penalty. Hernandez's second trial ended in a hung jury on May 11, 1990, and was followed by a conviction at his third trial on May 17, 1991.

Hernandez's sentencing hearing proved to be interesting. Rather than have his trial jury decide whether he should get the death penalty, Hernandez and his lawyers opted to have the trial judge, John Nelligan, sentence him. Judge Nelligan declined to impose the death penalty, or even give him a life sentence, and instead sentenced Hernandez to 80 years in the Illinois Department of Corrections.

To me, that spoke volumes about what he thought of the case. Think about it. I disagree with the death penalty, but if you're going to have one, if ever a case cried out for it, this was the one—as long as you think the guilty verdict was correct. It's clear Judge Nelligan backed off the death penalty because he had some doubt, though not enough to override the jury's verdict, as to Hernandez's guilt. This was supported by the comments he made in court while announcing his decision.

[There] **was no direct evidence presented in the trial of this case with respect to the physical evidence or circumstantial evidence, fingerprints, hairs or anything of that nature that would tie the defendant in with either the Nicarico home ... or at the prairie path scene where the body was recovered, or any other place. It was just a complete lack of evidence of that type in this case,** Judge Nelligan said, among other things.[58]

I testified at the sentencing hearing. Sort of. More accurately, I wrote a letter to Judge Nelligan asking him to spare Hernandez's life. The judge would not admit my letter into evidence—he ruled that the opinions I expressed were not relevant to the issues to be decided at the sentencing hearing—and, therefore, he did not consider it in determining punishment. But he did accept my reading of the letter, and the letter itself, for what is called an "offer of proof." An offer of proof allows the evidence to be heard or recorded in some way for the limited purpose of allowing the appellate court to look at it and see if it should have been admitted and considered substantively by the trial court. But even though Judge Nelligan didn't consider what I had written in determining his sentence, the offer of proof resulted in the public airing of my strongly worded rebuke of the entire Nicarico prosecution.

At the time I wrote and read the letter I was the elected Kane County State's Attorney, and I knew that my status added punch to what I said. I wrote the letter on Kane County State's Attorney's Office letterhead. I chose my words carefully, but I didn't hold back:

Dear Judge Nelligan:

From time to time, I have commented publicly regarding the Nicarico case. These comments have always been from my perspective as former counsel for Stephen Buckley, a co-defendant of Alex Hernandez. Although my views are affected by my experience as a defense lawyer in this case, I would like to share my opinions with you from my vantage point as a prosecutor.
I am of the firm belief that Alex, and his co-defendants Buckley and Cruz, are totally innocent of the crimes with which they were charged. Further, I believe that Brian Dugan is the party guilty of committing these offenses. And while it is arguable whether all

of this is relevant at a sentencing hearing, the credibility of the investigation and prosecution that got Alex to this stage is. While you struggle with the appropriate punishment to mete out, I submit to you that the character of the evidence in this case should cause you to reject the death penalty as an alternative.

You should consider that the prosecutors' illogical antagonism toward the Brian Dugan confessions is a complete mystery. Any fair-minded person who weighs the evidence against Dugan comes away convinced that he alone was the culprit. The state police, who investigated Dugan's confessions at the request of the state's attorney, have opined as much to the prosecutors. You should consider also the documented (in written and oral defense motions) allegations of prosecutorial misconduct made by each team of defense lawyers in this case. The instances of prosecutorial suppression of favorable defense evidence and of witnesses testifying to critical matters without that information being memorialized in some fashion are far too numerous to ignore. The credibility of the prosecution has been destroyed by these factors alone.

Judge Nelligan, time is on the side of truth in this matter. Someday, sooner or later, the public will realize what has happened in Nicarico, and it is important that Alex be alive to be able to experience that justice. Unfortunately, when the public does understand what has occurred, the prestige and credibility of prosecutors everywhere will be adversely affected. The Nicarico case will do to prosecutors what the Rodney King police beating tapes have done to the police. Please begin mitigating the damages of this ugly prosecution by rejecting the death penalty.

Sincerely,
Gary V. Johnson
Kane County State's Attorney

****

Even though Cruz and Hernandez lost their retrials, popular support for their causes, especially in the legal and journalism communities, kept gathering steam. Tom Frisbie of the *Chicago Sun-Times*, Eric Zorn of the *Chicago Tribune* and Rob Warden from the *Chicago Lawyer* all continued writing articles and columns pointing out the problems with the State's case.

That's also when the Nicarico case started to get national publicity. *The Los Angeles Times* magazine section ran a lengthy story describing our efforts on the defendants' end to get justice done.[59] Cruz's case drew the attention of Northwestern University law professor Larry Marshall, who took on Cruz's appeal, along with John Hanlon and others. Hernandez was represented on appeal by former federal prosecutor and best-selling author Scott Turow. Amicus curiae briefs—"friend of the court" filings by non-parties who have an interest in the case and are urging a particular result, and which assist the court in gaining information that it needs to make a proper decision[60]— also supported the two defendants in their appeals.

And then there was Mary Brigid Kenney. Ms. Kenney was the appellate lawyer in the Attorney General's Office who was assigned to Cruz's second appeal for the State—basically to defend the trial court's conviction and death penalty at the Illinois Supreme Court. She was excited about handling such an important and high-profile case—that is, until she immersed herself in it and saw the obvious injustice of his conviction.[61] So after a period of soul searching, in February of 1992,[62] in an incredibly gutsy move worthy of making her the fourth person in the Nicarico case whose conduct and courage made her stand out above the rest, she recommended to her bosses that the AG's office confess error in the trial of Cruz.

Ms. Kenney's request, in the form of a memo, stated in part, "... the execution of an innocent man would destroy confidence in our criminal justice system ... I cannot in good conscience allow my name to appear on a brief asking the Illinois Supreme Court to affirm this conviction. I submit, respectfully, that the Attorney General should not do so either."[63]

She was taken off the case. On March 5, 1992, in a letter to her boss, Illinois Attorney General Roland Burris, Ms. Kenney resigned, writing, "I was being asked to help execute an innocent man. Unfortunately, you have seen fit to ignore the evidence in this case."[64]

It was during this time, in April of 1992, that I met with several of Roland Burris's top assistants at their Chicago office. My mission was to convince them to confess error, as Mary Brigid Kenney had tried a couple months earlier. I talked for about 20 minutes, while the assistant AGs said next to nothing—though one appeared to be taking copious notes. It was a waste of time.

Although I failed, the efforts of Cruz's appellate lawyers paid off. The Illinois Supreme Court initially affirmed Cruz's conviction in a 4-3 decision,[65] but agreed to reconsider the matter after elections changed the makeup of the Court. They then, in July of 1994, in another 4-3 decision, reversed Cruz's conviction and remanded the matter for another retrial.[66] The Court found error regarding several evidentiary issues, the most important of which was the trial court's refusal to allow the defense to present evidence of Brian Dugan's other similar crimes—regarding victims Melissa Ackerman, Donna Schnorr and others—which he had committed alone. The Supreme Court ruled that this evidence was relevant to corroborate Dugan's Nicarico confessions and to prove that, like those other crimes, he acted without accomplices.

Hernandez's appeal was also successful, but for a different reason. On January 30, 1995, the Second District Appellate Court in Elgin—the Illinois Supreme Court did not hear the appeal because Hernandez had not received the death penalty—ruled that error occurred in his trial when the trial judge answered a question posed by the jury (by way of a note) outside the presence of Alex and his lawyers.[67] His case was also remanded for retrial.

****

May 10, 1994

"Please take your shoes off, gentlemen. I've got to X-ray them for contraband." It was my second trip to Menard Correctional Center to visit Rolando Cruz, but this time I was with Mike Metnick. Our goal was to get the green light from Cruz to allow us to represent him, as co-lead counsel, in the event that he got another retrial after his second conviction. His case hadn't been overturned yet, but we were hopeful that, due to the Illinois Supreme Court having reheard Cruz's appeal, a reversal was in his future. The prison guard who was screening us for entry was efficient, but she also had a friendly way about her.

Earlier that morning, just past midnight, John Wayne Gacy had been executed for the murder of more than 30 young men in Norwood Park (northwest Cook County), Illinois. The day before our visit with Cruz, Gacy had been transferred from Menard, where he had spent 14 years awaiting his fate, to Stateville Correctional Center near Joliet, for the purpose of carrying out his execution.

After Mike and I were cleared for entry into the prison and while we were waiting for our escort, Gacy's sister arrived to pick up the few possessions her brother had in prison.

Mike and I watched as the same guard who had requested our shoes produced a box containing a variety of personal belongings. As Gacy's sister was taking possession of the box, the guard gave her a sympathetic look and said, "I'm sorry for your loss, ma'am."

It was a small gesture that I would have, mistakenly, just let pass if Mike hadn't been so floored by it. "Can you believe that?" he asked me. "The sister of one of the most reviled men in history just got a few kind words from a prison guard—probably the only ones she'll ever hear about her brother. That was beautiful."

He was right. In the sometimes dark and depressing business I'm involved in, there are oases of humanity that restore my faith in people. Sometimes they're small and subtle, like the Menard guard's tender words. Sometimes they're plain as day. As the state's attorney, I prosecuted a reckless homicide case involving three fatalities. In Illinois, reckless homicide is the offense of involuntary manslaughter, but with an automobile, and it almost always involves an intoxicated driver. Various forms of DUI (driving under the influence) often accompany the reckless homicide charge. These cases are a little bit different, and very difficult, in that while the consequences of their actions are grave, people who have committed this crime had absolutely no intention whatsoever of hurting anyone. Often, they are young people who have just screwed up—royally.

In the case I prosecuted, the defendant was a college student who had just obtained a scholarship that would help pay for his tuition at Northern Illinois University. So he did what many college students do—he got hammered with friends. While drunk, he ran through a stop sign at a high rate of speed at an intersection in rural Kane County. Three other NIU students were in a car coming from the opposite direction and making a legal left turn in front of him. The defendant rammed the side of the victims' car, knocking it into a farm field and splitting it in two. All three victims were killed. As often happens in these situations, the defendant's injuries were relatively minor.

Now I've prosecuted and defended a number of these cases, and the family members of victims, unless it happens that they're also related to the defendant, almost always want blood. That's more than understandable, and I really don't know how I would react under those circumstances. But the NIU defendant's case was different.

His counsel was one of my favorite lawyers, Jack Donahue from DuPage County. Knowing there was no defense for his client, and having received only Department of Corrections offers from me, Jack had his client plead cold, or blind—meaning without any agreement as to a sentence from me. That would leave the sentence completely up to the judge after a sentencing hearing. These days, Illinois law would have all but required a decent-sized prison term, with little in the way of good time.

But back when this occurred, the sentencing judge, in this case Barry
Puklin, had more wiggle room.

As I prepared for the hearing, I spoke to the three victims' mothers
who would be testifying at the hearing. They were incredibly sympathetic. "He seems like such a nice young man," they all agreed, as did I.
"We don't really know what's right. Won't prison mess him up? And it
certainly won't bring our kids back. What should we say?"

"Say what you feel and think," I advised. "And I'll do the same."

So they did. At the hearing, the mothers repeated what they had told
me and even suggested that it would be all right if the judge showed
mercy. When it came time for the defendant to speak his piece, he turned
toward those very three mothers and gave an apology that caused me to
fight back tears. As for me, I said we were going to leave the sentence up
to the judge's discretion, and the defendant was a great kid whose lapse
in judgment, very sadly, ended in tragedy. But I also reminded Puklin
that unlike most other types of crimes, DUIs and reckless homicides are
often committed by regular, law-abiding people. "Regular folks can be
deterred by harsher sentences," I told him, "making this one of the few
types of crimes where deterrence of others as a sentencing rationale actually makes sense."

Judge Puklin was as moved by the proceedings as anyone, and he
went light. He sentenced the defendant to probation with six months in
jail, without good time. He also tacked on a bunch of community service
hours that the defendant had to serve by talking to students about his
experiences with the accident and this case.

After it was all over, the defendant's father approached me with teary
eyes and said, "Thanks for not making my son out to be a criminal."

****

Mike and I didn't represent Cruz on his second retrial. Cruz's appellate lawyer, Larry Marshall, who had Cruz's ear, made it pretty evident
that he wanted someone other than Mike or me to be lead counsel for
him. And he was pretty open about it. We even talked on a couple of
occasions about who might be good as Cruz's lawyers. So it came as no
surprise to me when I learned that Chicago lawyer Tom Breen would be
leading a team of lawyers to represent Cruz.

I personally made next to no money for my work in the Nicarico case.
But at the risk of sounding overly sentimental, I was able to meet and
become professional and personal friends with some truly outstanding
people, many of whom I've already written about in this book. And that's

been priceless. So my being mildly perturbed at being overlooked for becoming Cruz's co-lead counsel—and you should know that Larry Marshall had extended an invitation for me to be a part of the defense team, which I declined—was tempered for a handful of reasons.

First, it was 1994, and I had been involved in some way or another with the case for about 10 years. I reminded myself that I had dropped out of Steve's case once already as a result of burnout. So let's just say my bringing fresh ideas and energy to the case would have been a challenge. To go along with that, I knew Cruz's retrial would involve a pro bono commitment of time and effort that would tax not only me, but also the law firm I had been with for less than a year. Not getting directly involved in Cruz's defense actually brought a sense of relief.

Second, I couldn't stay angry at Marshall for long. He had sweated blood for the same goals as mine, and had advanced our cause as much, or more, than anyone else.

Third, over the years I had become friends with Cruz. We've spoken at forums together and we talk from time-to-time. He loves his children and always makes me laugh.

Finally, and most importantly, I quickly got to know Breen and his co-counsel, which included Larry Marshall, Nan Nolan, with whom I was already acquainted, and Matt Kennelly. I liked and respected all four of them. They are incredibly talented lawyers and wonderful people I'm still friends with today. And as I look back at it now, they were the right folks at the right time to bring this case across the finish line.

So I was proud of them and happy for Cruz when on November 3, 1995 their efforts paid off and DuPage County Judge Ronald Mehling directed a verdict of acquittal in favor of Cruz. As I noted earlier in this book, a directed verdict is a ruling by the trial judge, made after the State has rested its case, ordering the defendant to be found not guilty. In doing so, the trial judge must hold that, after considering all the evidence in a light most favorable to the prosecution, no reasonable juror could fairly conclude that the State had proved its case beyond a reasonable doubt. In other words, there wasn't enough evidence to require the case to proceed any further. Cruz was free.

A little over a month later, the State dismissed all charges against Hernandez.

After Cruz's acquittal, Mike Metnick and I discussed the happy results on the telephone. His attitude about not representing Cruz was similar to mine, and he summarized it with a metaphor I still get a chuckle over and reminds me that criminal litigators need to keep their egos in check. "Not everyone gets to light the Olympic flame at the opening ceremonies, Gary. Somebody has to carry the torch across Kansas, and that's what we did."

****

In 1995, over a dozen years after Jeanine's murder, the prosecutions against Buckley, Hernandez and Cruz were finally over. But litigation stemming from the case would go on for 16 more years. The prediction I had made to Amy regarding the duration of the case, way back at the beginning when I was nervous about taking on Steve's defense, had definitely proved accurate.

A year after the Hernandez dismissal, a special grand jury indicted four DuPage County deputy sheriffs, along with former prosecutors Knight, King and Kilander, for obstruction of justice-related charges. Among other things, the alleged Cruz vision statement took center stage.

Two-and-a-half years later, in the spring of 1999, they would all be acquitted, with Kilander and King receiving directed verdicts. While I was disappointed, I was not surprised. Charges, much less convictions, in these kinds of cases, especially against prosecutors, are extremely rare.[68]

On the other hand, in September 2000, DuPage County settled federal civil rights lawsuits that had been filed by Buckley, Hernandez and Cruz for a total of $3.5 million, to be split among the three. Not nearly enough, I thought, but it would certainly do.

Tom Knight had a beef with an article written in the *Chicago Tribune*, which resulted in his filing a defamation suit. A Cook County jury found in favor of the *Tribune* in 2005, a verdict that was affirmed on appeal in 2008.[69]

All that was left was Brian Dugan. What to do with the man who wreaked havoc on an innocent little girl and her family, who sat back and watched the prosecution and conviction of innocent young men, and who had a record of murder and violence in other cases for which he was serving consecutive life sentences?

In 2005, as word was getting out that then-DuPage County State's Attorney Joe Birkett was heading in the direction of indicting Brian Dugan, I wanted to voice my disapproval. I did so in an open plea to DuPage County prosecutors, by way of the *Chicago Tribune*. It never got printed in the paper, but *Tribune* columnist Eric Zorn did publish parts of it in his blog.

The letter, set forth in its entirety below, is self-explanatory and summed up my feelings at the time. As I said in the preface to this book, I am opening myself up to an accusation of hypocrisy in that then I was arguing to put the case behind us, while today I am writing this book. So be it.

Sparing Brian Dugan

Amid the rumors that the DuPage County State's Attorney will soon be indicting Brian Dugan for the rape and murder of Jeanine Nicarico, I thought I would make an attempt to convince those in DuPage, or elsewhere for that matter, of the senseless- ness of such an action. Before doing so, let me first say that I am not a neutral observer of this case. I represented Steven [sic] Buckley, one of the three original defendants (along with Rolan- do Cruz and Alex Hernandez) wrongfully charged with DuPage County's most notorious crime. Also, several years after Brian Dugan confessed that he was the sole perpetrator, Mr. Dugan's lawyer, Tom McCulloch, joined my law firm as a partner. Finally, I am the former elected state's attorney of Kane County. As such, I became accustomed to making decisions much like the one described here. That said, Joe Birkett should conclude this case by either refusing to prosecute Dugan or by offering him another sentence of life in prison.

Let's start with the obvious. It is clear from the evidence gathered over the many years this case has been investigated that Brian Dugan alone committed these atrocities against Jeanine Nica- rico. Moreover, Brian Dugan is a multiple murderer and serial rapist serving two consecutive life imprisonment sentences for similar crimes in neighboring Illinois counties. As a result, it can be said with complete certainty that Brian Dugan will, thank- fully, never be released and will eventually die in prison. The only reason to prosecute Dugan in DuPage County would be to attempt to give him the death penalty. Such a sentence, even if it is obtained and carried out (no sure thing), would also cause Mr. Dugan to die in prison. Therefore, the sole benefit of a Dugan prosecution would be to, at least theoretically, cause his death in prison sooner rather than later. Considering that Dugan is 47 years old, that there is currently a moratorium on the death penalty in Illinois, and that a successful prosecution and execu- tion of death would be measured more in terms of decades rather than years, such a benefit seems hardly worth it.

A cost-benefit analysis would also reveal that a Dugan prosecu- tion would cost a staggering amount of taxpayer money. As a result of the various prosecutions that have occurred over the years, it is likely that every DuPage County judge, the Public Defender, and even private criminal lawyers who practice regularly in DuPage, either could not or would not handle this case. Out-of-county defense lawyers and investigators would probably be appointed and paid to probe into every detail of this 20-year-old-case that has seen not only trials against the originally charged persons, but also against a number of former DuPage County assistant state's attorneys and deputy sheriffs. Under the new death penalty discovery rules, such a process would be very thorough (revealing?), time-consuming and expensive. Considering the vast amount of taxpayer money already spent in these investigations and prosecutions, not to mention the multimillion-dollar civil settlement the original three defendants received, DuPage County taxpayers would rightfully question the value of a Dugan prosecution. If achieved, a sentence of death for Brian Dugan would, at best, be a Pyrrhic victory.

Brian Dugan's motives for confessing have been vigorously debated. Some feel he confessed to cut a deal with the authorities in order to avoid the death penalty for Jeanine's murder. Others attribute a more generous motive—an attempt to prevent the prosecution and execution of three innocent men. Though we may never know for certain which is more accurate, few would doubt that his total cooperation with the police concerning this offense after DuPage County rejected his attempt to plead guilty to avoid the death penalty was for the purpose of preventing DuPage County from committing an irreversible and horrible tragedy. And fortunately, he succeeded, saving DuPage County from itself. If Dugan is prosecuted, such a motive should and would be a compelling argument for his life to be spared.

It's been said that in the law, there are no total victories. The Nicarico case has been investigated and reinvestigated, and prosecuted and reprosecuted, for the past 20 years. After many pitched and emotional battles, both sides have been left wanting. From my perspective, while I would like to see Buckley, Hernandez and Cruz publicly exonerated and apologized to by the DuPage County State's Attorney—something he has steadfastly refused to do—the realist in me figures that won't ever happen. I will have to be satisfied with the fact that these three men are not being punished for this crime, and that the public is at least vaguely aware of their innocence. On the other hand, if

Joe Birkett follows my suggestion, Brian Dugan will never get the death penalty. But he can be comforted by the fact that the authorities accused of bungling this case have been acquitted of criminal wrongdoing and Jeanine Nicarico's killer will die in prison, just not as soon as he had hoped. It's time to put this case, once and for all, in our collective rear view mirror.

Brian Dugan was indicted for the rape and murder of Jeanine Nicarico on November 25, 2005. After that, many of my predictions about the prosecution didn't come true as I had expected. Since Tom McCulloch could be a witness regarding the circumstances surrounding the various statements Dugan had made, it would have been impractical, if not impossible, for him to represent Dugan. So Dugan reached out to an excellent lawyer in Steve Greenberg from Chicago. Steve was then appointed by the court to represent Dugan, along with the DuPage Public Defender's Office and a lawyer from the State Appellate Defender's Death Penalty Assistance Unit.

I was glad on July 28, 2009, when Dugan pled cold (blind) and chose to leave his fate—in the form of either the death penalty or another life sentence—to a jury. But I have to say, had the case gone to trial, it would have been wildly entertaining to watch the State argue that he had committed these crimes after they had spent years saying how full of shit he had been. After a lengthy hearing on November 11 of the same year, the jury sentenced Dugan to death. In an interesting twist, the jury originally signed off on a verdict of non-death due to two jurors voting not to impose the death penalty. In Illinois death penalty hearings, the verdict of death had to be unanimous. Anything short of that required a non-death sentence. But as the lawyers were returning to the courthouse to hear the verdict, the jury informed the judge that they wanted to continue deliberations. The next day, the two jurors switched their votes, and the sentence was death.

The unusual way by which his death sentence was decided, plus a couple of other issues (including one which could have resulted in allowing him to withdraw his guilty plea), actually gave Dugan a decent appeal. But when Governor Pat Quinn, on March 9, 2011, signed a bill abolishing the Illinois death penalty and also commuting the sentences of all the current Death Row inmates to life in prison, including Dugan's, his appeal was pointless. Dugan was already serving two life terms—one more wouldn't hurt. Dugan requested that his lawyers drop his appeal.

Twenty-eight years after Jeanine was murdered, legal proceedings in the Nicarico case were over.

Epilogue

Prior to 1990 Election for Illinois Attorney General

"I can't do it, Dallas. Not unless he publicly exonerates Buckley, Hernandez and Cruz, which I don't see him doing. Sorry."

I had just received a call from Dallas Ingemunson. He was the long-standing and highly respected state's attorney of Kendall County, located just south of Kane. He was also well plugged into local and statewide Republican politics. And he was a friend. He had called asking me, as the Kane County State's Attorney, to endorse Jim Ryan for Illinois Attorney General. Even though most of the work done by the Illinois Attorney General's Office isn't criminal in nature, it does litigate some criminal prosecutions. But more importantly, it has the reputation of being a major prosecutor's office, so getting the support of the various county state's attorneys was important.

Dallas wasn't upset, but he was persistent. "You'll be the only Republican state's attorney in Illinois who isn't endorsing him," he gently warned. "You're going to stick out."

Buckley's case had been dismissed a few years earlier, but without a public exoneration, and Cruz and Hernandez were still incarcerated. So I was adamant. "I'm not changing my mind on this, Dallas. You know how I feel. Those three guys are innocent, and there's a mountain of evidence that Brian Dugan committed this crime alone. But I'd like to talk to him."

I had always wanted to talk to Ryan about the Nicarico case. I had this crazy idea that maybe I could change his mind. Stupid, huh? I think Dallas knew that, too, so I was surprised when a few days later he had arranged for the three of us to discuss our differences over lunch. Dallas would be the mediator.

We met at the Kendall County Courthouse, where Ryan and I got into Dallas's convertible for the short ride to his house. Dallas's wife made a nice lunch which we ate—but I don't think any of us were able to enjoy—on their back porch. Soon after lunch was over, and after a couple of minutes of nervous chatter, I got the ball rolling.

"Let's get into why we're here. Jim, Dallas says you want my support for the A.G.'s race. I really don't know that my endorsement means all that much except that I'm the only dissenting Republican state's attorney. But I can't support you as long as Cruz and Hernandez are locked up. Buckley, Hernandez, and Cruz are innocent, and Brian Dugan committed this crime alone. Until you publicly acknowledge that, that's where I stand."

"Gary, we've taken this case where the evidence has led us, and there has been probable cause to pursue these guys." Ryan was merely regurgitating his oft-repeated public defense of the prosecutions.

"Where are you getting your information from, Jim? Kilander?"

"Yeah. He's my First Assistant, and I trust him. I know that ultimately it's my decision, but I rely on my lawyers—especially Bob."

"Then he's giving you bad advice. Which leads me to ask, how much do you know about this case? I mean the facts, the details—everything."

"Well, I don't know as much as you do, Gary, and I can't be expected to. You tried the case. So I don't want to get into a debate over each and every detail. That's why I have assistants."

"In the normal course of things, I would agree. But not this case. You need to know everything. Seriously, Jim, this is the most important case you'll ever have. I think you should take a whole week off and go over all the evidence. Lock yourself in a room with the file. Get a list of phone numbers of people you can call for answers—from both sides. I can give you names and phone numbers from my side. Ask questions of everyone. Call Randy Garrett.[70] If you do that, I know you'll agree with me."

"I'm just not going to do that, Gary."

"Jim, I know you're interested in a political life beyond the state's attorney's office—even beyond the A.G.'s office. This is the kind of case that ends political careers. I'm telling you, you're fuckin' this thing up!"

"This has nothing to do with politics, Gary, and I take offense at that. I've had independent lawyers—former prosecutors who have no axe to grind—agree that I should go forward. And Dallas agrees with me, too."

"Jim, those guys aren't independent—they're connected to you politically. And why the hell are you talking to Dallas about this? He's the state's attorney of a small county that doesn't have that kind of crime. He doesn't have that much experience in this kind of prosecution. Why would you seek out his advice?"

"Because I trust him."

"I trust him too, Jim, mostly because he's one of the smartest political people around."

"What are you saying?"

"You went to him to get the political angle on this, that's what I'm saying. Besides, I talked to Dallas, and he agrees that politics are playing a part in this."

I heard Dallas groan. Dallas had told me that in one of our conversations leading up to the meeting, but I should have kept that under my hat. The tone of the conversation up to this point was barely controlled anger. That would soon end.

"Look, I don't really need your support, but I'll ask again to make it official—will you endorse me?"

"No—I can't. And if you insist on going ahead with this prosecution, that makes you one of two things. Either you're a fraud, or you're just plain stupid. I'll let you pick."

Ryan was stunned. Hell, I was stunned! It was a useless formality to announce that the meeting was over, but Ryan did so anyhow. Dallas drove us back to the courthouse. Thank goodness his convertible top was down. The air rushing by us, creating loud ambient noise, made our silence less uncomfortable. Ryan and I didn't say a word to each other.

****

Editorial, "Honor and Trust in the Cruz Case," *Chicago Tribune*, November 6, 1995:

> … Indeed, if the DuPage authorities had their way, Cruz and Hernandez would be dead now, executed by the State of Illinois on the basis of 'evidence' that was never more than a tissue of lies.
>
> That is an awesome thought that citizens in DuPage and throughout the state ought to carry into the voting booth at the next local and state elections.
>
> … Those who did wrong or were derelict must also be held to account. At the top of this list must be Illinois Atty. Gen. Jim Ryan, who as DuPage County State's Attorney mounted the first two prosecutions of Cruz. Ryan needs to explain why getting a conviction was more important to him than getting justice.
>
> … One thing is clear: None of those involved in the Cruz prosecution deserves ever again to enjoy a position of public honor or trust. They have demonstrated that they have no honor and they merit no trust.

Eric Zorn, "Buck Stops at the Top for Deceit in Cruz Case Prosecution," *Chicago Tribune*, November 7, 1995:

> … What Ryan has not acknowledged is that these juries

[hearing the various Nicarico trials] were deceived and fed
half-truths either by his prosecutors or the perjuring witnesses
they presented.

We're not talking subtle distortions of fact but, at key points,
whoppers—such preposterous tales and allegations that virtu-
ally every observer without a personal interest in the prosecution who took a full look at all the relevant information came
away shocked at what was happening in DuPage County.
Witnesses changed their stories, complained of threats made
to them by prosecutors and detectives and, in some cases,
recanted. Investigators 'remembered' incriminating but
unrecorded statements and conversations months even years
afterward. Prosecutors did all they could to ignore the mount-
ing evidence that Brian Dugan was, in fact, the only man
responsible for the crime.

If Doria, [the DuPage County Sheriff] Ryan and Ryan's suc-
cessor, Anthony Peccarelli, did not know this and its implica-
tions, they were derelict. If they did and let the case proceed
anyway, they were corrupt. And if they now deny it ... then
they are fools ...

Rick Pearson, "Jim Ryan Apologizes for Role in the Nicarico Case,"
Chicago Tribune, November 13, 2009:

Republican governor candidate Jim Ryan said Thursday he
was 'sorry' for his role in leading the wrongful death-penalty
prosecutions of two men in the killing of Jeanine Nicarico and
suggested voters be allowed to make their voices known on
whether Illinois should keep capital punishment.

... It marked the first time Ryan apologized for his role in
prosecuting Rolando Cruz and Alejandro Hernandez, who
were both sentenced to death, saw their convictions overturned and later were determined to be innocent of the murder.
Ryan ... previously had said he based his case against Cruz
and Hernandez on the best information available at the time,
though Dugan had long been a suspect in the crime.

On Thursday, Ryan said prosecutors, detectives and law
enforcement "acted in good faith in the Cruz and Hernandez
prosecutions and still came up with the wrong result."

... Ryan also said he supports a statewide advisory referendum asking voters if the state should continue to have capital
punishment ...

Jim Ryan took a beating politically because of his handling of the Nicarico case, but not at first. Even though he lost his bid for the A.G.'s office in 1990 (for which my refusal to endorse him had no impact whatsoever), Ryan went on to get elected to that office in 1994, and then re-elected four years later. But Ryan wanted to become governor, and by the time he geared up for that, the tide had turned irrevocably on the Nicarico prosecution, forcing him to backpedal.

Ryan defended his actions in the 2002 Illinois gubernatorial campaign, saying he "made decisions based on the totality of the evidence I knew at the time,"[71] but he eventually lost to Rod Blagojevich. By 2009, when he gave his half-hearted apology, it was probably as a strategy to blunt the criticism he knew he would get when he ran for governor again. But to say that law enforcement officials acted in good faith was ... well, let's just say from where I stood, good faith was a scarce commodity in the Nicarico prosecution.

Moreover, if Ryan really believed DuPage County got it wrong despite acting in good faith, then he also knew that the system was flawed, and you don't suggest an advisory referendum to ask Illinois citizens how they feel. You tell them what you learned from your experience as a prosecutor and lead them toward eventual abolition of the death penalty.

In the end, none of what Ryan said mattered. He didn't make it out of the March 2010 Republican primary.

Of the three major players I dealt with from the prosecution side of the Nicarico case, even though I didn't get to personally know any one of them all that well, it was Jim Ryan who I became most familiar with. My exposure to Bob Kilander was tied strictly to the case. While he was a pleasant enough person to deal with on a superficial level, I didn't appreciate his tactics as a prosecutor—as I've previously noted, some of them were unforgivable—and we stayed at arm's length. As far as Tom Knight goes, our dislike for each other was so apparent and intense, there was no way I even wanted to get to know him. But due to our being state's attorneys from neighboring counties, Ryan and I would occasionally meet under circumstances where we could let our guard down a little. Surprisingly, most of that occurred after the disastrous lunch at Dallas Ingemunson's home.

And here's the twist—I liked him.

I've often asked myself how I, as the state's attorney, would have handled Ryan's situation. It's similar, but not identical, to the question I asked myself in the sidebar to Chapter 3 of this book. The question I asked there was based on the hypothetical premise that I had obtained employment as an assistant state's attorney in DuPage County—something I believe almost occurred. How would I have reacted, if I had been asked to second chair the prosecution of Buckley, Hernandez and Cruz, once I absorbed the evidence that caused me, as a defense lawyer, to believe in their innocence? The difference, and it's a pretty big one, is the question I'm asking now is: "What would I have done had I been ulti-mately and finally responsible for the handling and decision-making of this case—as the elected state's attorney?"

To start with, even though there were enough red flags that good sense called for at least a suspension of the first prosecution (where all three defendants were tried together) until a thorough and renewed analysis of the case could be completed, I have never criticized Ryan for not do-ing so. The onset of that trial was like a train hurtling down the tracks at breakneck speed, and it occurred a mere five weeks after he took office. It would have taken elephant-sized nuts to stop it, or even slow it down. Knowing what Ryan knew at the time, I honestly don't think I would have done that. No, Knight and his boss, Michael Fitzsimmons, own that one.

It's afterward, when the Dugan confessions started gaining mo-mentum and their veracity became clear, where I got irate with Ryan. I realize he may have been looking at things a little differently because by the time Dugan made his statements, Cruz and Hernandez already had been convicted. But he needed to understand a concept that would, at a later date, become part of Rule 3.8 of the Illinois Rules of Professional Conduct: "The duty of a public prosecutor is to seek justice, not merely to convict."

How much did Ryan know? I've often wondered. Had he looked at the shoeprint reports, or even the print itself? Was he aware of the tainted and highly questionable evidence that his office had utilized? What the hell was Kilander telling him? Or not telling him? How much in the dark had Ryan allowed himself to get? Did he see this case as a botched burglary that ended in rape and murder, as Knight had? Or did he view it primarily as a sex-driven crime? Did his concern about a probable civil suit against DuPage County for wrongful convictions based on police and prosecutorial misconduct color his thinking? Remember, state's at-torneys in Illinois also represent their respective counties in civil suits. You have to figure the Nicaricos, who by their public statements sup-ported the convictions, were a presence in Ryan's mind. And who knows what Tom Knight was doing during all of this? Was he having an effect on the Nicaricos' public position?

And, of course, there would be political consequences for whatever decision Ryan made. He was conservative by nature. By that I don't necessarily mean ideologically. Even though he was a Republican, by today's standards I get the impression he probably wouldn't be considered conservative enough. I mean he wasn't one to upset the apple cart. I figured all of this, and more, was clouding Ryan's judgment.

Putting myself in Ryan's position at the Dugan stage of the case, though, I know I would have reacted differently. I was much more of a "hands-on" state's attorney than Ryan, something I would have been even in the larger DuPage County office. I would have followed the advice I gave Ryan at our meeting and talked to everybody on both sides. I would have read transcripts, examined the Dugan statements, looked at the shoeprint evidence, the "vision" statement, the DNA—everything.

And after that, I would have been terrified. Terrified, and confident, that I was about to send innocent men to their wrongful deaths.

My internal inquiry doesn't end there, however. Everything I've said above I'm absolutely sure of. But what I would have done with that information introduces an X factor—courage. How much of that would I have had? These days, I think partly because of the Nicarico fiasco and with the advent of DNA, prosecutors are at least a little more willing to admit the possibility of a wrongful conviction and take appropriate action. Back then, though, that wasn't very often the case. Would I have had the guts to do the right thing and outright dismiss the cases against the original defendants, publicly exonerate them, and offer my humblest apologies?

With the remotely possible exception of an alternative I will describe shortly, my answer is yes, that is exactly what I would have done. To put a reverse spin on the "courage" issue, the truth is I wouldn't have had the nerve not to end the prosecution. I would have called a press conference and surrounded myself with Ed Cisowski, John Sam, William Bodziak and maybe others. I would have had them explain the evidence from their respective vantage points. I would have criticized the original investigation, called the criminal justice system imperfect, and taken responsibility for not heeding the warnings that existed before the first trial. And then I would have hunkered down and prepared for the barrage of criticism from the Nicarico/Knight/original investigators' side of the case. Then, if there was enough usable evidence to prosecute Dugan, I would have done so. In all likelihood, I would have just offered him a plea to another life sentence in an effort to put the entire matter behind us. Nobody would have felt good. But it would have been the right thing to do.

There would have been another way to proceed—a candy-ass alternative to be sure, but a way out short of dismissals. That would have been, at a minimum, to give Dugan the protection he wanted. That could

212 / GARY V. JOHNSON

have been accomplished in one of two ways. The first would be to plead Dugan to another life sentence for the murder of Jeanine, allowing the double jeopardy clause to prevent further prosecution and the death penalty. The second way would be to request that the trial court grant Dugan immunity to testify. That would allow Dugan to explain in court how he committed these crimes with the guarantee that his words wouldn't be usable against him in a subsequent prosecution. Either way would allow Dugan to testify at any retrials of the original defendants without fear that his testimony would result in his execution. Beyond that, I would have agreed to the admission of Dugan's other crimes—evidence that would have provided a fuller picture. Then I would let the chips fall where they may.

The problem with this less courageous option is it would have required arguing a case against the original defendants—something I wouldn't have believed in, but under this scenario, I wouldn't have had the guts to say so. It would have necessitated telling the jury, in essence, "I'm not going to make this difficult call. Here's all of the evidence—you do it and, hopefully, let me off the hook." And for a prosecutor, that's not doing your job. The evidence that Dugan committed this crime alone was overwhelming, while the original investigation of Buckley, Hernandez and Cruz, which would have to be presented in the State's case in such a trial, was not credible.[72]

However, if you don't have the courage to do the right thing and dismiss the cases against the original defendants, as well as publicly exonerate them, at least the above "middle ground" option would have been better than the path Ryan took. Through his assistants, he just kept pounding away, trying to keep the Dugan evidence from the juries while at the same time shoving garbage down their throats. And sadly, he enjoyed a frightening degree of success, until ultimately his cases fell apart.

But now you know how my meeting with Ryan turned out when I got the opportunity to talk to him. I suppose I could have handled the situation at Dallas's house better—a little kinder, a little gentler—but it wouldn't have made any difference. Ryan had his head in the sand, and he was determined to keep it there. If only he'd had a dash of the courage of John Sam, Ed Cisowski or Mary Brigid Kenney. He was a good guy who trusted the wrong people and had an aversion to jumping head first into the Nicarico mess himself. In the short run, it resulted in a decent political career going down the drain. In the long run, and worse yet, he'll forever be known, more than any of the others, for prosecuting the wrong men for the murder of Jeanine Nicarico.

Soon after Illinois Governor George Ryan (no relation to Jim Ryan), a Republican, took office in 1999, he began to question various aspects of the death penalty, most notably the reliability of capital convictions.

In January of 2000 he declared a moratorium on executions until a commission he was about to create could recommend changes in the system. That commission was formed in March of the same year. In 2001, in an effort to increase the quality of death penalty litigation, Illinois established the Capital Litigation Trust Fund to pay for defense counsel, investigators and experts.

By 2002, the Illinois Supreme Court expanded the discovery rules and also mandated minimum levels of trial experience for first and second chairs for both prosecutors and defense lawyers in capital cases.

Then, on January 11, 2003, citing the state's high number of exonerations, including those in the Nicarico case, Governor Ryan granted executive clemency to all 167 inhabitants of Illinois' Death Row. Their sentences were reduced to life in prison.

By now, even the casual observer could hear the Illinois death penalty's own death rattle. Finally, on March 9, 2011, Governor Pat Quinn put the Illinois capital punishment machinery out of commission and out of its misery, and signed a bill abolishing the death penalty.

The Illinois death penalty was taken down by a quantity of wrongful convictions which, astonishingly, was greater than the number of executions since the re-establishment of capital punishment. And due to a variety of factors—timing, the egregious conduct of law enforcement, the resulting indictments of law enforcement officials, the length of the prosecution, and the number of trips to the Illinois Supreme Court—the Nicarico case was easily the most famous, or infamous, of those prosecutions.

It was, and still is, the Illinois poster child for wrongful convictions.

As Tom Frisbie wrote in the *Chicago Sun-Times Back Talk* blog on the 30th anniversary of the murder of Jeanine, in an article entitled, "Nicarico Case Was Beginning of the End of the Illinois Death Penalty," "[s]eeing Cruz and Hernandez sentenced to death on evidence that in retrospect was surprisingly flimsy encouraged lawyers and judges in other cases to be more open to the possibility that even in a major death penalty case, justice could go off the rails. A succession of Death Row exonerations followed."[73]

Opponents of the death penalty can look to the Nicarico case as the single most important event that led to the end of capital punishment in Illinois. And I was lucky to be a part of it.

Timeline

February 25, 1983
Jeanine Nicarico is kidnapped from her home in unincorporated Naperville, Illinois.

February 27, 1983
Jeanine's body is found on the Illinois Prairie Path.

March 8, 1984
Steve Buckley, Alex Hernandez and Rolando Cruz are indicted for the murder, abduction and sexual assault of Jeanine Nicarico.

March 20, 1984
Jim Ryan defeats J. Michael Fitzsimmons in the Republican primary election for DuPage County State's Attorney.

July 25, 1984
Cliff Lund and I enter our appearances to represent Steve Buckley. Alex Hernandez and Rolando Cruz are already represented by public defenders Frank Wesolowski and Tom Laz, respectively.

Early December 1984
Jim Ryan takes office as DuPage County State's Attorney.

January 7, 1985
Jury selection for the joint trial of the three defendants begins.

February 22, 1985
The jury returns guilty verdicts on all counts against Hernandez and Cruz. The jury is deadlocked and cannot reach a verdict as to Buckley. Buckley remains in jail.

February 29, 1985
Cliff Lund and I withdraw as lawyers for Buckley.

March 15, 1985
Hernandez and Cruz are sentenced to death by Judge Kowal after a sentencing hearing.

June 2, 1985
9-year-old Melissa Ackerman of Somonauk, Illinois is kidnapped and murdered. Later that month, Brian Dugan is arrested for those crimes.

November 8, 1985
Dugan's lawyer tells prosecutors that Brian Dugan admits to murdering Melissa Ackerman and Donna Schnorr, and that he also is solely responsible for the murder of Jeanine Nicarico.

November 19, 1985
As part of a plea agreement, Dugan is sentenced to two life terms in prison, without the possibility for parole, for the rapes and murders of Melissa Ackerman and Donna Schnorr.

June 16, 1986
FBI shoeprint expert William Bodziak reports that, after an examination of the evidence, Buckley's shoe probably did not make the shoeprint on the Nicarico front door. Shortly thereafter, he concludes definitively that Buckley's shoe did not make the print.

September 5, 1986
Judge Robert Nolan orders that Brian Dugan's confessions—that he alone kidnapped, raped and murdered Jeanine Nicarico—would not be admitted at Buckley's retrial.
I enter my appearance as co-counsel with Carol Anfinson to represent Buckley at his retrial.

February 20, 1987
A panel of forensic anthropologists and shoeprint experts from the American Academy of Forensic Sciences, along with judges and lawyers, convenes in San Diego and concludes unanimously that there is no scientific basis for the claims made by Dr. Louise Robbins regarding the uniqueness of human shoeprints.

March 5, 1987
All charges against Steve Buckley are dismissed.

January 19, 1988
The Illinois Supreme Court reverses the convictions of Hernandez and Cruz, and remands both for retrials.

December 1988
I am sworn in as Kane County State's Attorney.

Late May 1989
The first round of DNA testing on semen found in Jeanine Nicarico includes Brian Dugan as a possible donor, and excludes Buckley and Hernandez. Cruz cannot be definitively excluded as the source of the DNA.

February 1, 1990
Cruz is convicted for the second time and subsequently given the death penalty.

May 11, 1990
Hernandez's retrial ends with a hung jury.

November 12, 1990
DuPage County State's Attorney Jim Ryan loses Illinois Attorney General election to Roland Burris.

May 17, 1991
Hernandez is convicted of all charges after his hung jury from a year earlier. He is sentenced to 80 years in prison.

March 6, 1992
Assistant Attorney General Mary Brigid Kenney, assigned to represent the State on Cruz's appeal, resigns her position, stating she does not want to represent the prosecution on the appeal of an innocent man's guilty verdict and death sentence.

April 1992
I meet with several top assistant attorneys general in Chicago in an unsuccessful attempt to convince them to confess error in the Cruz appeal.

December 1992
I complete my term as Kane County State's Attorney and enter private practice.

December 4, 1992
In a 4-3 decision, the Illinois Supreme Court affirms Cruz's conviction and sentence.

May 28, 1993
The Illinois Supreme Court grants Cruz a rehearing.

July 14, 1994
In a 4-3 decision, the Illinois Supreme Court reverses Cruz's conviction and remands for retrial.

January 9, 1995
Jim Ryan becomes the Illinois Attorney General.

January 30, 1995
The Second District Appellate Court reverses Hernandez's conviction and remands for retrial.

September 21, 1995
A second round of DNA testing on semen found in Jeanine Nicarico conclusively excludes Cruz, as it had done earlier for Hernandez and Buckley, as possible donors, and includes Brian Dugan as the likely donor.

November 3, 1995
Cruz is acquitted of the abduction, rape and murder of Jeanine Nicarico.

December 8, 1995
Charges against Hernandez are dismissed.

December 12, 1996
Three former DuPage prosecutors (Tom Knight, Pat King and Bob Kilander), along with four deputy sheriffs, are indicted by a special grand jury for criminal charges related to their conduct in the Nicarico case.

May 13, 1999
King and Kilander are acquitted by a directed verdict of not guilty at the end of the special prosecutor's case. On June 4, Knight and the other four defendants are acquitted after completion of the trial.

January 30, 2000
Governor George Ryan declares a moratorium on executions until he can be morally certain that innocent persons don't get executed. In March, Ryan forms a commission to make recommendations to improve the Illinois capital punishment system.

September 27, 2000
DuPage County settles federal civil lawsuit previously filed by Buckley, Hernandez and Cruz. The three are awarded $3.5 million to split.

January 1, 2001
The Capital Litigation Trust Fund is created to pay fees for defense lawyers, investigators and expert witnesses.

November 4, 2002
Jim Ryan loses to Rod Blagojevich in Illinois gubernatorial election.

January 11, 2003
With just a few days left in his term, outgoing Governor George Ryan commutes the death sentences of 167 inmates to life in prison, and pardons four. Illinois' death row is cleared of inmates.

May 20, 2005
A Cook County jury finds in favor of the *Chicago Tribune* in the defamation suit filed against it by Tom Knight.

November 29, 2005
Brian Dugan is indicted for murder of Jeanine Nicarico.

September 10, 2008
Appellate court affirms trial court's finding of no liability in *Knight v. Chicago Tribune* defamation suit.

July 28, 2009
Brian Dugan enters a cold plea to the murder of Jeanine Nicarico. A jury will determine whether he gets the death penalty.

November 11, 2009
Jury sentences Dugan to death.

March 9, 2011

Governor Pat Quinn signs bill abolishing the Illinois death penalty and commutes the sentences of all of the state's death row inmates (those sentenced to death after then-Governor Ryan's commutations and pardons), including the death sentence of Brian Dugan, to life in prison.

March 2011

After learning of the commutation of his death sentence to life in prison, Brian Dugan drops the appeal of his guilty plea and sentence.

Main Characters

Melissa Ackerman
Murder and rape victim of Brian Dugan.

Carol Anfinson
The assistant public defender appointed to represent Steve Buckley after I withdrew from Steve's case. When I re-entered the case, I was her co-counsel.

William Bodziak
The FBI shoeprint examiner who examined the shoeprint evidence after the joint trial and concluded that Buckley's shoe could not have made the print on the Nicarico door.

Tom Breen
Lead counsel for the third team of trial lawyers to represent Rolando Cruz.

Stephen Buckley
My client and one of three men originally charged with the murder of Jeanine Nicarico.

Ed Cisowski
Lead investigator from the Illinois State Police who investigated Brian Dugan and his confessions that he alone kidnapped, raped and murdered Jeanine Nicarico.

Rolando Cruz
One of three men originally charged with the murder of Jeanine Nicarico. He was Buckley's co-defendant.

Brian Dugan
The man who confessed, after the first trial of the three original defendants, that he alone kidnapped, raped and murdered Jeanine Nicarico.

Dugan is currently serving several life sentences for the murder of Jeanine Nicarico, as well as the murders of Melissa Ackerman and Donna Schnorr.

Larry Essig
Hernandez's appellate lawyer for his first appeal.

J. Michael Fitzsimmons
The elected DuPage County State's Attorney whose office oversaw the Nicarico investigation and who left office just prior to the first trial.

Tom Frisbie
Co-author, with Randy Garrett, of *Victims of Justice* and *Victims of Justice Revisited*, and reporter for the *Chicago Sun-Times* who wrote extensively on the Nicarico case.

Tim Gabrielsen
One of Cruz's appellate lawyers for his first appeal.

Isaiah "Skip" Gant
Co-counsel on Cruz's second team of trial lawyers.

Randy Garrett
Co-author, with Tom Frisbie, of *Victims of Justice* and *Victims of Justice Revisited*.

Ed German
Shoeprint examiner for the Illinois State Police Crime Lab.

John Gorajczyk
The DuPage County Crime Lab shoeprint examiner who compared Buckley's shoe to the shoeprint on the Nicarico door and came to the preliminary opinion that the Buckley shoe could not have made the print. Once he made his preliminary findings, the evidence was taken from him and he was not able to complete his examination.

John Hanlon
One of Cruz's appellate lawyers for his first appeal and co-counsel on the second appeal.

Alejandro "Alex" Hernandez
One of three men originally charged with the murder of Jeanine Nicarico.
He was Cruz and Buckley's co-defendant.

Matthew Kennelly
Co-counsel on Cruz's third team of trial lawyers.

Mary Brigid Kenney
Appellate lawyer for the Illinois Attorney General who was assigned to
prosecute the second appeal of Rolando Cruz (i.e., to defend the conviction). She resigned in protest, believing Cruz to be innocent.

Robert Kilander
DuPage County First Assistant State's Attorney who became lead counsel
for the prosecution of the original three defendants after Tom Knight left
the office.

Patrick King
The DuPage County Assistant State's Attorney who second-chaired (assisted) Tom Knight in the prosecution of the three original defendants
in the first trial, and also assisted Robert Kilander in preparation for the
retrial of Buckley.

Thomas Knight
Lead prosecutor for the investigation and first trial of the original three
defendants.

Judge Edward Kowal
Judge during the first trial of the three joined defendants, and also for
Cruz's and Hernandez's first retrials.

Thomas Laz
The DuPage County Assistant Public Defender who represented Rolando
Cruz in his first trial.

Robert E. Lee
The Cook County Assistant Public Defender and member of their Homicide Task Force who tutored me in the defense of death penalty cases.

Owen Lovejoy
Anthropologist from Kent State University who testified for the defense as a shoeprint expert in Buckley's case.

Cliff Lund
Steve Buckley's counsel, along with me, in the first Nicarico trial.

Barb Mahany
Reporter for the *Chicago Tribune* who wrote extensively on the Nicarico case.

Larry Marshall
Lead counsel for the second appeal of Rolando Cruz and co-counsel on Cruz's third team of trial lawyers.

Tom McCulloch
Assistant Public Defender from Kane County who was Brian Dugan's lawyer.

Judge Ronald Mehling
Presiding judge for Rolando Cruz's third trial.

Michael Metnick
Lead counsel for the second and third trials of Alex Hernandez.

George Mueller
Assistant Public Defender from LaSalle County who was Brian Dugan's lawyer.

Judge John Nelligan
Judge who presided over the last of Alex Hernandez's retrials.

Jeanine Nicarico
Victim in the case that is the subject of this book.

Tom and Pat Nicarico
Parents of Jeanine Nicarico.

Joseph Nicol
Criminologist instrumental in starting the Illinois state crime lab system and who testified as a shoeprint expert for the defense in Buckley's case.

Nan Nolan
Co-counsel on Cruz's third team of trial lawyers.

Judge Robert Nolan
Judge assigned to handle Steve Buckley's retrial.

Robert Olsen
Shoeprint examiner from the Kansas Bureau of Investigation.

Jane Raley
Co-counsel for the second and third trials of Alex Hernandez.

Louise Robbins
Anthropologist and shoeprint examiner from North Carolina.

Jim Ryan
The elected DuPage County State's Attorney who took office just prior to the first Nicarico trial.

John Sam
DuPage County investigator who concluded that Buckley, Hernandez and Cruz were not involved in the crimes against Jeanine Nicarico. He resigned after making his opinions known.

Don Schmitt
DuPage County Crime Lab quartermaster who testified for the State as a shoeprint examiner in the trial against Buckley.

Donna Schnorr
Murder and rape victim of Brian Dugan.

Rick Stock
DuPage County Assistant State's Attorney and Chief of the Criminal Division who assisted Robert Kilander with the prosecution against Hernandez and Cruz after Pat King left the office.

Jed Stone
Lead counsel for Cruz's second team of trial lawyers.

Scott Turow
Appellate counsel for Alex Hernandez's second appeal.

Jeff Urdangen
Co-counsel for the second and third trials of Alex Hernandez.

Susan Valentine
Co-counsel on Cruz's second team of trial lawyers.

Rob Warden
Writer, editor and founder of the *Chicago Lawyer*, who wrote extensively on the Nicarico case.

Frank Wesolowski
The DuPage County Public Defender who was Alex Hernandez's first lawyer.

Eric Zorn
Columnist for the *Chicago Tribune* who wrote extensively on the Nicarico case.

Endnotes

1   I would come to learn that Drew Peterson was a year behind me at Willowbrook High School in Villa Park, Illinois.

2   Of course, starting with the recent 2016 and 2018 elections, many suburban voting areas in the country, like the one I live in, are now opening up to Democrats.

3   In *Furman v. Georgia*, 408 U.S. 238 (1972), the United States Supreme Court held that the Georgia death penalty statute violated the 8th Amendment's prohibition against cruel and unusual punishment. Consequently, there was a nationwide hiatus in executions while Georgia and other states, Illinois among them, retooled their capital punishment laws to make them less arbitrary in their application. In *Gregg v. Georgia*, 428 U.S. 153 (1976), the Supreme Court ruled that the new Georgia death penalty statute was constitutional and executions there and in other states resumed.

4   In the last version of the Illinois death penalty, this aggravating factor could be found at 720 ILCS 5/9-1(b)(7).

5   Formerly 720 ILCS 5/9-1(c)(d)(e)(f)(g).

6   *Witherspoon v. Illinois*, 391 U.S. 510 (1968).

7   www.deathpenaltyinfo.org.

8   *Frye v. United States*, 293 F. 1013 (D.C. Cir. 1923).

9   *Brady v. Maryland*, 373 U.S. 83 (1963).

10   Illinois Supreme Court Rule 412(c).

11   In a July 28, 2004 deposition of Tom Knight taken in the case of *Thomas Knight v. Chicago Tribune Co. et al.,* Knight testified he hadn't heard about the Gorajczyk examination until he read about it in a newspaper article subsequent to our filing the motion to dismiss and subpoenaing Gorajczyk. The following are questions and answers taken from that deposition:

Charles Babcock: I think in your affidavit in this case you said you learned about the examination by Gorajczyk of the boots in a newspaper article; but in the grand jury, you testified that you heard about it at the—at the lab?

Thomas Knight: Right.

Babcock: Which—which is it?

Knight: It's—it was the—the—the fact that I first heard something about it in the newspaper.

And at the time that I testified in the grand jury, which was, you know, sometime quite a bit earlier, I think what I was recalling is that, after I found out whatever I was—learned from the newspaper, which wasn't much, that I went to the sheriff's crime lab, and that must be the meeting that was sticking in my mind when I testified, where I talked to someone else. It's just putting it together at this point.

I definitely remember both of those things; and I think the construction of that is that I read about it in the newspaper, either I got a call from Gorajczyk or I called him or I just went over to the lab. But at some point, that's what I was remembering earlier, was that I went to the lab to find out about the details about what this was.

Must have talked to somebody else at that point before I talked to Gorajczyk, and then ended talking to Gorajczyk.

Babcock: Okay.

Knight: But it's a spotty memory at that point after so long.

12   Illinois Supreme Court Rule 412(f).

13   In 2003, the Illinois legislature, in one of a series of enactments passed to improve the state's overall criminal justice system and dismal capital punishment record, imposed the requirements of *Brady* on law enforcement, requiring them to turn over any potentially exculpatory information in all felonies to the prosecuting authority. Ch. 725 ILCS 5/114-13.

14   Former Illinois Supreme Court Rule 416(h).

15   725 ILCS 5/114-6 (current Change of Place of Trial statute).

16   I'm using a fictitious name to protect this person's privacy.

But anyone who reads this and is familiar with the legal community in Kendall County will have no difficulty at all figuring out her identity.

17   Pucky Zimmerman, "Judge Denies Defense Motion for Dismissal in Nicarico Case," *Naperville Sun*, December 19, 1984.

18   Of course, John Doe is not his real name, but for obvious reasons, I've made him anonymous. Also, the person named was not Steve Buckley.

19   *Bruton v. United States*, 391 U.S. 123 (1968) is a landmark United States Supreme Court case dealing with the issue of severance.

20   *Batson v. Kentucky*, 476 U.S. 79 (1986).

21   *J.E.B. v. Alabama ex rel. T.B.*, 511 U.S. 127 (1994).

22   *Georgia v. McCollum*, 505 U.S. 42 (1992).

23   Thomas Frisbie and Randy Garrett, *Victims of Justice Revisited*, (Evanston, Illinois: Northwestern University Press. 2005), 100-101.

24   Donald Johanson and Maitland Edey, *Lucy—The Beginnings of Humankind*, (Simon and Schuster 1981), 246-248.

25   See William J. Bodziak, *Forensic Footwear Evidence*, (Boca Raton: CRC Press, Taylor and Francis Group. 2017), 303-304.

26   *Wilson v. Clark*, 84 Ill.2d 186, 417 N.E.2d 1322 (Ill. 1981).

27   Based on *People v. Prim*, 53 Ill.2d 62, 289 N.E.2d 601 (Ill. 1972), the instruction reads as follows:
> The verdict must represent the considered judgment of each juror. In order to return a verdict, it is necessary that each juror agree thereto. Your verdict must be unanimous.
> It is your duty, as jurors, to consult with one another and to deliberate with a view to reaching an agreement, if you can do so without violence to individual judgment. Each of you must decide the case for yourself, but do so only after an impartial consideration of the evidence with your fellow jurors. In the course of your deliberations, do not hesitate to reexamine

your own views and change your opinion if convinced it is erroneous. But do not surrender your honest conviction as to the weight or effect of evidence solely because of the opinion of your fellow jurors, or for the mere purpose of returning a verdict.

You are not partisans. You are judges—judges of the facts. Your sole interest is to ascertain the truth from the evidence in the case.

-Illinois Pattern Jury Instruction 26.07.

28   It was at about this time that Randy Garrett, one of the co-authors of *Victims of Justice* and *Victims of Justice Revisited*, met with former DuPage County detective John Sam. Sam also told Garrett that whoever committed the Ackerman murder should be looked at for the Nicarico murder as well.

29   *People v. Bowel*, 111 Ill.2d 58, 488 N.E.2d 995 (Ill. 1986).

30   Thomas Frisbie and Randy Garrett, *Victims of Justice*, (New York: Avon Books, Inc. (1998), 148.

31   Frisbie and Garrett, *Victims of Justice*, 138.

32   Frisbie and Garrett, *Victims of Justice*, 168; Art Barnum, "Expert Supports Dugan Confession," *Chicago Tribune*, August 29, 1989; Testimony of Dr. Michael Baden (May 4, 1990).

33   Report of Illinois State Police Polygraph Examiner Thomas M. Walsh (Dec. 5, 1985).

34   Ch. 725 ILCS 5/114-5(a)(d).

35   Illinois Supreme Court Rule 414.

36   Barbara Mahany, "Expertise of Expert On Trial," *Chicago Tribune*, August 18, 1986; Thomas Frisbie, "Expert's Methods Studied in Nicarico Murder Trial," *Chicago Sun-Times*, December 8, 1986.

37   Stephen Fischer, "Expert Witness? Convention Casts Doubt on Nicarico Witness' Theory," *Naperville Sun*, February 25, 1987. Stephen Fischer, "Defense to Try to Disqualify Nicarico Witness,"

Naperville Sun, February 27, 1987.

38   Editorial, "Murder On Trial," *Chicago Sun-Times*, March 22, 1987.

39   Barbara Mahany and John Schmeltzer, "Nicarico Death Suspect Freed," *Chicago Tribune*, March 6, 1987.

40   Barbara Mahany, "Extradition Sought for Witness in Nicarico Case," *Chicago Tribune*, April 15, 1987.

41   Barbara Mahany, "Slaying Witness 'Tired of Running,'" *Chicago Tribune*, March 27. 1987.

42   Jim Fisher, "Dr. Louise Robbins: The Shoe Print Expert From Hell," *Jim Fisher True Crime* (blog), March 11, 2012, jimfisher-truecrime.blogspot.com/2012/03/dr-louise-robbins-shoe-print-expert.html.

43   Fisher, "Dr. Louise Robbins: The Shoe Print Expert From Hell."

44   *People v. Dennis Ferguson*, 172 Ill.App.3d 1, 526 N.E.2d 525 (2nd Dist. 1988).

45   Thomas Frisbie, "Nicarico Parents Rap Confession by Dugan," *Chicago Sun-Times*, April 14, 1987; Jim Peters, "Nicaricos Break Silence on Murder Investigation," *Aurora Beacon News*, April 14, 1987.

46   *People v. Stephen Buckley (Carol Anfinson et al., Contemnors-Appellants)*, 164 Ill.App.3d 407, 517 N.E.2d 1114 (2nd Dist. 1987).

47   Ch. 735 ILCS 5/2-1401.

48   *People v. Alejandro Hernandez*, 121 Ill.2d 293, 521 N.E.2d 25 (Ill. 1988).

49   *People v. Rolando Cruz*, 121 Ill.2d 321, 521 N.E.2d 18 (Ill. 1988).

50   Before the first trial, a forensic scientist from the Illinois State Police crime lab, using pre-DNA technology, attempted to type the

semen collected, but was unable to exclude any human male as a possible donor.

51   Lisa Calandro, Dennis J. Reeder, and Karen Cormier, "Evolution of DNA Evidence for Crime Solving—A Judicial and Legislative History," *Forensic Magazine*, January 6, 2005. https://www.forensicmag.com/article/2005/01/evolution-dna-evidence-crime-solving-judicial-and-legislative-history.

52   Thomas Frisbie,"Nicarico Case DNA Test Asked," *Chicago Sun-Times*, January 27, 1988.

53   Art Barnum, "Blood Samples Taken in Nicarico Case," *Chicago Tribune*, May 4, 1989.

54   Barnum, "Blood Samples Taken in Nicarico Case."

55   Thomas Frisbie, "Test Said to Implicate Dugan," *Chicago Sun-Times*, May 23, 1989.

56   Ted Gregory and Peter Gorner, "Cruz Didn't Rape Nicarico, DNA Expert Says," *Chicago Tribune*, September 23, 1995 (Dr. Blake determined that the DNA characteristics of the donor of the semen found in Jeanine occurred in three out of every 10,000 males, and Dugan was one of them); M.A. Farber, "Presumed Guilty," *Vanity Fair*, October, 1996, 166; In 2009, when Brian Dugan pled guilty to the crimes against Jeanine, then DuPage County State's Attorney Joseph Birkett teased that improved DNA testing yielded a Dugan connection between the semen *and a hair* that was linked to the crime. Christy Gutowski, "Dugan Admits Nicarico Murder Without Deal to Save Own Life," *Daily Herald*, July 28, 2009.

57   Maurice Possley, "The Nicarico Nightmare," *Chicago Tribune*, November 5, 1995.

58   Frisbie and Garrett, *Victims of Justice Revisited*, 271, quoting from the court transcript.

59   Barry Siegal, "Presumed Guilty: An Illinois Murder Case Became a Test of Conscience Inside the System," *Los Angeles Times*, November 1, 1992.

60   Steven A. Gifis, *Law Dictionary*, (Woodbury, N.Y.: Barron's Educational Series, Inc. 1975), 11-12.

61   Siegal, "Presumed Guilty."

62   Ted Gregory, "I'm Just Very Confused Why the Thing Took This Long: For 3 Early Critics, Long Wait Is Over," *Chicago Tribune*, Nov. 30, 2005.

63   Siegal, "Presumed Guilty."

64   Gregory, "I'm Just Very Confused Why the Thing Took This Long."

65   Frisbie and Garrett, *Victims of Justice Revisited*, 287.

66   *People v. Rolando Cruz*, 162 Ill.2d 314, 643 N.E.2d 636 (Ill.1994).

67   Frisbie and Garrett, *Victims of Justice*, 257, 262.

68   Maurice Possley and Ken Armstrong, "Prosecution on Trial in DuPage," *Chicago Tribune*, January 12 1999. http://truthinjustice.org/dupage.htm.

69   *Knight v. Chicago Tribune Company*, 385 Ill.App.3d 347, 895 N.E.2d 1007 (1st Dist. 2008).

70   Randy Garrett was one of the co-authors of *Victims of Justice* and *Victims of Justice Revisited*. He had an encyclopedic knowledge of the entire Nicarico case, from start to finish—even more than any of the lawyers. Though he made no secret that he believed Brian Dugan was the sole actor in the crimes against Jeanine, he would give accurate information to anyone who asked him about the case.

71   Dave McKinney and Abdon Pallasch, "Ryan Sorry for Wrongful Convictions," *Chicago Sun-Times*, November 13, 2009.

72   I suppose a parallel could be drawn when I, as state's attorney, authorized the capital prosecutions of two defendants whose guilt I

was convinced of, but while still being against the death penalty. See *Becoming a Defense Lawyer—Sidebar*. But the difference between these situations is huge. As the Kane County State's Attorney, I was merely seeking a legal and available penalty I was not in favor of. In the hypothetical where I place myself in the shoes of the DuPage County State's Attorney, I would have actually believed in the innocence of the people I was prosecuting.

73   Thomas Frisbie, "Nicarico Case Was Beginning of the End for Illinois Death Penalty," *Chicago Sun-Times Back Talk* (blog), February 25, 2013, re-posted November 20, 2013. https://chicago.suntimes.com/politics/2013/11/19/18618257/nicarico-case-was-beginning-of-the-end-for-illinois-death-penalty.

About the Author

Gary V. Johnson is a former prosecutor and a longtime criminal defense attorney. He served as Kane County State's Attorney in suburban Chicago from 1988 to 1992.

He and his wife Amy have two adult children.

This is his debut book.

All profits from *Luck is a Talen*t benefit Colleen's Dream Foundation, which raises funds for ovarian cancer research and education.